THE SEARCH FOR
LOST AMERICA

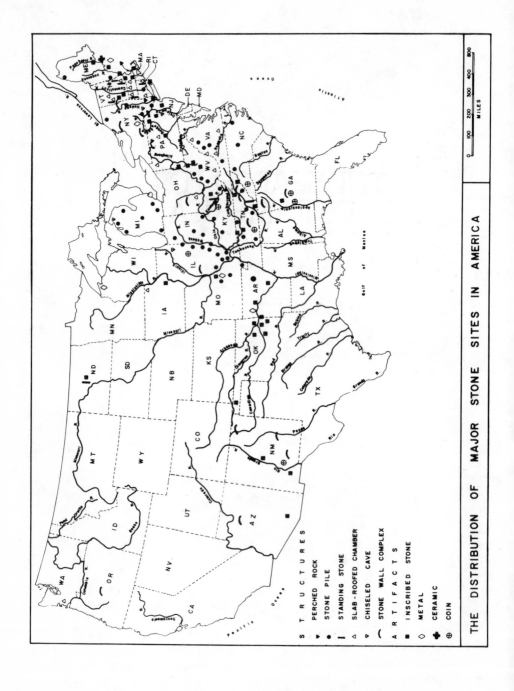

S T R U C T U R E S

▼ PERCHED ROCK
● STONE PILE
▌ STANDING STONE
△ SLAB-ROOFED CHAMBER
▽ CHISELED CAVE
(STONE WALL COMPLEX

A R T I F A C T S

■ INSCRIBED STONE
◆ METAL
◇ CERAMIC
⊕ COIN

THE DISTRIBUTION OF MAJOR STONE SITES IN AMERICA

0   100   200   300   400   500
        MILES

THE SEARCH FOR LOST AMERICA
The Mysteries of the Stone Ruins

Salvatore Michael Trento

Contemporary Books, Inc.
Chicago

Library of Congress Cataloging in Publication Data

Trento, Salvatore Michael.
   The search for lost America.

   Bibliography: p. 251
   Includes index.
   1. Man, Prehistoric—North America.   2. North
America—Antiquities.   3. Megalithic monuments—
North America.   4. America—Discovery and exploration
—Pre-Columbian.   I. Title.
E71.T7   1978   974   77-91180
ISBN 0-8092-7852-9

Published by Contemporary Books, Inc.
180 North Michigan Avenue, Chicago, Illinois 60601
Manufactured in the United States of America
Library of Congress Catalog Card Number: 77-91180
International Standard Book Number: 0-8092-7852-9

Published simultaneously in Canada by
Beaverbooks
953 Dillingham Road
Pickering, Ontario L1W 1Z7
Canada

TO
Bill, who taught me how to see,
Jesse, who showed me how to laugh,

AND
Tina, who heard my cry.

Contents

How sweet I roam'd from field to field . . .
WILLIAM BLAKE

Introduction

Thousands of large stone structures stand throughout America with little or no documentation as to what they are. Radial lines of stone piles, perched rocks, alignments of boulders, hewn granite slivers, and slab-roofed chambers, among others, tower in mute testimony to past activity. Obscure exploratory groups—some for the past fifteen years—have consistently and obstinately searched for and located hundreds of flat-faced rocks bearing ancient inscriptions. Hunters, fishermen, hikers, and farmers have repeatedly reported the existence of balanced boulders, standing stones, giant field walls, and other puzzling man-made stoneworks. What are these ruins?

In the town of North Salem, New York, a peculiarly perched stone rests not more than 10 yards from the main road. A nearby wooden sign erected by the town Historical Society implies that at the end of the last Ice Age, as a local glacier melted, a 90-ton, pink granite boulder neatly plopped atop a few smaller, cone-shaped rocks. In short, the sign suggests it was a natural geological phenomenon.

Near the Hudson River city of Poughkeepsie, New York, a long rectangular slab of stone juts out of the ground in a well-defined direction. Local residents say an Indian chief is buried beneath it. Local geologists say it was placed there by the glaciers. "Besides," they claim, "the local Indians didn't use tombstone markers." The scientists are right about the known Indian burial customs, but—another glacial phenomenon?

A report from a book published in 1892 described a mysterious mountaintop formation high above the Delaware River, near northeastern Pennsylvania. It spoke of large rocks placed on geometrically arranged "pillars." Scientists at the time attributed the strange event to a freak of nature beyond the comprehension of man.

Are all these rocks monuments to accidents of nature? Who left them and why? How old are they? What do the inscriptions say? How many times has America really been settled?

In the past million years the earth has experienced at least ten Ice Ages. During the last glaciation huge sheets of ice, some more than 2 miles thick, spread across North America. Because a great deal of the ocean was locked up in glaciers, sea levels dropped and exposed vast tracts of ocean floor. The previously submerged continental shelves now connected the hemispheres, making Asia, America, Europe, and Africa a single, gigantic land mass.

Almost twenty thousand years ago nomadic bands of big game hunters trekked across the Bering land bridge from Siberia to Alaska. Successive migrations of these ancient Asians moved into a strange and wild countryside. There they slaughtered unsuspecting herds of wooly elephants, giant sloths, and bighorn elk. Each year the animal supply dwindled as a consequence of overkill, and hunters were obliged to push further and further south in search of new game.

Around ten thousand years ago, when the great ice masses finally melted and released billions of gallons of trapped water into the world's oceans, the bridge from

Asia to America was covered up. The newly formed Bering Strait isolated the continent from further land migrations. Groups of hunters remaining in the Western Hemisphere spread into widely divergent climates as the last uncomfortable stages of the Ice Age trickled to a halt. In a few centuries, then, the entire Western Hemisphere from Alaska to the southern tip of America was traversed and occupied by men who much later in time would erroneously be called Indians.

In 1975 I heard that Harvard Professor Barry Fell, a marine biologist and president of an inscription society, had made the astounding discovery that over four hundred stone slabs unearthed from a field in Pennsylvania were etched with Punic scribblings. Punic, a Semitic-style script, was the mother tongue of the Phoenicians, a merchant, seagoing people who sailed the Mediterranean around 1000 B.C. The Phoenicians, he said, had been to America. Fell also claimed that he had found in this country and deciphered Egyptian hieroglyphics, Roman Latin, and a hitherto unknown form of Ogam, an ancient Celtic alphabet.

At the time I assumed the reports resulted simply from a combination of eager news reporters in search of a story and a wildly imaginative scholar. After all, professional archeologists assumed the Americas had been isolated from the rest of the world for well over ten thousand years. And anthropologists had shown long ago that similarities between geographically separate cultures could be easily explained as parallel development. Besides, prior reports of inscribed stones and pre-Columbian artifacts had always turned out to be well-executed forgeries, so why waste time on meaningless drivel?

As time passed, though, I realized that a strange and provocative controversy was brewing in America's learned institutions. The rebuttals published by other scholars seemed to be overly antagonistic towards Dr. Fell's claims. Furthermore, a survey of the professional literature showed that the university community was simply setting aside the site reports of many archeological groups which had been finding Old World material in America.

Thus, despite my doubts, I found myself asking these questions: was there really enough data in this country to suggest that men had sailed across the Atlantic and established actual settlements centuries before Columbus's epic voyage? Did Columbus know where he was going? Why hadn't the academic community studied these problems in the past? Had Barry Fell and others opened up a new door for American archeologists, or had they merely overstated their claims? I chose to examine *de novo* all material—documentary and field reports—and let the data speak for itself. I saw no reason to waste time either in academic contradiction or support of the pre-Columbian contact theories, since it appeared obvious that too much emotionalism, at both the professional and amateur level, had clouded the issue.

In order to independently investigate and assess the inexplicable ruins, I organized an archeological research center in January 1976. Taking its name from my hometown in southern New York, the Middletown Archeological Research Center (MARC) started out as an informal, weekend gathering of college friends. But within a few months, as stacks of site reports gathered in file folders and more people joined our Friday through Sunday miniexpeditions, I devised a formal research plan to make maximum use of the great number of people wanting to contribute their special and necessary skills to the problem of unraveling the stone mysteries. Under my guidance as executive director, a core team of research assistants trained in both archeological survey and archival retrieval coordinated the work of over two hundred volunteers in a seven-state, eighteen-month site survey expedition. Land surveyors, architects, geologists, archeologists, anthropologists, graduate students, and pilots, as well as housewives, businessmen, politicians, and high school students roamed hills, valleys, and stream beds finding, recording, and measuring megalithic-style (from the Greek *mega=-*

large, and *lithos*=stone) rubble and rock-cut inscriptions. Local, regional, and national historical references, farm charts, deeds, and survey reports, as well as seventeenth-, eighteenth-, and nineteenth-century antiquarian letters were analyzed and cross-referenced. MARC researchers obtained and quantified all data that might explain the origin and function of scattered and oftentimes isolated stonework.

Although we concentrated our initial efforts on the eastern sector of the country, it soon became clear that the problem of mysterious stone structures is a common one throughout America. As more people took to mountain trails, sketchy reports from practically every part of the country reached our center telling of similarly designed stoneworks. Photographs of rock slabs and cliff faces from Texas, Oklahoma, Arizona, and New Mexico, to name just a few states, showed structures and markings that looked as if they could have been found in a New England meadow. From the Mississippi River and its many tributaries crisscrossing the Midwest came accounts of towering standing slabs and "altar stones." Slowly the implications of our eastern work took on a much wider geographical meaning.

Evidence gathered from the major river valleys, tributaries, and coastal lowlands of the Northeast surprisingly proved very suggestive of tiny groups, possibly of late Bronze-Age people[1] from the Mediterranean and northwestern Europe, who, having sailed here from their native shores, roamed the prehistoric forests of America. Inscriptions etched on hundreds of New England and Mid-Atlantic field stones bore a striking affinity to slabs found in countries ranging from Morocco to Sweden. After months of surveying, map plotting and aerial photography, only one conclusion could be drawn: many of the stone structures in eastern America are not the products of chance weather erosion but instead appear to be of the same handiwork as the stone monuments erected in the Old World. Sixty miles from New York City, for example, is a host of lithic artifacts which appear to have been deposited centuries ago by a highly skilled, technologically advanced people. All this points to the possibility that a variety of ancient explorers portaged up the Mississippi, Susquehanna, Delaware, Hudson, Housatonic, Connecticut, and Merrimack Rivers and, among other things, set up open-air chambers as well as small tombstone slabs for their dead. These, along with other material MARC was uncovering in the eastern states—presumably the regions of first Atlantic sea landings—compare admirably with the remains of prehistoric Europe.

Along the western edge of Europe, in the lands bordering the ocean, giant, cut-rock structures lie in fallow fields. These megaliths are the ruins of a civilization long since forgotten. Some date back to 4000 B.C.—close to 6,000 years ago. How did "cavemen" cut, move, and erect these monoliths without iron or electromechanical power? Why did they bother at all? Are these the people who left behind America's stone ruins?

The answers to these questions have only begun to be understood. During the past several years, megaliths have come under the scrutiny of astronomers, engineers, and other scientists outside the realm of archeology. The results of their work have shown us that prehistoric society was a good deal more sophisticated than we had imagined. Revised interpretations of various megalithic constructions suggest that these were also used as solar and lunar observatories. Astro-mathematical computations concerning the orientation of stone placement indicate an advanced awareness of cosmic order. For these early farmers it would have been pertinent to know, for example, when the shortest and longest day of the year occurred; their planting and harvesting success demanded it. Prehistoric man wasn't a lumbering sot given to raising club and bone at every clap of thunder. Rather, he was a clever engineer-priest-politician quite capable of mobilizing hundreds of people to do his bidding.

This ancient sophistication was first reported in the 1950s, when astronomer Alexander Thom measured the diameters of over one hundred fifty prehistoric stone circles in Great Britain and concluded that there had been one standard unit of length in use from the north of Scotland to the south of England. Thom's analysis showed that, in a geographical area covering over seven hundred miles, ancient workers laid out boulders at specific distances from each other with an accuracy far exceeding the technological level attributed to them by modern archeologists. The unit was 2.72 feet or any multiple of that. The length was so accurate it seemed as if a prehistoric "yardstick" was used to lay out and construct the megaliths. Archeologists have since termed this unit of 2.72 feet the megalithic yard, and it has been discovered in many parts of the Continent and the Mediterranean as well. Thus, it has become somewhat routine for a megalithic archeologist to first measure the number of "yards" between stones at an excavation.

At North Salem, New York, there is a 200,000-pound capstone resting on top of a few conical stones. The area between the foundation stones forms an isosceles triangle with a base that's twice the megalithic yard. The chances of a glacier causing this arrangement are very slim. Within a mile of the dolmen (from the Breton *dol* = table, and *men* = stone) researcher John Williams of the Epigraphic Society has found stone slabs inscribed with markings identified as the Celtic Ogam alphabet. Aerial photography of the surrounding fields has also exposed circular impressions with diameters of over 100 yards.

The menhir (from the Breton *men* = stone, and *hir* = long) sticking up out of the ground near Poughkeepsie, New York, points southwest towards an ancient ceremonial site. Nearby a slab inscribed with a script used over twenty-five hundred years ago rests in a field wall, unnoticed by all who pass by.

An interesting rock formation above the Delaware River was surveyed on land and from the air by MARC researchers. The survey showed a series of perched boulders in the form of a triangle. Extending from the apex of the triangle was a linear arrangement of stones in an alignment pattern.

Near the Susquehanna and Delaware River Valleys a cache of inscribed blocks was discovered at the confluence of two streams. The markings on them are not of Indian origin. A good number of them are believed to speak of burials, with phrases of mourning and other poignant lamentations.

It is evident, then, that the problem is not who arrived on our shores and when, but rather, how often and how influential were such newcomers? The implications are vast: do human groups, if given enough time, develop independently, or do they rely on stimulus contact from advanced societies? Is parallel development of culture in isolated sections of the world an intrinsic part of the history of mankind, or is it merely a random phenomenon?

Cross-culturally, stones have always symbolized strength, power, and fertility, the qualities admired by and necessary for the survival of human groups confined to hunting, gathering, and farming. Monolithic pillars were frequently mentioned in older parts of the Old Testament. Among the ancient Semites the sacred pillar was universal, for it had a ritualistic purpose as well as a memorial function. That the stones were often erected near springs and rivers suggests that convenience was not the only factor. The presence of water made the site fit for consecrations inasmuch as water was indispensable for absolutions.

It has been argued that the fire altars of various ancient Mediterranean peoples were located on high mountain peaks and summits not only because they were open to the cosmos and nearer to heavenly gods but also because barren, unfrequented hilltops above a town or village offered some practical safety from the burning holocaust. It is much more difficult for a fire to spread uncontrollably on an unwooded mountain peak than on a heavily forested plain. Curiously, many perched rocks in southern New York State were initially discovered on hilltops by the colonists, who first described them as "Indian altars."

Other cultures have used stones for a variety of rituals. Polynesians and Fiji Islanders were great stone worshippers, but so were other peoples like the Egyptians, Celts, Greeks, Romans, and Persians. The Tharus and Bogshas, hill tribes living at the base of the Himalayas, often placed vertical slabs in front of their homes to signal divinities.

Knowing the significance of stones in other cultures does not justify assuming that a connection exists between these and the American ruins. This is the trap many earlier investigators fell into. Societies very often adjust to their respective physical and psychological surroundings in ways that, on the surface, appear to be similar. Closer inspection, however, usually reveals that the similarity is only visual. Distinctions have to be made between similarities that are homologous (derived from a common source) and those that are analogous (alike in function and superficial structure, but independently derived). A connection between traits in cultures should not be assumed unless, as a noted British archeologist has pointed out, we can show the traits to be functionally the same and can establish a plausible chronological and geographical connection between them.

Today only a few American scholars are willing to accept the idea of even limited trans-Atlantic crossings; most, instead, regard America's stone ruins as analogous to those of other cultures. Critics ask why, if they are homologous, past excavations have not revealed any definitive artifacts. This is an important question, since it points to the very backbone of archeology in America: the systematic study of human debris such as broken pottery, tools, and food scraps. Perhaps the answer lies in the perverse weather conditions of the east. The rainy climate, damp swamps, highly acidic soil, and seasonal frost-thaw upheavals tend to obliterate structures. Indeed, hidden within forest thickets, it is not uncommon to find Colonial stone foundations which have lain unnoticed for only two hundred years but look like they have been there for two thousand.

The best answer, however, comes from the archeological record. Very little digging has been done in eastern America. Coordinated professional excavation has little more than a twenty-year history in the Mid-Atlantic and New England states. Too few spades have entered the soil, and when they have, they've not penetrated the proper places to fully appreciate the meaning of the obscure stone ruins. Sometimes when an inexplicable artifact is found in an "Indian" burial site, it is termed either "intrusive, *post mortem*," or "provenance unknown." Inevitably an American generic name is attached to it. In other words, when archeologists label something a "boatstone" because it resembles a boat, they and future students "see" and "understand" the artifact as simply a "boatstone," nothing more. Their cognitive perception has been indexed and shelved. Furthermore, an American archeologist is not trained to identify and therefore may not recognize a prehistoric, west European artifact, even when he sees it *in situ* (in place) at his dig site. Similarly, it is all too likely that the megalithic specialist who might recognize a megalithic structure in America rarely goes there and spends enough time to look. His or her reputation as a serious scholar might be placed in jeopardy.

Another problem in uncovering artifacts is knowing where to dig. River valleys, fields, lakesides, rock shelters, and caves must all be examined for telltale debris. Prehistoric communities, be they American Indians or British Druids, chose their settlements on the basis of the accessibility of food, water, and shelter. The modern researcher must be able to project himself into the past world of the ancients, imaginatively searching for land areas which might have made a comfortable settlement site thousands of years ago. Futhermore, once it became obvious to MARC that we were working with the remains of a people who were quite knowledgeable about the movement of the sun and the moon across the sky, it was easier to find more stone structures. Predictability patterns developed, allowing us to locate similarly aligned sites.

The point is obvious: seek and ye shall find. Without firsthand investigation, no one, whether expert or layperson, should rule out the possibility of pre-Columbian, trans-Atlantic crossings.

When Christopher Columbus sailed into the Caribbean, more than one hundred centuries had passed since the last Ice Age. What had happened during the interval between the last glacial stream and 1492? Were both North and South America unknown to the rest of the world for over ten thousand years? Were the American Indians ever visited by men from other lands during this enormous time lapse?

When the pragmatic pioneers pushed into the wilderness felling trees and clearing fields, they incidentally noticed buried stone chambers, monstrous boulders balanced on smaller rocks, massive earthen mounds, and other stone ruins (see Plates 1 and 2). They didn't dwell on the matter too long, though, for they were busy scratching out an existence from a frightening and hostile country. Distinguished savants of the time, however, observing the chaotic and what they thought to be barbaric customs of the native red man, reasoned that a different people must have erected the curious field stones. The savages weren't capable of such feats, they thought.

In the early 1800s, after the initial problems of settlement had been worked out, scholars began roaming around America in search of something to study. Fur trappers and settlers had reported the existence of earthen ruins and stone debris, and naturalists and geologists were telling the same story. Based on the findings, many assumed quite matter-of-factly that an extinct civilization had inhabited early America. Books and lectures on a hypothetical ancient race sparked public imagination for decades. The title of an 1853 best seller by William Pidgeon, a fur trader and explorer, pretty much sums up the attitude of the period: *Traditions of Dee-Coo-Dah and Antiquarian Researches: Comprising Extensive Explorations, Surveys, and Excavations of the Wonderful and Mysterious Earthen Remains of the Mound Builders in America; the Traditions of the Last Prophet of the Elk Nation Relative to Their Origin and Use; and the Evidence of an Ancient Population More Numerous Than the Present Aborigines.*

By the late nineteenth century, as a reaction to popular

literature which had just about everyone from Noah and his Ark to Caesar and his legions storming across America, the Smithsonian Institution began its first systematic exploration of this country's earthen heaps. It gave Professor Cyrus Thomas five thousand dollars and three field workers to compile "the most definitive and comprehensive report to date" on the mounds. While Thomas spent a good deal of his time in Washington coordinating the attack, his assistants routinely prodded, dug, and contaminated over 2000 mounds in the states of Alabama, Arkansas, Florida, Georgia, Illinois, Iowa, Kentucky, Louisiana, Michigan, Minnesota, Mississippi, Missouri, New York, North Dakota, North Carolina, Ohio, Pennsylvania, South Carolina, South Dakota, Tennessee, Wisconsin, and West Virginia (See Plate 3).

The field team was not looking for anything special. It was simply interested in recording the major contents of each structure and sending the report to Washington. Thomas faithfully relied upon his diggers' reports for a good many of the gutted earthworks. He concluded among other things that "nothing found in the mounds justifies the opinion that they are uniformly of great antiquity" and that "the links of evidence connecting the Indians and mound-builders are so numerous and well established as to justify archeologists in assuming that they were one and the same people."[2]

In 1894 the Smithsonian issued the *12th Annual Report of the Bureau of Ethnology to the Secretary of the Smithsonian Institution* which flatly denied, based on Thomas's work, that any evidence existed for a non-Indian people visiting America before the fifteenth-century discovery by Columbus. The framework of the report eventually became the official doctrine and dogma behind American archeological thinking. A rigid scientific paradigm was established. With its publication, and for many years afterwards—indeed, up to the present day—archeologists who spoke up for the Smithsonian were curiously able to demand and receive funds for their own ideas and projects. Those who disagreed with the Institution found themselves outside the academic ball park. Furthermore, although many universities in the early twentieth century had ample opportunity to examine potential dig sites, after the report most archeology departments cautiously ignored eastern America and concentrated on more exotic lands like Egypt and the Middle East. As a result, only a minute section of the country east of the Mississippi River has been excavated. Work on the earthworks was also considered taboo for many professionals. And local ordinances in mound-building counties frequently restricted further excavation and destruction of the sites. As a result, to some extent, the *actual mounds* were and still are considered artifacts.

By the early 1930s, however, various people began to advance theories designed to bring substance to the intellectual vacuum created by the delinquent scientific community. The usual crop of ancient peoples was listed on America's guest list: the Jews, the Phoenicians, the Carthaginians, the Greeks, the Scythians, the Chinese, the Swedes, the Welsh, and the Celts. While a few theories offered a starting point for scientific scrutiny, many of the ideas created real difficulties. The problem lay in the way the arguments were presented. Authors accepted certain assumptions as true and then built their respective cases around them. In their earnest efforts to prove their theories, they played a Rorschach game, projecting their pet ideas into ancient legends, scripts, and artifacts. The unfortunate part was that the unknowing public readily accepted such flotsam as established dogma. Myth was elevated into fact.

Given the almost carnival atmosphere surrounding the study of America's dim past (outside the realm of the Indian), very few reputable archeologists and historians in the 1940s and '50s dared tread on such academically dangerous ground. The feeling has endured even into the present day. Coupled to this has been the increasingly specialized education the young archeologist gets in graduate school. He is trained to see America's past in terms of isolated cultural development. In the Western Hemisphere everything found in the context of a prehistoric setting must, *a priori*, be the result of clever aboriginals.

But it is often forgotten that this is a mere hypothetical construct.

Throughout the 1960s several writers suggested that dozens of prehistoric ethnic groups had all sailed to and settled in America. But the facts were speculative, and the arguments weak. Various publications made it a point to outdo each other by presenting wild and exotic ideas about these "facts." Theories are easy to come by, and authors were quick to fantasize on a kaleidoscope of new and old topics. Thus, the Americas were visited by spacemen in god drag, misplaced monks in junks, adventurous Arabs, and wandering Israelites. Most of these accounts read like so much pastry for the brain, and they are partially responsible for the negative attitude of the American archeological community. Such an attitude has made it exceedingly difficult for serious students to specialize in this area, and few have. MARC has, unfortunately, come directly up against this problem.

In July 1976 MARC sent a collection of photographs, surveys, charts, and diagrams to the Smithsonian along with a cover letter asking if certain Mediterranean parallels were indeed correctly made in our interpretation of locally found inscriptions and stone structures. We were reaching out for an opinion. We were asking the top archeological institution in the United States for help in explaining the New York, New Jersey, and Pennsylvania stone enigmas. The initial response from the assistant secretary for museum programs was quite cordial and interested. But the final letter lamented:

> I have now had an opportunity to investigate the possibility that someone on the Institution's staff might be able to give you some advice in response to your letter to me of July 7th. Unfortunately, it develops that *there is no one familiar enough with the history of the megalithic structures in the Mediterranean area, or with the various stone remains in the United States, to give you useful advice.* I regret I cannot be more helpful.
>
> I am returning the material that you sent, enclosed.[3]

The present-day, short-staffed museum is not to blame for this outrageous lack of information. They are working under a bureaucratic credo established long before they were born. Painfully, this attitude of benign neglect and total indifference has left the unexplained American stone remains to the ravages of time, the fantasies of reckless adventurers, and the macadam of progress. This must stop soon.

Current interest in America's past is shaking up the nation. The discovery and appreciation of ancient monuments and inscriptions has become a preoccupation for many. People are starting to notice stone mysteries which prior generations passed by with indifference. Perhaps changing demographic and social patterns are contributing to this renewed interest in the past. Perhaps it is part of America's search for roots. In either case it is clear that noticing a ruin reflects the prevailing concepts of the time, the *Zeitgeist*.

This book was written with the objective of exposing and putting on record the vast amount of undocumented stone mysteries which literally lie in the backyards of America. It is an attempt to synthesize and systematically categorize the preliminary field reports filed by MARC participants and others. The data set forth will hopefully promote immediate and critical investigation of long neglected and newly discovered, potentially viable archeological sites.

If *some* of the stone structures reported in this writing, after future archeological analysis, turn out not to be the work of prehistoric people from across the ocean, then we will, nonetheless, still be faced with the questions: who built them, and why? It is frustrating that up until very recently no university has investigated these ruins. An entire segment of our prehistory and history has been lost. This is tragic, for as Eric Sloane has mused, "When a man has lost sight of his past, he loses his ability to look forward intelligently."

A good many of the stone structures lie on top of pine-clad hills and ice-scarred peaks. The people who placed them there are long gone. Now only the wind blows across their harsh, eroded surfaces. Occasionally a mountain man or a weekend backpacker passes by, and if he's sensitive enough, he will stare at the cluster of stones and wonder what the perched rocks and jutting slabs were for. But the ruins offer no answer. He only hears the soft murmuring of a distant brook or the light tapping of rain splashing across gray, weather-beaten stone.

But we are fortunate that the ravages of civilization have not yet destroyed all evidence of pre-Columbian activity. We are now in a position to unravel the true purpose of America's stone structures. We can now discern how often our country has been explored and perhaps settled—for the rocks left behind by mariners long before Columbus hold the answers, if we can read them.

"Time, which antiquates Antiquities, and hath an art to make dust of all things, hath yet spared these minor monuments." Although the British antiquarian Sir Thomas Browne wrote these words over three hundred years ago in reference to England's megalithic remains, they are quite applicable to the stone mysteries of America.

1

Goodbye Columbus, Hello Hanno

The physical debris left by an invading people usually becomes the dominant element recovered at an archeological site, for whenever a troop of soldiers enters a foreign land, part of their culture inevitably remains long after they leave. All too often, however, modern scholars have developed migration or invasion theories from a land orientation viewpoint. While it is not to be denied that man has traveled far and wide by the power of his foot—great empires were built by men who had the courage to fight and the energy to walk—the subtle cultural and/or oral imprints left by sea-going peoples have often been either overlooked or else cast aside as spurious by land-based academics. This philosophy is bound to change, however, for in many parts of the world there is mounting evidence that prehistoric man was worth his salt on the high seas. In the western Mediterranean, for example, on the island of Mallorca, the largest and most cultivated of the Balearic archipelago, Dr. William Waldren, director of an archeological museum in the village of Deya, has

1

shown that man lived here close to 6,000 years ago. It is possible that similar, though less dramatic, discoveries may be made about America.

There is a curious void in our knowledge about prehistoric, seagoing peoples. For instance, we know that crafts must have been used to reach the island of Malta in the central Mediterranean because we find some of the oldest megalithic monuments there (close to 4000 B.C.). But thus far, no such vessels have survived the centuries, no doubt due to their perishable wood construction. Similarly, along the coast of western Europe, we find five-thousand-year-old megalithic communal tombs that are indicative of very old communication and trade via the sea; yet we find no boats.

One of the few sailing peoples we know anything about is the Phoenicians—and they were probably latecomers to the ancient maritime tradition. Nonetheless, the Phoenicians have been dubbed the sea lords of antiquity. Their homeland originally lay in the central part of the Levantine coast, about where the country of Lebanon exists today. This region had long been influenced by the adjoining Mesopotamian and Egyptian civilizations, but it wasn't until the first millennium B.C., when the Mycenean and Hittite empires of the eastern Mediterranean fell apart, that the Phoenicians distinguished themselves as powerful and daring sea merchants. Their far-flung voyages and strong-arm naval tactics allowed them to corner the ancient market for commercial goods like Canary Island purple dye, African gold, and British tin. Their skill in building and navigating seaworthy vessels eventually led them to conquer, rule, and trade with an empire that may have extended across the Atlantic to the Americas. The Phoenicians may, in fact, have sailed here long before Columbus. A look at their history supports this notion.

Whatever is known about these enterprising people is based on the writings of the Hebrews, Greeks, and Romans, nations which were not always on the best of terms with them. Plutarch, a Greek of the first century A.D.

wrote that "they are a people full of bitterness and surly, submissive to rulers, tyrannical to those they rule, abject in fear, fierce when provoked, unshaken in resolve, and so strict as to dislike all humour and kindness."[1] On the other hand, Pomponius Mela, a Spanish contemporary of Plutarch, had kinder words. "The Phoenicians were a clever race, who prospered in war and peace. They excelled in writing and literature, and in other arts, in seamanship, in naval warfare, and in ruling an empire."[2] It is ironic that we have no full-length documents written by the Phoenicians themselves, for their major contribution to western civilization was their alphabetic script, from which evolved the Hebrew, Greek, Latin, and Arabic alphabets. Inscriptions we do have tend to be bland dedications, simply stating the name of the dedication, the deity, and the purpose of the sacrifice.

Sea trade was started by the Phoenicians as early as the twelfth century B.C. By 900 B.C. they had established a wealthy and secure string of colonies in the Mediterranean ranging from Malta to the Iberian Peninsula. In time, however, it occurred to the Phoenician rulers that their empire was getting too big to control from their capital city of Tyre at the extreme eastern end of the Mediterranean. So in 814 B.C. the North African city-state of Carthage was built to keep watch over the western colonies.

Phoenician enterprises in the west declined in the seventh century B.C. as a result of Assyrian assaults on their homeland of Tyre. Consequently, Greek maritime powers stepped into the poorly defended areas and established their own trading posts along the Mediterranean coastline. But Carthage had also been extending her sphere of influence. In fact, the Carthaginian power base on Iberia's southern shore rivaled the Greeks. Within a few years the city-state and Greece were fighting over the lucrative Iberian copper and silver mines. By 500 B.C. Carthage had obtained complete control of the western Mediterranean and destroyed the last Greek stronghold in Spain. For the next few centuries up until the Punic Wars, when Carthage was destroyed by the emerging Roman Republic, the

Carthaginians prevented all vessels from sailing past the Strait of Gibraltar into the Atlantic Ocean.

The rationale for this was simple. Once competing nations were cut off from the Atlantic sources of gold, ivory, tin, and slaves, a very profitable monopoly was left for Phoenician-Carthaginian merchants. The profit incentive was so strong that it promoted the strictest secrecy among these early mariners. They never revealed their sources of merchandise. Strabo tells of a Phoenician captain who was being trailed by a Roman vessel intent on learning where the Phoenicians got their tin. The captain sailed his ship into rocky waters so that both vessels were destroyed. For this act he received from the state the full value of his cargo. He had kept a Phoenician secret from the Roman competitors.

The key to understanding the maritime success of the Phoenician-Carthaginians becomes evident when we recall that sailing procedures were already an ancient and established tradition by 1000 B.C. A fifth-century B.C. description of a Phoenician merchant vessel readily testifies to the sophistication of ship construction.

> I remember, said Ischomachus to Socrates, I once went aboard a Phoenician ship, where I observed the best example of good order that I ever met with: and especially, it was surprising to observe the vast numbers of implements which were necessary for the management of such a small vessel. What numbers of oars, stretchers, ship-hooks, and spikes, were there for bringing the ship in and out of the harbor! What numbers of shrouds, cables, halsers, ropes and other tackling, for the guiding of the ship. With how many engines of war was it armed for its defense. What variety, and what numbers of arms, for the men to use in time of battle. What a vast quantity of provisions were there for sustenance and support of the sailors. And, besides all these, the loading of the ship was of great bulk, and so rich that the very freight of it would gain enough to satisfy the captain and his people for their voyage; and all these were stowed so neatly together, that a far larger place would not have contained them if they had been removed.[3]

As Henriette Mertz has added, "It must be borne in mind that organization of one small ship such as this must presuppose centuries of experimentation."[4]

A few records of early Phoenician exploration have miraculously survived the centuries; and though Rome's annihilation of Carthage during the Punic Wars of the second and third centuries B.C. undoubtedly destroyed many records of commercial activity, some accounts still do exist. For example, in 600 B.C. Pharaoh Necho II of Egypt commissioned a fleet to circumnavigate Africa. It took the Phoenician sailors more than three years to sail down the Red Sea and around the west coast of Africa. As the mariners rounded the Cape of Good Hope, they observed the sun rising on their right instead of on their left. This curious phenomenon eventually led the Greek chronicler Herodotus to discount the story as a sailors' yarn; but in fact, the tale substantiates the accuracy of the trip, for that is exactly what is seen as one sails south around Africa. The extreme southerliness of the African continent makes the sun *appear* to be rising in the west when in actuality it is not.

The voyages of the Carthaginians, Himilco and Hanno, as recorded by the Roman, Avienus, and the Greek, Pliny the Elder, also testify to the highly sophisticated skills of the ancient sailors. According to these and other sources, Carthage had sent out Himilco to search for a western tin route, as the Spanish tin mines were being rapidly depleted. Although no complete account of his North Atlantic journey around the Iberian Peninsula exists, sections of it do crop up in many classical writings. We can be reasonably certain that the Cornish (southwest Britain) tin-trade route via the Atlantic Ocean was originated by Himilco.

Hanno, king of the Carthaginians, took greater pains than Himilco to record his voyage, but as usual only the more sensational passages have survived. Some scholars even claim that later Carthaginians actually garbled versions of Hanno's report so that other nations wouldn't be tempted to follow his lucrative path. The state supposedly

decided that their king should sail beyond Gibraltar with
about thirty thousand men and women to colonize parts of
the West African coast. The account is interesting and
probably contains some truth, because many of the passages describe geographical and zoological features peculiar to the African continent. Comments about volcanoes
and gorillas (probably chimpanzees) testify that the trip
was actually made. The idea of taking thirty thousand
people to establish a series of cities would create night-
mares for the modern urban planner. But Hanno, if his
text is true, carried it off superbly.

Sailing near a continental land mass is no easy matter.
Breakers created by land winds, as well as shallow
coastal waters and razor sharp ridges, made ventures in
sight of land extremely hazardous, and for the experienced
navigator, totally unnecessary. Oceangoing mariners had
learned long ago to sail in westerly arcs into the Atlantic
after leaving Gibraltar. To get back to the coast, all they
needed to do was swing back in an easterly direction. It is
very possible that wider and wider sea arcs initially led to
an accidental crossing of the Atlantic Ocean. And when
we consider the thousands of years man must have been
sailing along the Atlantic coast (as is evident from the
megalithic monuments), then we must seriously entertain
this thought.

Another early people whose skill on the high seas had
gone unnoticed up until very recently were the Celtic
tribes of western Europe. The Celts known to antiquity—
the Romans called them *Galli,* the Greeks, *Galatai* or
Keltoi—were a strange and barbaric people. They were
described as blond giants who "filled the whole region
with their wild singing and horrible and diverse yelling"
and who, when they arrived, "covered a vast area with
their horses, men, and carts."

Their terrifying way of going into battle did little to
soothe the civilizations of the Mediterranean. The Greek
historian Diodorus Siculus tells us that Celtic men often
gained the upper hand in a battle by challenging the
bravest of the enemy to a duel.

At the same time they swing their weapons about to intimidate their foe; if anyone accepts the challenge, the Celtic warriors break into a wild singing, praising the deeds of their fathers and their own prowess, while insulting and belittling their opponents, to take the edge off them before the battle begins.[5]

The Celts have been called by writer Gerhard Herm, and with good reason, "the people who came out of the darkness." Despite their extensive migrations out of south Germany through Yugoslavia, Greece, and Italy and their settlements in Iberia, France, Britain, Scotland, and Ireland, little is known about their activity before 400 B.C. And the classical historians who wrote of them recorded only information about tribes living in northern France and the British Isles. Celtic communities inhabiting the interior of Galicia, the geographically distinct, northwest region of the Iberian Peninsula, were virtually unknown to the ancient writers. Their doings went unnoticed for thousands of years.

This northwestern section of the peninsula is marked by heavy rainfalls and a natural forest cover that extends down the western seaboard. The whole of this Atlantic coastal strip has, as it were, turned its back on the dry plains of Portugal and Spain and looked out to the seaways leading to the Mediterranean and to Northern Europe. That ancient contact between this region and the fringes of Great Britain was a common matter is undeniable—the archeological record as well as the biologically similar gene pools of contemporary populations in both areas readily attest to this fact. Furthermore, there is new evidence emerging which suggests that Celtic sea power during the first century A.D. was much more extensive and sophisticated than previously believed possible. Newly excavated forts flanking the northwestern English shoreland near Lancaster imply that an elaborate defense system was needed to guard against amphibious attacks. The enormous quantity of Roman fortification along the Cumberland coastal region, where Roman legionnaires were welcome, means that Celtic sea raiders from Ireland were a constant threat.

Fig. 1.1. An eighteenth-century illustration of a huge T-shaped stone structure (*taula*) found only on the Balearic island of Menorca, and a cone-shaped mound of cut limestone blocks (*talayot*). The little known about the *taula* suggests that it may have been constructed as late as 300–400 B.C. as a lunar-calendar temple. The *talayot* dates to 1500 B.C. and is believed to have been used as a defensive watchtower. From Armstrong, John. *The History of the Island of Minorca.* 2nd ed. London: The Royal Society, 1756.

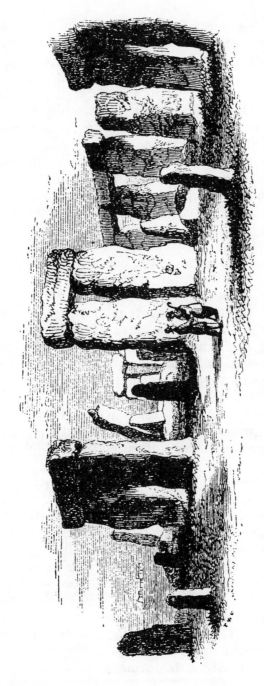

Fig. 1.2. Stonehenge, England, as it appeared in the mid-nineteenth century. This megalithic solar-calendar dates from 2000 B.C. From Wright, Thomas. *Wanderings of an Antiquary*. London: J. B. Nichols and Sons, 1854.

From these excavations we can speculate that if the
military genius of Rome felt it necessary to construct
blockades against Celtic naval tactics, then surely, during
peaceful times, Celtic merchants and explorers must have
roamed far and wide. This may very well have been so,
for we are finding stone inscriptions on American soil
which appear to have been made by a people familiar with
an early style of Celtic writing.

Now then, given this background for an extensive
maritime tradition among specific Mediterranean and
northern European peoples, one would expect to find a
host of oral and/or written traditions which speak of far-
ranging sailing ventures. Interestingly, this is just what
we do find in the writings of the early Greeks and
Romans. There are innumerable accounts of land existing
somewhere beyond the Atlantic Ocean.

One of the earliest methods used in this country to
illustrate that America was regularly visited in early
times was to dig into these classical writings. To Plato
and Aristotle did America's antiquarians turn as they
carefully dissected passages and joyfully claimed to have
found the literary *proof* of ancient contact. The hundreds
of books written since that time have in one way or
another focused upon these references. While hardly con-
clusive, this approach is nonetheless salient in light of
renewed interest in and interpretation of New World
inscriptions.

If ever the classical historians wrote detailed accounts
of the Americas, we shall never know. The burning of the
library of Alexandria, Egypt, in 396 A.D. destroyed much
of our potential knowledge of the ancient world. During
its most flourishing period this remarkable collection of
the literature of Greece, Egypt, and India is said to have
contained as many as seven hundred thousand volumes.
Due to the fires only enticing morsels of the Greek and
Roman accounts have survived.

The earliest existing reference to land beyond the Strait
of Gibraltar comes from Herodotus. Writing in the fifth
century B.C., the Greek historian speaks of the trading

methods adopted by Phoenician merchants who did not speak the language of their customers. Strabo, the most astute Roman geographer of the first century B.C. writes, "For wherever it has been possible for men to reach the limits of the earth, sea has been found and this sea we call 'Oceanus'." He stresses that "the ancients will be shown to have made longer journeys, both by land and by sea, than have men of a later time."[6] The most quoted and fascinating reference comes from Diodorus Siculus, a Greek contemporary of Caesar and Augustus who lived in Rome and worked for thirty years on his voluminous *Historical Library*. Writing in the first century B.C., he describes an intriguing place beyond the Pillars of Hercules (Strait of Gibraltar).

For there lies out in the deep off Libya an island of considerable size, and situated as it is in the ocean it is distant from Libya a voyage of a number of days to the west. Its land is fruitful, much of it being mountainous and not a little being a level plain of surpassing beauty. Through it flow *navigable rivers* which are used for irrigation, and the island contains many parks planted with trees of every variety and gardens in great multitudes which are traversed by streams of sweet water. . . .

In ancient times this island remained undiscovered because of its distance from the entire inhabited world, but it was discovered at a later period for the following reason. The Phoenicians, who from ancient times on made voyages continually for purposes of trade, planted many colonies throughout Libya and not a few as well in the western parts of Europe. And since their ventures turned out according to their expectations, they amassed great wealth and essayed to voyage beyond the Pillars of Heracles [Hercules] into the sea which men call the ocean. . . . The Phoenicians, then, while exploring the coast outside the Pillars . . . were driven by strong winds a great distance out into the ocean. And after being storm-tossed for many days they were carried ashore on the island we mentioned above, and when they had observed its felicity and nature they caused it to be known to all men. Consequently the Tyrrhenians, at the time when they were masters of the sea, purposed to

dispatch a colony to it; but the Carthaginians prevented
their doing so, partly out of concern lest many inhabitants
of Carthage should remove there because of the excellence
of the island, and partly in order to have ready in it a place
in which to seek refuge against an incalculable turn of
fortune, in case some total disaster should overtake Carthage. For it was their thought that, since they were masters
of the sea, they would thus be able to move, households and
all, to an island which was unknown to their conquerors.[7]

For our purposes it is unnecessary to detail all of the
Greek and Roman sources. Some further references appear
in Table 1, but simply pointing out two themes occurring
most often will suit our purposes here: (1) an early group
of seamen discovered islands somewhere beyond the Pillars of Hercules and (2) the islands had navigable rivers.
These remarkable items seem to imply that a sophisticated maritime tradition existed years before the classical
geographers recorded their stories. This must be the case,
for west of Africa no islands with navigable rivers are
encountered until Haiti, Cuba, and the Americas. This
extremely important point takes on additional significance
when we learn that Christopher Columbus guided his
ships, with the aid of sea charts depicting islands, into
this very part of the Caribbean. Could Columbus have
known, in fact, where he was going?

On Friday, 12 October 1492, seventy days after leaving
the port of Palos, Spain, Admiral Christopher Columbus
and a crew of ninety men landed on Watlings Island in the
Bahamas and said hello to India. That is, traditional
history tells us, he at first thought the sandy beach was
India, land of silk, spices, dazzling palaces, and jeweled
Maharajas. The Genoese mariner who for twenty years
had wandered around Europe trying to convince some
king or queen to fund a questionable ocean venture to the
exotic East, had finally made contact with the people he
was sure Marco Polo had described three hundred years
earlier. And what did he present to the wealthy Asians to
gain their respect? Worthless glass trinkets and colored
cloth. He dipped into his ship's coffers and produced

beads, bells, and bangles—awfully strange currency to bring to the relatively sophisticated people of the Far East, a people known to European merchants since the thirteenth century. Glass beads were a perfect choice to razzle-dazzle the natives on Watlings Island, but it would seem that an intriguing sense of resourcefulness was responsible for taking these trinkets on board "to charm into Christian ways the simple heathen."

Christopher Columbus merits special attention. He was the first recorded European to sail across the Atlantic Ocean. His initial voyage catapulted Spain into the position of a sixteenth-century superpower and led other countries to quickly follow. He opened up a new cultural dimension and added another half to the world. But who was Columbus? How on earth did he manage to convince Spain's King Ferdinand and Queen Isabella to pay out some fourteen thousand dollars to finance and equip a trip that all contemporary scholars thought absurd?

Columbus was a visionary who worked in mysterious ways. Ever since his logbook became public reading almost four hundred years ago, controversy has raged over whether he knew where he was going. Throughout the years skeptical scholars have pored over the admiral's notes, searching for telltale scribblings on book margins and supply sheets that might support this theory. But only recently, in light of the revised interpretation of America's prehistoric past, have certain details of the mariner's entries become meaningful. Similarly, his pre-voyage conversations, travels, and sailings all suggest that Christopher Columbus may have obtained information, in the way of maps and eyewitness accounts, of a land mass west of the Portuguese Azores. It was land the clever mariner might have known was neither India nor the China of Marco Polo. It is possible that Columbus was only the most recent practitioner of a maritime tradition that may have extended back some four thousand years.

The son of a poor weaver, Columbus was born in 1451 at the Italian city of Genoa. Besides learning how to tailor from his father, the boy studied voraciously and spent

TABLE 1
Some Ancient References to Land
Beyond the Atlantic Ocean

Name	Approximate Date	Comment
Herodotus	ca. 480 B.C.	Tells of Phoenician trading customs beyond the Pillars of Hercules.
Avienus	ca. 450 B.C.	Mentions the journey of Himilco and Hanno.
Plato	ca. 400 B.C.	Writes dialogues of Atlantis and other continents beyond.
Aristotle	ca. 360 B.C.	Says the country outside the Pillars of Hercules is fertile, well-wooded, fruitful, and has navigable rivers.
Theopompus	ca. 378 B.C.	Describes an island of immense size out in the ocean, inhabited by strange people quite different from the Greeks.
Strabo	ca. 100 B.C.	Speaks of Phoenician traffic outside the Strait of Gibraltar and hints of circumnavigation.
Diodorus	ca. 21 B.C.	Describes a great country many days' voyage through the Atlantic, with navigable rivers, big houses, forests, and fruits. Says the Phoenicians had discovered the country long ago but had kept its whereabouts a secret.

Name	Approximate Date	Comment
Seneca	ca. 30 A.D.	Speculates that there might be land on the other side of the Atlantic.
Mela	ca. 44 A.D.	Reports that "Indians" had been carried by high winds across the sea and cast upon the shores of Germany.
Plutarch	ca. 70 A.D.	"Far west in the ocean in the latitude of Britain, lie islands beyond which stretches a great continent. Greek language is spoken there."
Pausanias	ca. 150 A.D.	"West of the Atlantic are a group of islands whose inhabitants are red-skinned and whose hair is like a horse."
Aelianus	ca. 200 A.D.	Reports that among the Phoenicians of Cadiz it was common knowledge that a huge "island" existed out in the Atlantic.
Proclus	ca. 440 A.D.	Claims that the new land had stones and pillars erected by Egyptians and that inscriptions often found on the pillars told of the history of the people.

years learning enough mathematics and astronomy for proper navigation. When he was only twenty-three or twenty-four years old, he wrote to the Florentine physicist-cosmographer Paolo Toscanelli, requesting information about the shortest route to India. Evidently in 1474 King Alfonso of Portugal had asked Toscanelli to prepare a map of a possible sea route to the Orient. Inspired by the idea, Columbus asked the famed mapmaker for a duplicate report. Toscanelli sent Columbus a copy of his letter to the king in which he gave an elaborate and detailed description of what to expect in Asia. He said that the islands of the East were heavily populated by merchants and sailors. Numerous cities were under the rule of a prince called the Great Khan; and large quantities of gold, silver, gems, and "knowledge" were easily obtainable. In short, the Florentine painted a picture of a "splendid" land peopled by traders, seamen, astrologers, and scholars. (And yet, for his later voyage, Columbus saw to it that his ship conveyed "some grosse and slight wares fit for commerce with barbarous people.")

Sometime around 1472 Columbus moved to Lisbon, then the center of geographical and navigational science. The exciting port city held many attractions for the young Genoan. To Lisbon were drawn all of Europe's most illustrious wise men, mariners, mapmakers, and adventurers. While there, Columbus is believed to have joined many Atlantic sailing expeditions. Although there are still some nagging questions about the extent of his travels, some scholars are convinced that he sailed as far as Africa, England, Ireland, and possibly Iceland. If he did, then he must have ventured into numerous bars and taverns in search of stories and legends to support his desire to sail the Atlantic. Old salty dogs must have spun many a yarn for the Italian. Considering the sea route later taken by Columbus, we can be reasonably sure that he was a good listener.

Perhaps it is a little difficult to fathom how a poor boy from Genoa eventually came to have audience with the aristocracy of fifteenth-century Europe. Perhaps Columbus fretted over the same thought; we will never know. But one thing is certain: around 1480, he solved all of his social problems by marrying Doña Felipa Moniz, the daughter of an established, aristocratic sea family. Soon after the marriage, his father-in-law introduced him to important royal and scholarly figures. He also set him up with a library of nautical charts and a batch of navigational instruments. The son of a tailor was now in a position to talk himself into glory. His newfound, wealthy friends would soon be hearing all about the information he had gathered during his youthful sea voyages. They would soon tire of the indefatigable sailor and his stories of an exotic land mass beyond the ocean sea.

Columbus also read. We know a few of the documents which, apparently, deeply impressed him. During the Middle Ages, the Franciscan friar Roger Bacon of Oxford University became the first scholar to compile all of the classical Arabian and Hebrew sources which told of land beyond the Atlantic Ocean. One hundred fifty years later the French philosopher Cardinal d'Ailly, Bishop of Cambrai, wrote a massive work entitled *Imago Mundi* in which he repeated Bacon's summation. Although d'Ailly finished the manuscript in 1410, it was not published in book form until 1490. But unbound copies had been widely distributed and were quite familiar to scholars in the mid-1400s.

The impact of the *Imago Mundi* on Columbus is clear from the many marginal notes he wrote in his copy, now preserved in Seville.

> D'Ailly's chapter on India (Asia) is heavily annotated. . . . The mighty rivers, the gold, silver, pearls and precious stones, the elephants, parrots, gryphons and monsters excite him. One postil accompanied by an index finger calls attention to the innumerable islands around India, full of pearls and precious stones.[8]

Columbus was not only sensitive and aware of the classical writers, but he probably took their descriptions of land beyond the Atlantic at face value—until otherwise disproven. This is clear from a letter he wrote after his first voyage in which he described his astonishment when he observed the world to be "pear shaped," not spherical as the ancient writers had said.

Thus inspired by Toscanelli's map, the Greek and Roman writings, legends, and, probably, by his own sailings in the North Atlantic, Columbus first tried to enlighten the king of Portugal with his scheme. The crown's maritime committee had practical doubts about the plan and advised King John II to send the Italian on his way but to borrow his navigation charts for "future study"—a fifteenth-century don't-call-us, we'll-call-you routine. Left with his notes, the committee attempted a secret crossing, but a stormy Atlantic foiled them. The failure was enough to convince the king not to waste any more time on the idea. Besides, scholars in Lisbon were now talking about reaching the East by sailing around Africa.

Undaunted, Columbus gathered his notebooks and journeyed to Spain, spending the next eight years collecting more information on ancient trans-Atlantic sailings. Within two years of his Portuguese mistake, the dogged Italian was courting the Spanish royal family with the same story, but he didn't fare too well in Spain either. University scholars at Salamanca thought him to be boastful and generally untrustworthy. At Seville a maritime counsel reported that "his promises and offers were impossible and vain and worthy of rejection." They advised the court "that it was not a proper object for their royal authority to favor an affair that rested on such weak foundations, and which appeared uncertain and impossible to any educated person however little learning he might have."[9]

Sea captains and savants alike did not accept his vague and exaggerated claims about the East. They also did not agree on the actual mileage to be traveled. Columbus proposed that Asia extended into the Atlantic much further east than generally thought, thereby narrowing the ocean distance to be traversed. Learned men in Europe all contended that the distance of 3,000-plus nautical miles which Columbus projected between the Canary Islands and the Orient was a gross underestimate. They were right. The distance is 10,600 nautical miles. But the stretch from Las Palmas, capital of the Canaries, to the Bahamas is some 3,500 miles—a span well within the range mysteriously anticipated by Columbus.

The Italian sailor couldn't get anyone but his closest friends to listen to him. Part of the problem, as he wandered from city to city, lay in his exorbitant demands. Columbus wanted two types of royal grants from the monarchies he visited: economic concessions and jurisdictional rights. Aside from asking for men, ships, and supplies, Columbus insisted that he be appointed admiral, viceroy, and governor-general of all islands and territories that he might discover on his voyage. He also wanted a share in the profits of all future expeditions. The Portuguese threw him out in part on these grounds, as did the Spanish court of Ferdinand and Isabella in 1489.

Two years passed before Queen Isabella would again see the vociferous Genoan. During the autumn of 1491, after constant requests, she had his proposal reviewed once more by a special advisory committee of astronomers, sailors, and professors. The scheme was accepted by the team, which then passed it on to the royal council, which, after much debate about the even higher-priced demands incorporated by Columbus into this new bid, finally rejected it. The king and queen were reluctant to give in to the stringent conditions. For some unknown reason Columbus was apparently giving more thought to the rewards of the voyage than either Ferdinand or Isabella believed necessary.

There is ample evidence that, as each year wore on and he obtained new sailing information, Columbus's desire for wealth became more acute. A letter written by him in 1485, for instance, indicates that at first he wanted very little from the voyage. But as he gathered yellowing maps and documents from the musty libraries of Europe, as he sought out age-old tales of sea crossings, as he studied the

"Brazil Wood" found off the west coast of Ireland (drift-wood from the Americas brought to the North Atlantic via the Gulf Stream), Columbus must have realized that a New World lay before him—a world filled with the riches of antiquity. It has even been suggested that Columbus concealed his intentions to visit the New World by argu-ing for a westward sailing to India.

Perhaps after years of struggling for an underwriter and getting nowhere, Columbus thought the time was ripe to let someone else in on his secret, if he did in fact have one. This might have happened, for in January 1492 the most mysterious event of the Columbus story unfolded. A few months before, he had been told by the royal council to never again bother the court with his crazy plans. As a result, he set off for France hoping to gain audience with King Charles VIII. But just as he was preparing to cross the Pyrenees, a message suddenly reached him declaring that the queen had changed her mind—Spain would fund a westward voyage to India! Quite unexpectedly, it seems, Queen Isabella, after absolutely and definitely rejecting the proposal three times, now agreed to gamble away her wealth and position on some bizarre Italian's dream.

It has been argued that this sudden change of heart was the work of Luis de Santangel, the court treasurer whom Columbus had befriended during his Spanish stay. But perhaps the glib treasurer was only one carefully placed confidant in a plan masterminded by a desperate opportu-nist. It is difficult to believe that the mere persuasive powers of Santangel influenced Isabella, while Columbus's lucid arguments, which obviously contained many more nautical details, did not. Besides, Columbus's delivery had taken on an impressive style over the years. His speeches unwound with all the intensity of a Greek drama. Still, it almost seems as though a classic setup had been insti-gated against the crown: Columbus presents his case before the royal family; makes huge demands with full knowledge that they'll be rejected; and leaves for another country while his friend, at exactly the right moment, confides in the queen that more might be at stake than she realizes. Columbus again appears before the court, rehashes the "same" story, and then comes to terms with the king and queen for financial backing. Of course we will never know if this really happened, but the little we do know about his return to Spain gives some credence to the theory.

At any rate, after twenty years of study, research, and travel, his dream came true in April 1492, with an agreement known as the Treaty of Capitulation. Did Columbus present new evidence to Ferdinand and Isabella during the three months it took to negotiate the agreement? This certainly seems to be what happened, for the treaty says absolutely nothing about a westward route to India! Instead, it specifically mentions discovering land in the Atlantic.

> Whereas you, Cristobal Colon, are setting forth by our command . . . *to discover and acquire certain islands and mainland in the ocean sea* . . . it is just and reasonable that, since you are exposing yourself to this danger in our service, you be rewarded therefore. . . . it is our will and pleasure that you shall be our Admiral . . . and shall be empowered henceforward to call and entitle yourself Don Cristobal Colon, and his heirs and successors forever may be so entitled, and enjoy the offices of Admiral of the Ocean Sea, Viceroy and Governor of the said islands and mainland.[10]

Was not Columbus exposing himself to the same dangers four years before when he first proposed his scheme to the Spanish court? Why did his exorbitant demands of 1491 for titles, honors and money seem "just and reasonable" in 1492? Perhaps Columbus finally specified that a mainland existed across the ocean where some of the people dwelt in golden splendor. Whatever document or chart Columbus may have shown the king and queen as the *pièce de résistance*, it must have been a powerful incentive, because on 22 May 1492 the Genoan sailor arrived at Palos de la Frontera in southern Spain to begin five months of preparation and recruitment for his first voyage.

Scholars have soberly insisted that the lands referred to in the Treaty of Capitulation were simply Japan and China. They argue that pearls, precious stones, gold, silver and spices were products of the Orient and that no Atlantic tradition of these items existed at the time. We do know, however, that these goods did exist in the New World. Indeed, when Cortez later discovered Mexico City, he was dazzled by the casual display of so much glorious gold. The Spanish conquistador De Soto, in his fruitless wanderings around the Gulf Coast, time and again encountered Indian villages where pearls "were as thick as fat chick-peas."[11] The extensive gold lode existing in the mountains and river valleys of Central America could not have escaped the ancient mariners. Columbus may have read some obscure reference to these riches, but he also must have known about the other riches to be obtained in the form of primitive tribes—tribes that could be easily tapped for slaves.

On Friday, 3 August 1492, Christopher Columbus and three ships sailed for the "islands and mainland" beyond the ocean sea. Samuel Eliot Morison, the late historian and chronicler of the admiral, once asked: "Granted that [Columbus] had to hit land if he kept on going, how did he get back to Spain and what's more, how did he find 'The Indies' again? In other words, how did Columbus know where he was on the surface of the globe?"[12] These are important questions, for once out in the middle of an ocean with no land in sight, some very special skills are needed to find one's way. Did Columbus have talents that other sailors lacked? Hardly. Morison points out that, of the two methods existing in the 1400s for keeping a ship on course—celestial navigation and dead reckoning—Columbus probably knew very little about the former.

Celestial navigation (observing the stars and other heavenly bodies and applying their position to a chart) was a relatively new art in Columbus's day; whereas dead reckoning ("laying down your compass courses and estimating distances on a chart")[13] was a very common and popular navigational method. But its implementation in uncharted waters is quite difficult, because accurate sea charts and compass orientations are needed for plotting course; and for an ocean crossing, an error of only half a degree translates approximately into a 250-mile discrepancy for the expected landfall. We know that a magnetized mariner's compass was taken aboard the Santa Maria, but what type of maps were used? Did the admiral have special charts that other sea captains were lacking? Or did he have what both the French sailor Jean Charcot and Samuel Morison called "*le sens marin*, that intangible and unteachable God-given gift of knowing how to direct and plot 'the way of a ship in the midst of the sea'"?[14]

Whether the gifts Columbus actually took with him were God-given or not is unknown. What we do know is that extracts from his logbook indicate that maps helped him navigate. Eleven days out from the Canary Islands, Columbus

. . . conversed with Martin Alonso Pinson, captain of the other caravel Pinta, *respecting a chart which he had sent to the caravel three days before, on which, as it would appear, the Admiral had certain islands depicted in that sea.* Martin Alonso said that the ships were in the position on which the islands were placed, and the Admiral replied that so it appeared to him: but it might be that they had not fallen in with them, owing to the currents which had always set the ships to the N.E., and that they had not made so much as the pilots reported. The Admiral then asked for the chart to be returned, and it was sent back on a line. The Admiral then began to plot the position on it, with the pilot and mariners.[15]

What islands on what chart? The traditional explanation places Toscanelli's map on board, but there is no evidence for this. These critical questions were raised as early as 1906 by Yale history professor Edward Gaylord

Bourne. Bourne applied the actual mileage Columbus had traveled by 19 October to the Toscanelli map. He found that no islands existed in the region where Columbus reported he was. The professor then went to the ship's log and discovered that the sailors "had been frequently told by [Columbus] that he did not look for land until they had gone 750 leagues (3000 miles) west from the Canaries."[16] But, as Bourne points out, according to the Toscanelli letter, China (or the Orient, the East, India, etc.) was

> . . . 4,500 miles west of the Canaries. Columbus then seems to have expected to find Cipango [China] some 1500 miles to the east of where it was placed on the Toscanelli map. These considerations justify a very strong doubt whether Columbus was shaping his course and basing his expectations on the data of the Toscanelli letter and map.[17]

Columbus had said all along that the distance between the Canaries and the "mainland" was some 3,000 miles. According to his accounts, he expected to find land at that distance, regardless of Toscanelli's 4,500 miles.

The figure touted by Columbus takes on new meaning when we look at a map of the world. The distance from the Iberian Peninsula to America is approximately 3,300-3,500 miles. Was the admiral using information known to no one but him? A few pages later in the journal, there is talk about several other charts and documents. We will never know to which maps Columbus was referring, for only the charts of Martin Behaim and Paolo Toscanelli have survived the centuries. But the admiral's mysterious comments remain to haunt us: "On the spheres that I saw and on the paintings of world-maps . . ."[18]

Soon after arriving in the Caribbean some of the crew scouted Watlings Island in search of water. Not only did they find an adequate supply to quench their thirst, but they also spotted something that whetted their appetites as well. They "found a man who had a piece of gold in his nose, . . . on which they saw letters."[19] The sailors accompanying Columbus were keen-eyed men whose very

life depended upon the close observation of naure's nuances. They were also given to utter fascination with gold.
Seeing a gold piece in a native's nose would alone have
been sufficient information to tell Columbus, but they also
described markings on the nose ring. This detail obviously
impressed the sailors enough to tell their captain. According to all contemporary accounts, the people Columbus
met had no metallurgy, let alone a writing system; so
what letters did the men see? Did any other Indian tribes
use symbols for conveying messages? Our work in northeastern Pennsylvania and northern Maine suggests that
quite a number of tribes had a system of written communication. The intriguing part, however, is that the symbols
used by the Algonquins and the MicMacs, for example,
were the *same* symbols used by certain ancient Mediterranean peoples.

Within thirty years of Columbus's epic voyage, European adventurers had discovered and explored still newer
islands and continents in the Western Hemisphere. Many
Spanish colonies were soon established in the lush valleys
and hillsides of the New World. By 1520 the entire eastern
coast of North America from Labrador to Florida had been
scouted. During this contact period, a good many of the
last vestiges of pre-Columbian civilizations in Central and
South America were surely destroyed by gold-crazed
cavalcades and God-fearing priests. Conquistador Cortez
obliterated the highly sophisticated Mexican Aztecs. His
reaction upon arriving in the New World was typical of
the period: "I have come to get money for myself, not to
till fields like a peasant." Pizarro murdered the Inca rulers
and subsequently destroyed a continental empire. De Soto
wandered throughout Florida and the Gulf Coast ruth-
lessly killing thousands in his vain search for riches.
Within a few years after the arrival of the first Spaniards,
virtually all was destroyed. The Spanish chronicler Bernal
Diaz ominously described a scene which was to plague
Central and South America for decades. "Everything lies
shattered on the ground. Not a thing is left standing
upright."

If ever Central America held the key to the question of a

prehistoric maritime race, it is either still hidden in the jungle or else in ruin. There are, however, some intriguing figurines that somehow managed to survive the wanton destruction of the Spaniards. Ceramic statuettes found in Mexico have features which, according to some researchers, define different population types. So-called Negroid, Nordic, Mediterranean, and Asiatic characteristics have been identified on a wide variety of art pieces. Curious stone statues also exist in the highly inaccessible plains of Peru. Students of the art figurines are convinced that the facial characteristics indicate direct knowledge of people from across the ocean. But just as Samuel Eliot Morison once expressed his weariness of reading so many modern accounts of Mediterranean sailors being blown off course to America (and subsequently planting the seeds of "civilization"), so also should we be weary of the barrage of books whose sole evidence for trans-Atlantic contact consists of legend and artwork.

Though it is certainly true that stories relating to "white gods" and "sailing saints" exist both in Europe and Central America, caution is advised in dealing with them. Briefly, the tradition of a white god in ancient America was a legend first recorded by the Spanish conquistadors. It told of a Great White God who came among the Indians' forefathers, ministered for a while, and then left, vowing to return. The legend had been preserved through generations of Indians from Chile to Alaska, and had likewise been significantly persistent among the Polynesians from Hawaii to New Zealand. Although the traditions differed in name and minor details from island to island and from country to country, the overall outline remained essentially the same. The Great White God of the Americas and the South Pacific was described as a tall white man, bearded and with blue eyes, who wore loose flowing robes. He came from the sea and went back to the sea.

This god was known as Quetzalcoatl in parts of Mexico, primarily in the Cholula area. He was Votan in Cipas and Wixepechocha in Caxasa, Gucumatz in Guatemala, Viracocha and Hyustus in Peru, Sume in Brazil, and Bochica in

Columbia. To the Peruvians he was also known as Con-
tici or Illa-Tici, *tici* meaning both 'creator' and 'the light'.
To the Mayans he was principally known as Kukulcan. In
the Polynesian Islands he was Lono, Kana, Kane, or Kon,
and sometimes Kanaloa, the Great Light or Great Bright-
ness. He also was known as Kane-Akea, the Great Progen-
itor, or Tongaroa, the God of the Ocean Sun.

The enormous geographical range of the white god
legend should give us pause. To believe, as some scholars
do, that the legend is merely the result of an initial story
being diffused upriver via the wanderings of Indian tribes
repeating the mythical tale to other tribes over generations is stretching a rational explanation. Would this one
legend have the greatest distribution of all American
Indian myths if there were not some truth to it? Of course
it is possible that the various traditions all reflect an
ancient memory of the intrepid sailor(s) blown off course.
But legends alone do not prove anything. In fact, if we had
nothing more than a whitewashed story to go on, then we
could easily dismiss the tale as a collective fantasy, as the
Smithsonian did in the last century. In order to substan-
tiate it, we would have to look for material remains which
would suggest a widely spread and long-term physical
presence in the Americas. We would have to look to areas
of the Western Hemisphere that were not systematically
plundered by sixteenth-century Spanish zealots. We
would have to look to North America.

In the Northeast, for example, we have the artifactual
debris of a literate people who built slab-roofed chambers
on mountaintops; we have standing stones in deserted
fields with a full view of the constellations and the
seasonal positioning of the sun; we have partially hidden
passage rooms with entranceway orientations that suggest
a detailed knowledge of astronomy. We have all these
things and more in North America, and when we find a
complex of similar cultural traits in close conjunction
with one another, then the possibility that each trait is a
separate, unassociated phenomenon becomes less and less.

Archeological excavation along the coast of southern

Spain has exposed numerous Phoenician standing stones dating back to the fifth century B.C.—the period when ships from nations other than Carthage were restricted to Mediterranean sailings (see Plates 4 and 5). The dates for the Phoenician stelae are significant; for stones discovered in America along the routes of the major river valleys are inscribed with a Punic script which is stylistically similar to the script found on the Phoenician stelae. The American stones speak of the famous fifth-century navigator, Hanno, Prince of Carthage.[20]

That an Old World writing people visited the major river valleys of North America appears to be so, for other such inscriptions and artifacts have been discovered throughout the northeast. Ceramic jugs found off the coast of New England are identical with amphorae recovered from the Iberian Peninsula at Lagos and Evora, Portugal. Portuguese archeologists have classified their jars as belonging to the Roman period (see Chapter 6). From North Salem, New Hampshire, came a piece of broken pottery which revealed, under an "X-ray, mineral-content analysis," that the composition of the clay had a Mediterranean or Near East geographical provenance.

Now, if Old World travelers actually did sail to America in antiquity, then we must provide some reasons for them to do so. Apart from a possible chance crossing or the throes of wanderlust, what incentives could have persuaded generations of Mediterranean peoples to brave the stormy waters of the Atlantic Ocean? Since the beginning of time, money, in one form or another, has created its own power drive. During Phoenician times great wealth was offered to mariners who ventured forth into unknown territory and returned with new markets or new goods. If a profit was to be made, then no obstacle was too great for a Phoenician merchant.

During the height of Phoenician expansionism, around 1000 B.C., bronze, an alloy of copper and tin, was still an important metal for civilized nations. Although iron smelting was rapidly taking the lead in the production of weaponry, bronze still occupied an important religious and decorative niche in European and Mediterranean cultures, and the necessary tin was probably obtained from three western localities: Cornwall in England, the mouth of the Loire River in France, and the northwestern portion of Spain and Portugal.

For many years, academics assumed that the only way tin could have traveled from Britain and Spain to the Mediterranean was by the overland route. Archeologists and historians had ancient miners loading barges at Land's End, Cornwall, for a 20-mile channel crossing. On the Continent side, Brittany longshoremen, in turn, unloaded the cargo and packed it away on mule caravans en route to the south. This ridiculous scenario was and still is presented in most textbooks to explain the passage of northern tin into the Mediterranean region. Incredibly, most landlubber scholars find a North Atlantic journey by Phoenician seamen to be preposterous and beyond the navigational skills of the sea merchants. Those who doubt the skill of the Phoenicians would do well to recall Strabo's narrative of the secretive Phoenician sea captain, or the exploits of Himilco and Hanno.

Copper was obtained from a number of places. The island of Crete must have been one of the earliest sources, and Spain was another site. But many of the Mediterranean mines—those from Cyprus, Crete, Sinai, and the Rio Tinto River Valley of Iberia, for example—produced a low-grade ore insufficient in quantity to meet the great demands of the Phoenician market. On a global basis, there are relatively few places where a high grade of copper ore exists in large, easily accessible quantities. One such place is North America. Among the regions that yield good copper are Virginia, North Carolina, Tennessee, Georgia, Alabama, and Arizona. Interestingly enough, at each of these locales there is detailed evidence of ancient mining activity. The most active region, however, appears to have been the upper Michigan Peninsula.

On Isle Royale in Lake Superior and in northern Michigan, thousands of worked copper mines were discovered as early as the sixteenth century by French Jesuit missionaries, who reported that the Indians of the peninsula knew absolutely nothing about their origins. In 1849 Dr. Charles T. Jackson, in his geological report to the United States Government, gave the first systematic description of the upper Michigan-Wisconsin mining works. Of one mine approximately 30 feet in depth, Dr. Jackson wrote:

> . . . not far below the bottom of a trough-like cavity, among a mass of leaves, sticks, and water [lay] a detached mass of copper weighing nearly six tons. It lay upon a cob-work of round logs or skids six or eight inches in diameter, the ends of which showed plainly the marks of a small axe or cutting tool about two and a half inches wide. They soon shriveled and decayed when exposed to the air. The mass of copper had been raised several feet, along the foot of the lode, on timbers, by means of wedges.[21]

Within the trench was a 35-pound stone maul and a 25-pound copper sledge. "Old trees showing 395 rings of annual growth stood in the debris, and the fallen and decayed trunks of trees of a former generation were seen lying across the pits."[22]

Jackson went on to detail another remarkable mining site. In the face of a vertical bluff, some ancient people had dug a shaft 25 feet in length, 15 feet high, and 12 feet deep. He reported that some of the stone blocks removed from the recess must have weighed 2-3 tons and required some type of lever to get them out. Once the surface rubbish was cleared away Dr. Jackson found

> . . . the remains of a gutter or trough made of cedar, placed there to carry off water from the mine. At the bottom of the excavation a piece of white cedar timber was found on which were the marks of an axe. Cedar shovels, mauls, copper gads or wedges, charcoal, and ashes were discovered over which "primeval" forest trees had grown to full size.[23]

Although nineteenth-century scholars were totally perplexed by these mines, it was evident that they were all dug by a common people a very long time ago. The mines were said to show the same methods of excavation, the same implements, the same peculiarities both of knowledge and lack of knowledge, and the same amount of debris and growth covering up the openings. But the scientists of the last century were at a loss to identify the "common people" who dug the shafts. In fact, after one hundred years of investigation, the deep tunnels and gaping storage pits of Michigan and Wisconsin remain an intriguing archeological mystery.

The most provocative explanation for the copper mines has been put forth by Henriette Mertz. In her book, *Atlantis: Dwelling Place of the Gods,* which has been prematurely dismissed as nonsense by academics, Ms. Mertz makes a powerful case for ancient Mediterranean activity in North America. Among a great many other items, she points out details about the shafts which are so painfully obvious that it is embarrassing to realize no one else before her noticed them. According to Ms. Mertz, metallurgical engineers estimate that more than a billion pounds of copper were mined out of the Michigan Peninsula and the Isle Royale. She writes:

> This incredible amount of copper has not been accounted for by American archeologists—the sum total according to archeological findings here in the states amounts to a mere handful of copper beads and trinkets—float copper. Five hundred thousand tons of pure copper does not disintegrate into thin air—it cannot be sneezed away—it must be somewhere and, to date, it has not been located in the United States.[24]

Recent carbon-14 dating of organic matter taken from the shafts places them back around 1000 B.C.—just about the time of major Phoenician naval power during the Bronze Age. Ms. Mertz argues that American copper was mined for extensive shipment (presumably by Phoenician ships) to various Mediterranean civilizations.

> At this period of time, Egypt required incalculable amounts
> of copper for tools necessary in pyramid and temple con-
> struction; Greeks likewise stood in need of almost unlimited
> quantities of copper for copper lined the entire interior of
> such structures as the 50 foot dome of the Treasury at
> Mycenae and that at Orchomenus—while roads leading into
> these magnificent edifices blazed with gleaming copper—so
> Schliemann found.[25]

Regardless of how spectacular this hypothesis at first may
seem, its beauty lies in its testability. Samples of copper
saws from the Museum of Cairo or from Crete need only
be analyzed and compared with copper ore from the
American mines in Michigan. There is every reason to
suspect that comparative metallurgical tests would show
remarkable similarities in copper (impurity) composition.

Although not as famous as the Michigan shafts, many
inexplicable mining pits are scattered along the rivers and
tributaries of America's Northeast. There is good reason
to suspect that these obscure mines represent exploratory
tunnels carved out by a people who were searching for
veins rich in minerals sometime before the arrival of the
first settlers. Surrounding these copper, iron, and lead
mines we have been finding personal amulets and inscribed stones. The inscriptions have been identified as
part of a writing system that was used on the Iberian
Peninsula close to three thousand years ago.

It seems that if Christopher Columbus, during his
twenty-year search, found the documents or charts which
pointed the way to the Western Hemisphere, then the
admiral, although a great sailor and exquisite navigator in
his own right, was merely, as it were, a late pupil of
Hanno. The journey across the Atlantic, which added
another half to the world and which eventually led to the
founding of America, may well have been made possible
not by a crafty Renaissance navigator, but rather by a
skilled sailing people thousands of years removed from us.
If so, then to them we should pay our deepest homage.
They have left their ruins all around us.

2

The Structures: Shapes of Time Past

When we speak of America's stone ruins, what structures, exactly, do we mean?

Stone Piles

Historically, stone piles (also called heaps, stone mounds, and cairns) have been found since the earliest white settlements. The first surveyors used them as reference stations, while colonial farmers found the piles very convenient as a source of building stone. Mostly an East Coast phenomenon, stone piles have been reported in a geographical area ranging from Kentucky to northern Canada (see Figure 2.1).

Stone cairns have been found elsewhere in the world. Fifty years ago Bedouin tribes traveled across the Sahara by following little piles of rock set up along caravan routes. Edwardian hunters in darkest Africa often witnessed their cargo bearers adding stones to cairns on ridge tops before descending into a jungle valley. The natives said it assured their safe return. Biblical notations led some to believe that the American and the Middle Eastern cairns were connected. (See Plates 6 and 7). It is easy to understand this, since stone piles are frequently mentioned in the Old Testament as resting near a sacred place where an ancient hero once worshiped.

Stone heaps come in many shapes and sizes. Some are as large as 60 feet in diameter and 8 feet in height, while others are little more than 2 feet by 2 feet. There is good indication that smaller American cairns are merely the result of colonial field clearance. Ox-driven sleds were used in the early 1700s for gathering construction stone. As a wooden platform slid across a field, farmers would collect and pile miscellaneous rocks to be used eventually to construct property walls. Many of the smaller heaps are found near such boundaries. The larger piles, however, are more difficult to explain.

Endless speculation has arisen over the origin and function of the cairns. James Adair, whose *History of the American Indians* appeared in 1775, felt that the Indians "raised those heaps merely to do honour to their dead, and incite the living to the pursuit of virtue."[1] Earlier books all mentioned passing Indians throwing rocks onto existing piles. And even Washington Irving, high above the Hudson River at his dreamy Sunnyside Estate, told a similar story in a fanciful essay entitled "Traits of the Indian Character."

Inevitably, as more men took to the forest, other explanations arose. Richard Smith, writing of the New Jersey Indians in the eighteenth century, noted that "to know their walks again, in infrequent woods, they heaped stones or marked trees."[2]

The insidious thing about these early descriptions is the questionable accuracy of the material and the amount of information borrowed among writers. A fellow would venture into the woods for a few years, return to civilization, and then write a book about his travels. Because it was practically impossible to verify the stories—in the

1700s all land west of Pennsylvania was uncharted wilderness—firsthand accounts were simply accepted as fact; and publishers, realizing the potential market for exciting adventure stories, printed almost anything that would satisfy public hunger for information about the newly settled country. Regardless of descriptive accuracy, if a story contained enough spice, it was widely distributed. Less adventurous, but more imaginative authors then applied these "Indian customs" of popular opinion to a particular tribe in question, and *voila*—another mystery solved and another fortune made.

Explanations miraculously changed with time. A newspaper account from the 1920s spoke of thirsty Indians crouching behind the piles to site various horizon points where water was to be found. Modern property owners often assured MARC investigators that the piles were of recent origin. They dogmatically recited illogical family legends which told of country doctors erecting the stones as animal lookouts and band platforms. Aging mountain men spoke of retarded neighbors who repeatedly heaped stones, knocked them down, and piled them up again. Deer hunters said the old loggers piled them up, while others claimed the charcoal burners of the last century erected them. And some land owners were as surprised as we were to discover cairns on their property. That some piles were revered and were added to by a few Indian tribes has finally been confirmed by modern anthropological work, but the ethnographic data still has not explained the origin and meaning of the custom.

One of the more striking features about stone piles is the great amount of care that went into their construction. Specific stones were selected, chinked, and laid into place. Evidently in many cases the builders took great pains to keep the piles from toppling, for they frequently placed them on top of flat boulders, regardless of the soil condition. (A base rock acts as a platform which prevents piled stones from sinking into the ground and falling over.) Colonial writers reported that Indians *threw* stones on the place of their ancestors. Clearly the good Mr. Adair and others were confusing all stone heaps with the carefully erected piles we are now describing.

In the late 1880s the Smithsonian excavated a mound on a farm near Patterson, North Carolina, and discovered some surprising remains. Agents for the Institution showed that several skeletons and stone piles had been simultaneously buried beneath the earthen mound. The cairns accompanying the skeletons seemed to confirm age-old legends about the sites being repositories for the dead (see Plate 8). One might assume that archeologists would have flocked to other stone pile sites en masse—such obvious "burial markers" rarely occur in American archeology. Yet more than fifty years elapsed before any professional team took on the problem; and when they did, they discovered that all piles are not created equal. In fact, only the odd cairn was a burial site. Almost all others were simply heaps of stone, totally mysterious and without explanation. Archeological interest rapidly faded as the problem was brushed aside and efforts were invested in sites with a far grander provenance.

Now MARC workers have compiled significant character differences between stone piles. Three size categories have been defined:

1. *Small.* Size varies from 3-by-10-foot conical piles to randomly placed 3-by-3-foot compost heaps, probably left by early loggers. Commonly found on old Indian trails.

2. *Medium.* Oval in shape with heights ranging from 2 to 4 feet. Long axis of the mounds runs east-west in the New England states, and north-south in southern New York. Length varies from 10 to 30 feet and width ranges from 10 to 20 feet.

3. *Large.* Usually great circles of rocks and small boulders of varying sizes. Diameters range from 20 to 60 feet with heights varying from 3 to 8 feet at the center. Usually found on top of high ridges.

Conical cairns were found to share some intriguing features (see figure 2.2):

1. Most were erected on large surface boulders.
2. They occur in clusters, ranging from ten to several dozen.
3. A water source—stream, river, swamp, or lake—is always nearby.
4. They're usually found at the upward slope on the east side of hills and mountains.

The quantity of conical piles found in southern New York and New England allowed us to develop predictability patterns for the location of other sites.

Stone piles very often have mysteriously large stone walls nearby. Researchers from Illinois, Tennessee, and West Virginia report that some of these walls are 30 feet wide and 6 feet high. Cairn-wall sites, too, share common characteristics: (1) they are of dry stone construction, (2) they are usually situated on high bluffs, and (3) all excavations completed have yielded no data to suggest they were ever used as burial pits. They are thought to be the remains of some unknown type of ceremonialism.

An archeology report hidden for twenty years surfaced in 1973, a few years after its author's death. In the early 1950s, Frank Glynn, a former editor of a New England journal, excavated two stone heaps along Connecticut's coast. The results of his study, one of the earliest professional excavations of a stone pile complex, were intriguing. For one thing, Glynn found that the heaps were *not* used for burials. At the bottom of a middle-sized heap he found bits of pottery from the Woodland Period (a particular phase of American Indian culture, circa 1000 B.C.-700 A.D.) in conjunction with Late Archaic (7000-1000 B.C.) stone tools. Repeated fires, as well as clam and oyster shells found in successive layers, suggested that the medium-sized oval heaps in southern Connecticut were used for cooking shellfish—kind of oversized barbecue platforms. The purpose of the smaller and larger piles, however, remained obscure.

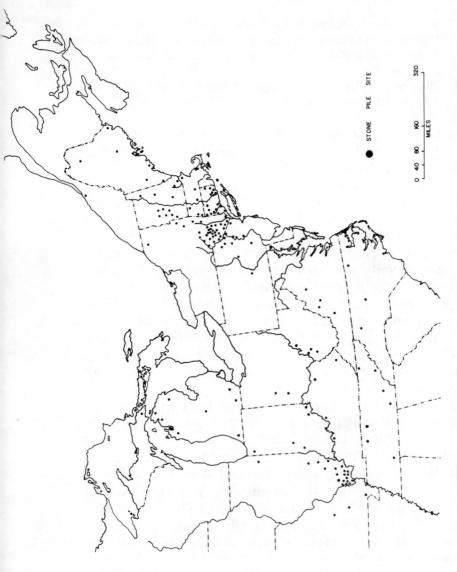

STONE PILE SITE

● STONE PILE SITE

0 40 80 160 320

MILES

Fig. 2.1. Distribution of stone piles in eastern America. (Map by Kalpana R. Shah)

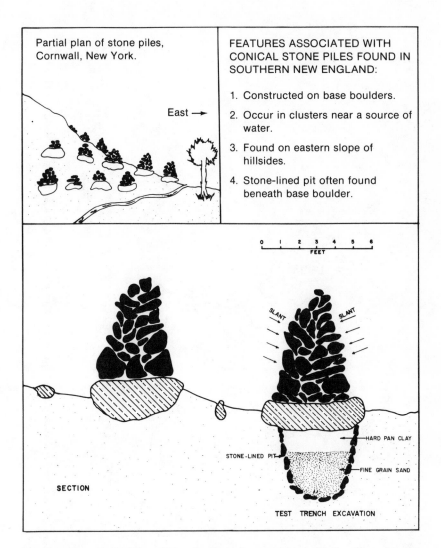

Partial plan of stone piles, Cornwall, New York.

East →

FEATURES ASSOCIATED WITH CONICAL STONE PILES FOUND IN SOUTHERN NEW ENGLAND:

1. Constructed on base boulders.

2. Occur in clusters near a source of water.

3. Found on eastern slope of hillsides.

4. Stone-lined pit often found beneath base boulder.

0 1 2 3 4 5 6
FEET

SLANT

SLANT

HARD PAN CLAY

STONE-LINED PIT

FINE GRAIN SAND

SECTION

TEST TRENCH EXCAVATION

Fig. 2.2. Conical stone piles, Orange County, New York. (Drawing by Kalpana R. Shah)

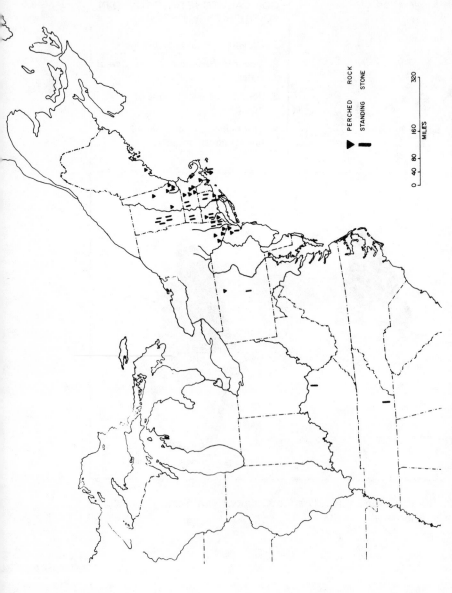

Fig. 2.3. Distribution of perched rocks and standing stones in eastern America. (Map by Kalpana R. Shah)

PERCHED ROCK
STANDING STONE

0 40 80   160   320
MILES

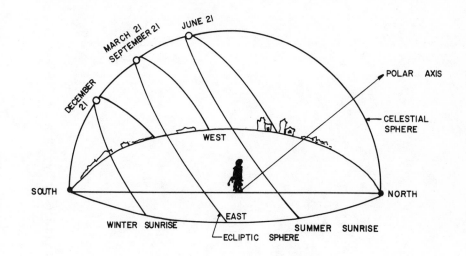

June 21:   Summer   Solstice, $+23.5°$ Declination

March 21:   Vernal   Equinox,   0° Declination

December 21:   Winter   Solstice, $-23.5°$ Declination

September 21:   Autumnal   Equinox, 0° Declination

Fig. 2.4. Daily path of the sun. (Drawing by Kalpana R. Shah)

Fig. 2.5. Distribution of slab-roofed chambers in eastern America. (Map by Kalpana R. Shah)

△ SLAB-ROOFED CHAMBER

0 40 80   160   320

MILES

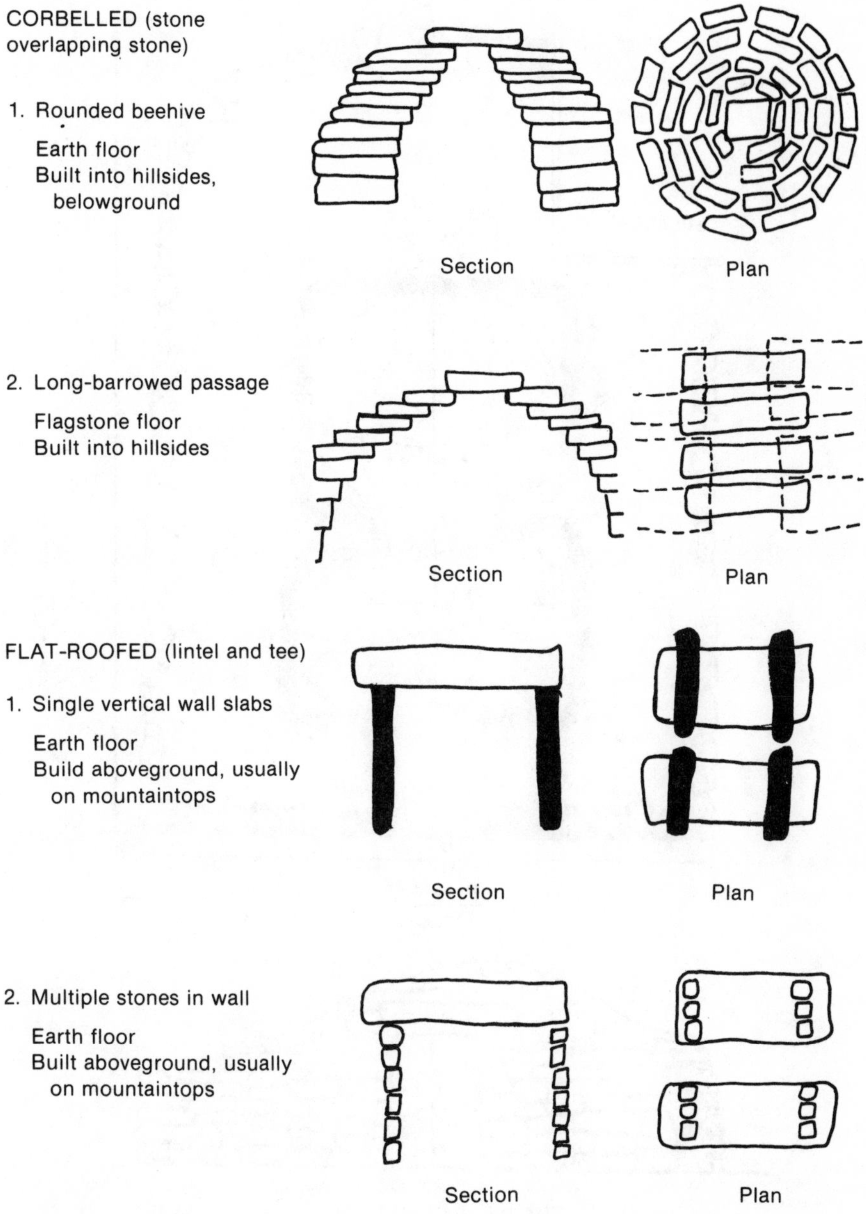

CORBELLED (stone overlapping stone)

1. Rounded beehive

    Earth floor
    Built into hillsides, belowground

Section   Plan

2. Long-barrowed passage

    Flagstone floor
    Built into hillsides

Section   Plan

FLAT-ROOFED (lintel and tee)

1. Single vertical wall slabs

    Earth floor
    Build aboveground, usually on mountaintops

Section   Plan

2. Multiple stones in wall

    Earth floor
    Built aboveground, usually on mountaintops

Section   Plan

Fig. 2.6. Tentative categorization of slab-roofed chambers. (Drawing by Kalpana R. Shah)

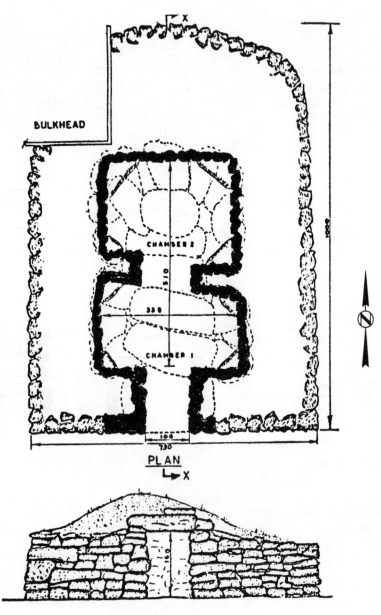

BULKHEAD

CHAMBER 2

CHAMBER 1

PLAN

X

FRONT ELEVATION

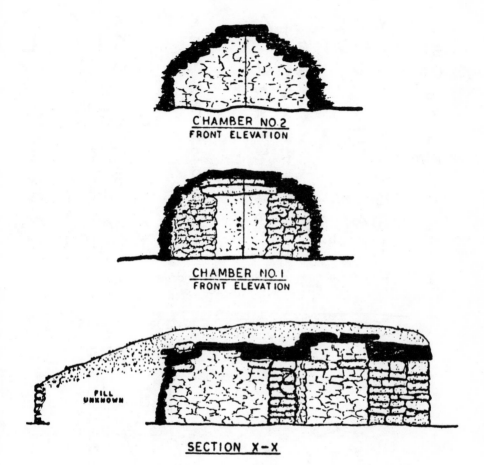

CHAMBER NO. 2
FRONT ELEVATION

CHAMBER NO. 1
FRONT ELEVATION

FILL
UNKNOWN

SECTION X-X

Fig. 2.7. Corbelled stone chamber, North Salem, New York. Nearby barn and farmhouse were constructed in 1710 and 1730 by the ancestors of the family that presently owns the land. Family records indicate that at the time of the first field clearings, the chamber was already standing. (Courtesy of James Whittall and ESRS)

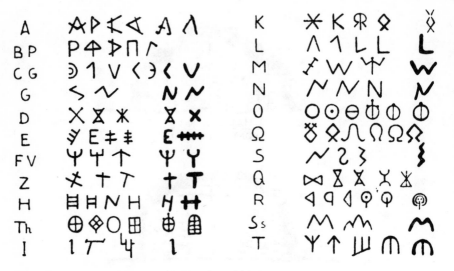

Fig. 2.8. Ancient Iberic signs (Courtesy of Waldemar Fenn)

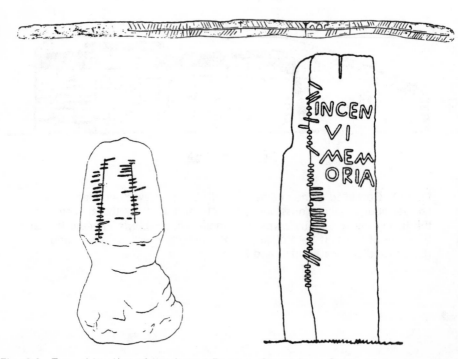

Fig. 2.9. *Top,* side view of the famed Bressay Stone from Scotland showing Ogam script markings. On the face of this slab is an intricate series of bas-relief Celtic carvings. (Daniel Wilson, *Prehistoric Annals of Scotland) Left,* Ogam stone from Silchester, Great Britain, circa 300 A.D. *Right,* Ogam stone from Lewannick, Cornwall, Great Britain, circa 300 A.D. (Horsford, *An Inscribed Stone)*

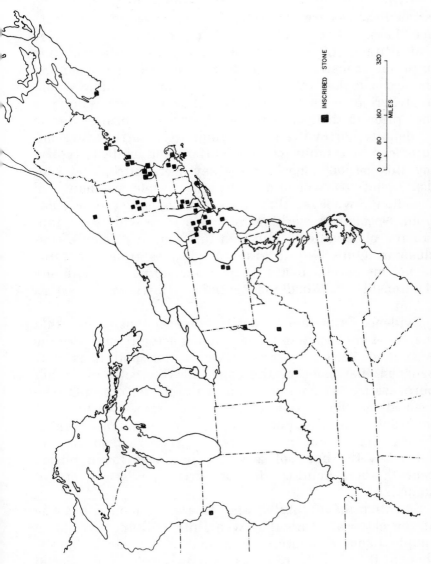

Fig. 2.10 Distribution of inscribed stones in eastern America (Map by Kalpana R. Shah)

INSCRIBED STONE

0 40 80   160   320

MILES

An interesting point about Glynn's work is the association of Woodland ceramics with the piles. Not much is known about the origins of the Woodland peoples who roamed the eastern forests of America close to 3000 years ago. Less is known about their curious style of pottery and artifacts. Elsewhere in the world a definite evolution of pottery construction and design can usually be found in the archeological record. Ceramics from the Middle Woodland Period of eastern America, however, are unique in that prior to their occurrence no stages of local evolution or definite borrowing (or copying) from surrounding cultures can be established. The pottery and artifacts typifying this period suggest that they were introduced suddenly and overwhelmingly by the people we now call Woodland, whoever they were and wherever they came from. Specialists working in this field provide some tantalizing observations, although far from any definite conclusions. Only two geographical locales from about the same time period, 1000 B.C., bear ancient pottery with any relationship to Woodland ceramics: Siberia and western Europe.

Evidence from the far north, however, has shown that the act of constructing stone mounds actually precedes the Woodland Period by several millennia, and it is now believed that some of the cairns were erected for other purposes by yet another unknown prehistoric people who roamed the North American continent some two to seven thousand years ago. For example, near the small village of l'Anse Amour on the eastern edge of Forteau Bay in Labrador, the body of a young boy was found buried beneath three hundred tiny boulders—almost 3½ tons of stone.

Scientists have puzzled over this stone mound because of the elaborate care that went into building it. That a simple band of hunters—presumably Archaic Indians—thought it important to invest so much effort into a burial is amazing. Simply surviving the cold Labrador winters must have been taxing enough. Yet, for some unknown reason, these people got together and left a memorial to their dead. So apparently, over thousands of years, different groups of people saw fit to erect stone heaps. Judging from the meager evidence at hand, however, we cannot simply assume that a filial relationship exists between all American heaps. Just as there are different tools for different chores, there must have been different stone piles for different purposes. And given their worldwide distribution, through vastly unrelated time periods, the act of piling stones may have arisen independently, many times, in many places throughout the history of mankind.

And yet, the problem remains to plague us: *Who* erected the eastern American stone piles and for *what* purposes?

Perched Rocks, Balanced Rocks, Dolmens, Standing Stones, Alignments

Glaciers had a savage effect on America. Some thirty thousand years ago drastic changes in the earth's climate brought arctic weather to the Northeast. An ice sheet thousands of feet thick crept southwards across eastern Canada and New England. Bedrock was scraped, gouged, and carried off by the advancing ice. Each year layers of unmelted snow hardened and added further weight to the glaciers. Ice eventually covered most of northern New Jersey and Manhattan Island before it stopped its southward advance on Long Island. Although it has been over thirteen thousand years since the end of the last Ice Age, the effects of the epoch are still relatively clear.

All glaciers did not melt uniformly when the earth's temperature increased. As the partly frozen sheet retreated northwards, massive chunks of ice broke off and lay isolated, strewn about on bedrock like soil-filled ice cubes scattered across a patio floor. Glacial debris, often consisting of large boulders known as erratics, was deposited over vast areas when the stagnant ice melted. Rocks formerly encrusted within the ice sheet fell free, smashing into each other and creating perfect conditions in the ensuing centuries for rapid soil formation. Steep-sided hills of stratified sand and gravel, known as glacial kames, were formed while potholes in the glaciers filled up with debris.

Glacial ice did melt quite rapidly, however. Heavy rains coupled with increasing meltwater transported large volumes of soil and rock into lowland regions. The abrasive action of weathering wore down many sharp-edged, soft stones into gravel, while hard boulders composed of granite and gneiss often survived into the present period. Boulders tumbled and slid down hillsides, while larger erratics deposited on clifftops remained in place, undisturbed for centuries.

Throughout the millennia, wind, streams, and the destructive effects of repeated freezing and thawing removed much of the base soil beneath many glacially deposited erratics. Erosion left only the more resistant rocks underneath the boulders. Thus perched rocks are very commonly found in areas of past glacial activity, like the Berkshires of New England and the Highlands of southern New York; they are features which the Indians regarded as sacred and which the early white settlers disregarded as meaningless. In fact, quite a number of these structures were probably pushed over cliffsides by good-humored explorers and pioneers. But as geological writer Jerome Wyckoff has stated, "Enough oddly placed rocks remain ... to prompt some people to say 'now who could have done that?'"[3]

Who indeed? When reports of balanced rocks first filtered into MARC's offices, we decided to investigate firsthand, to determine whether these boulders had been perched by nature or by man. On the basis of the archeological work that had been done on Indians in the Mid-Atlantic region, we could only assume that the eastern Algonquin tribes *never* had a tradition of stone placement. And since it is definitely known that melting glaciers did deposit thousands of oddly placed boulders, standing rock slabs, and rows of stones, we initially favored the glacial cause rather than the human cause. It was the simplest explanation, after all.

However, as more and more reports reached our center,

the glacial argument seemed less reliable. An examination of early records and trail guides yielded enticing accounts. For example, Captain Smith in his description of Virginia—a state well below the reaches of the last glaciation—mentions that many Indians had "altar stones" scattered throughout the wilderness; most were erected to offer sacrifices upon after returning from war, hunting trips, or other special occasions. Among the Blackfoot Indians of northwest Canada, says an early encyclopedia, were sacred standing stones, as well as sacrificial altar stones. Human blood was smeared on them in honor of a god. Some were also rubbed against as a cure for barrenness, just as peoples of other cultures, like the Irish and the Syrians, laid themselves on stones to cure a variety of childbearing ailments.

Circles of stones, also thought to be products of glacial erosion, were described in an 1824 issue of the *American Journal of Science.* A geologist reported that a stone circle on a high hill outside the town of Hudson, New York, attracted attention "many years ago on account of the remarkable size of the stones, and their position."[4] The same geologist cited another account of stones he was sure had been placed by ancient man. Termed the Sacrifice Rocks, they were said to be on the side of the road between the town of Plymouth and Sandwich in Massachusetts. Standing between 4 and 6 feet high, they were frequently visited by Indians who made numerous offerings there.

Henriette Mertz, a Chicago attorney who has written extensively about ancient sailing routes to America, uncovered some impressive reports of early pioneers in the Pennsylvania State Archives. In a recently published book she writes:

> When modern man pushed into the interior from Chesapeake Bay someime late in the 17th century and up the Susquehanna beyond Harrisburg, two important markers had been discovered—one standing near the old site of Frank's Town and the other just beyond Huntingdon, marking the proper fork of the river at the confluence. Hunting-

don stands today on a site which in Revolutionary war times was known as Standing Stone. Here at this spot an ancient stone marker once towered on a promontory. Amazed explorers described the stone as an obelisk— fourteen feet high, broad of base, tapering to six or seven inches at the top, covered on all four sides with undecipherable letters, believed by some who first saw it to have been Egyptian hieroglyphics. This stone has frequently been mentioned in Pennsylvania archives—the original disappeared about 1755. This is only one of a great many recorded standing stones that earliest travelers and explorers found marking the trail from the Atlantic to the Ohio by water—a trail of standing stone markers found as far west as Lancaster, Ohio.[5]

These and many other descriptive accounts of peculiar rocks prompted us to search area libraries for more reports on balanced rocks, standing stones, and alignments of boulders. We found that most contemporary scientists simply dismissed many of the accounts as antiquarian folly—reading too much into rocks. Could glaciers have dropped so many rock slabs and big boulders on so many smaller stones on so many mountaintops—even in areas of no glacial activity? (See figure 2.3.) Geologists all along have answered simply, "Yes, they could."

We went to the woods and looked ourselves. MARC workers collected as much field information as possible on balanced boulders, standing stones, and boulder circles, to see if the amassed data suggested either a glacial or nonglacial origin for the stones. Although some of the rocks resting in the valleys of southern New York and Connecticut were found to have been definitely deposited by the glaciers, the positions of many of them could not be attributed to melting ice. Significant, nonrandom details and patterns cropped up time and again (see Plates 9, 10, 11, and 12).

On cliffs high above the rivers of southern and northern New England, surveys revealed triangular configurations of perched rocks. The axes of many balanced boulders and stone circle sites were oriented towards the position on the local horizon where the sun sets on December 21 (the winter solstice). Measurements suggested that a common unit of length was used in placing the stones. Gradually a combination of features hinted at possible astronomical functions for many arranged stones. The positions of nearby cairns and curiously marked rock slabs which later were interpreted as inscriptions implied that something more than nature's playful hand had been at work. As data accumulated, the sites gave the distinct impression of being the ruined vestiges of an ancient solar calendar system.

In the course of twelve months, the sun moves across the horizon on a regular journey (see figure 2.4). On the first day of spring and the first day of autumn, known respectively as the vernal equinox (March 21) and autumnal equinox (September 21), the sun rises due east and sets due west. As summer approaches, sunrise moves further north each day until late June, when it appears to slow, stop, and begin moving southward again. June 21, the day its northward motion stops, is the summer solstice. Half a year later the winter solstice, December 21, signals the end of its southward movement along the horizon. The solstices are unique moments of the year. As soon as two or more sticks or stones are placed in the ground, a visual vantage point is created from which the sun's movement across the sky can be observed. The blatant beauty of such an event becomes acutely obvious as each season's sunlight shifts shadows, changing the tone and character of a land. But the act of marking out the sun's path is not only aesthetic; it is functional as well. The two solstices, once plotted out via some permanent marker, become reference points for devising a solar calendar.

From southern New York, western Connecticut, and central Vermont, came site reports depicting similar arrangements of placed boulders. There were stones protruding out of the ground in clear view of the equinox sunrises and sunsets; perched rocks lying in conjunction with stone semicircles on high bluffs above waterways; and massive dry stone walls running due north-south or towards solstice sunrises and sunsets. Moreover, in Woodstock, Vermont, Byron Dix, an aerospace engineer specializing in the design of sophisticated, high-altitude instruments, uncovered impressive stone ruins which hinted at a sophisticated astro-alignment observatory.

A few scientists in Vermont have reported that most standing stones are probably the result of natural stone erosion. They base their theories on a little known weathering phenomenon associated with a particular type of New England stone, phyllite. Phyllite erodes very rapidly and in a vertical fashion along cracks and natural joints. Standing stones consisting of this type of rock have been routinely dismissed as a by-product of tombstone weathering—so called because sustained erosion splits phyllite into segments resembling tombstones. However, New England standing stones have been found to consist of at least six other types of stone not subject to the unique decomposition pattern of phyllite. These stones must have been shaped and deposited by man.

Our teams discovered that the megalithic yard (2.72 feet) and its divisions and multiplications appear to have been the measurement units used for laying out certain lithic configurations. Along the Shawangunk Mountain Ridge in New York, for example, stone semicircles and cairns were found to zigzag across high hill tops in predictable intervals. It appeared very unlikely that glaciers were responsible for the complex arrangement of perched rocks, standing stones, and alignments we were finding in unique patterns and placements around the countryside.

So we weren't working with glacial debris. But what were we measuring?

When first erected some four thousand to six thousand years ago, the Old World parallels to American structures, known as dolmens (stone tables), often functioned as massive, earth-covered stone tombs. The Balanced Rock in the town of North Salem, New York, rests on limestone supports which extend deeply into the ground. In light of the arrangement of the base stones, as well as the association of nearby inscriptions and stone chambers, the possibility of a prehistoric burial beneath the support stones is extremely high. Similar dolmenlike balanced rocks were found to exist in West Port, Massachusetts, and elsewhere.

On the other hand, many significant arrangements of balanced stones rest on bedrock, thereby excluding the possibility of burial. How are these to be explained? What purpose did perched stones serve? It is clear that a different category of structure exists in many parts of the Northeast, one paralleling western European dolmens on only a very superficial level. The key feature, ground soil for burial, is missing. Unraveling this mystery demanded that we collect and synthesize as much information from the sites as possible, cautiously keeping in mind that, given enough imagination, ostensible similarities from widely separate lands can easily be found.

When all the stone data is seen together, it is strongly suggestive of a homologous, not an analogous, relationship between North America and Europe in prehistoric times. Could a people have sent explorers across the sea and given us a part of their culture, however scattered, however small? Are the stones of America a testament to that ancient crossing?

Slab-roofed Chambers

With slab-roofed, drystone (mortarless) chambers we are out of the category of glacial happenstance and into the domain of man-made certainty. These dirt-covered chambers have gone by many names (See Table 2). Dutch fur traders called them Indian houses. English pioneers knew them as stone huts. William Pidgeon believed the ones he saw were Indian tombs. Late nineteenth-century New Englanders assumed the structures were merely the ingenious product of their ancestors' labor. As a result, generations of Yankee children knew the stone caves as

TABLE 2
Different Names and Functions Ascribed to Slab-roofed Chambers

Name	Function
1. Stone cave	Undetermined, but a common expression among landowners is, "They've always been there"
2. Hermit's shelter	It is believed that during the Great Depression of the 1930s scores of unemployed people took to the woods and set up tiny housing societies
3. Farm outbuildings	Believed to be shelters for nineteenth-century animals and/or farm equipment
4. Slave quarters	Shelters built either by New England slave owners to house the large slave population, or else constructed by freed slaves setting up residence in the North after emancipation
5. a) Colonial house	Temporary shelter for first settlers
b) Colonial root cellar	Storage cellar for vegetable and dairy products
c) Colonial icehouse	Storage of ice blocks
6. Witch hovels	Some New Englanders like to think the Salem witch trials were actually exposing black magic. According to this theory, the stone chambers were the focal point of hideous covenants with Satan; they were "demon huts"

Name	*Function*
7. Iron smelter dwellings	The theory is that in colonial America there was a powerful guild of secret iron forgers who hid away in the forest plotting to overtake the thirteen colonies. The stone chambers were their homes
8. Soldiers quarters	Barracks built by the Continental Army to house the troops
9. Spanish caves	Temporary shelter for fifteenth- and sixteenth-century Spaniards who searched America's shores for gold
10. Fisherman huts and/or fur storage chambers	Supposedly during the thirteenth and fourteenth centuries A.D. Normans, Bretons, Basques and Portuguese fishermen were regularly visiting America's shores in search of good fishing territory and fur producing animals. The chambers were either used as homes for the fishermen-traders or for the preservation of animal skins
11. Irish churches	A band of Irish Culdee monks were believed to have set up a monastery in New England to convert the heathens in the tenth century A.D.
12. Viking houses	Winter quarters of the Norsemen

Name	Function
13. Solar and lunar temples	The preliminary epigraphic work of Fell and others suggests the chambers may have been used for astroreligious rites by Celtic mariners, circa 800 B.C.
14. Neolithic Bronze Age structures	Some investigators see similarities between European stonework such as that at Skara Brae, Scotland, and New England slab-roofed chambers. The Scottish structures date to 3000 B.C.
15. Indian huts	Two variations of the theory: a) function unknown, but thought to be the work of an abortive native culture which attained the ability to work in stone; b) believed to have been used as hideouts by Indian Mastodon hunters!

colonial root cellars—storage pits for vegetable and dairy products.

Around the turn of the century, good-natured, weekend antiquarians offered other explanations for the mysterious stoneworks often found deep within densely overgrown, isolated tracts of the countryside (see figure 2.5). The slab-roofed chambers were thought to be everything from the Spartanlike hovels of tenth century A.D. Irish Culdee monks to the temporary shelters of runaway slaves.

Not surprisingly, the wilder ideas about the chambers have come from the ranks of the romantic and untrained explorer, who sometimes, but not always, has created an exotic atmosphere not palatable to the objective investigator. As a result, the structures have not been adequately dealt with in professional archeological and historical journals.

.Slab-roofed chambers can be divided into two general types: corbelled and flat-roofed. Corbelled chambers (stone overlapping stone in steplike projection so that two converging walls are formed), can be further subdivided into rounded beehive and long-barrowed passage types. Flat-roofed chambers can be subdivided into those whose walls consist of single vertical slabs of stone and those having multiple stones in the walls. They are usually much larger than the corbelled type (see figure 2.6). Corbelled chambers are often constructed with massive slabs of granite, granular quartz, gneiss, or slate, the choice apparently dependent upon the local availability of stone. Floors in most of the barrow-type chambers are covered with thick, 10-20-foot-wide flagstone, while the ground of the smaller beehive and flat-roofed varieties is usually matted with earth. The flat-roofed, boxlike structures are built above ground, usually near the mountaintops, while the corbelled varieties are usually built below the ground and into the upper crests of hills.

On first impression, slab-roofed chambers have all the superficial appearance of Old World megalithic structures. In fact, various similarities have been pointed out between the American structures and Greek Tholos houses of the fourth millennium. But then again, they also remind one of the seventh century A.D. christian churches scattered around the countryside of Ireland and elsewhere. (During the sixth and seventh centuries A.D. single-room dry-stone buildings were quite widespread throughout Europe and the Mediterranean.)

In the past the similarity, with respect to roofing, between New England's stone chambers and Europe's prehistoric megaliths had been touted as the key to a singular example of diffusion, the transmission of ideas from one culture to another. Corbelled vaulting was thought to be evidence of Old and New World cultural exchange. This is simply not so, for corbelling occurred in many different parts of the world in many different time periods. Thus a visual analogy has hindered, rather than aided, objective investigation and understanding of the American stone ruins.

Early in our fieldwork it became obvious that all reported structures had to be examined and measured. A plan was devised to record their respective distances from one another to determine if site location influenced architectural design. We needed to know if there existed local and regional distributions of chamber types in order to see if the same construction techniques were used. We also needed information pertaining to the farmlands where many of the sites were located. Entranceway orientations were also collected at most chambers in the event that the data might be useful. This last piece of information later proved to be the most valuable of the data amassed by MARC workers.

What, then, are these mysterious, slab-roofed monuments? Some of the many conjectures as to their origins and functions are summarized in Table 2. In recent years, however, few of the theories and speculations put forth by archeologists have adequately explained them. Unfortunately there are not many firsthand accounts from the colonial period to refer to. Only a few documents speak of chambers at all, and those are buried deep within musty archives and filled only with the vaguest references to "man-works."[6] Months of searching by our library teams produced only a handful of definite notations. This is odd. If the structures are provisional, storage, animal, or slave shelters from the colonial period, then the vast number of similarly built chambers found in a geographical area ranging from New York to Canada suggests that a very popular construction design was used in each case. That in two to three hundred years of American growth absolutely no recollection of this technique, either written or oral, has come down to us is extemely puzzling and disturbing. If the structures are from the seventeenth, eighteenth, or nineteenth centuries, what does this say about cultural amnesia?

On the other hand, if the colonists did not erect the slab-roofed chambers, but simply took advantage of their presence, why didn't more people write about them? Perhaps the pioneer's view of existence precluded any serious introspection. Perhaps later generations of settlers "forgot" the structures were even there—they knew them as always having been there. The chambers were ordinary, common, and as unworthy of detailed description as a barn side. Add to this the massive emigration to the Midwest following the poor crop yields of the early 1800s, and we have the perfect social conditions for lost knowledge.

The first pioneers had to contend with severe environmental conditions. Dwellings had to be erected as quickly as possible in order to ward off inclement weather and hostile Indian groups. Vast expanses of densely wooded forest had to be cleared, plowed, planted, and nurtured before any food could be coaxed from the land. As a result, the earliest rural buildings in America reflect the original, home-country traditions of the first colonial people who settled each locale—if they were able to erect buildings. According to Thoreau's account, many of New York's earliest Dutch settlers built and occupied pit dwellings long before they were able to afford above ground accommodations. "They burrow themselves in the earth for their first shelter under some hillside, and casting the soil aloft upon *timber*, they make a smoky fire against the earth, at the highest side."[7]

In 1650 the Dutch Secretary of the Province of New Netherland released information to those settlers who wished to take up land in the New Amsterdam and New England area but who had no means to build a farmhouse. He stated that a square pit should be dug, cellar fashion, 6-7 feet long and as broad as they needed. The interior of the hole should then be lined with wood and bark to prevent the earth from caving in. Wooden planks were to be placed on the floor and overhead. The entire structure was to be then covered with green sod. It was said that the first "wealthy and principaled" men of New England built initial homes in this fashion "in order not to waste time in building, and not want food the next season, and in order not to discourage poor laboring people whom they brought over in numbers from the Fatherland."[8] The details of home construction listed in the report preclude any supposed similarity between slab-roofed structures and the earliest pit dwellings—a lot of time and energy went into the building of the former edifices, and the latter were of wood, not stone.

While the fundamentals of building construction originated in Europe, regional conditions and the amalgamation of nationalities in the New World produced unique and sometimes puzzling situations. New England, for example, which had as much stone as the Mid-Atlantic region and which was settled almost entirely by the English, never had a house tradition of stone construction. Wooden mortise and tenon techniques were the primary home-building heritage of these settlers. The first English, Scottish and Irish farmers, who were already well acquainted with drystone work—as the numerous walls crisscrossing the mother country testified—seemed to prefer the hardwood of chestnut trees for their earliest homes. The Dutch and German settlers of the Mid-Atlantic states, however, after leaving their Manhattan dugouts, insisted upon stone as a building material wherever it was available. Much later, in the 1850s, stone ceased to be common material for house construction, except for foundations. These curious ethnic details have often been overlooked by past investigators.

If we are to believe the "root-cellar hypothesis" (that is, that the structures were built by the colonists merely to store root crops like onions and radishes), then surely we should find numerous remnants of stone chambers on land originally occupied by Dutch immigrants, given their penchant for stone construction. Interestingly, MARC researchers discovered that the highest frequency of slab-roofed chambers occurred east of the Hudson River in New England terrain, while the lowest frequencies occurred west of the river in the Mid-Atlantic region—the area of initial Dutch settlement. It seems odd that the

English farmers would build their homes out of perishable wood and their storage areas out of durable stone, while the Dutch farmers built their homes of mortared stone and had their root cellars below the foundations (see Plate 13).

The scant records available eventually gave us the distinct impression that New England farmers were blessed with hundreds of existing stone chambers. An interesting report from Maine, for example, appeared in Eaton's *History of Rockland and South Thomaston*. On the property of an early settler in what is now the town of Cushing on the Georges River, an "old cellar" 40 feet in length and 9 feet in depth was found on a point projecting into the river. A "subterranean passage" led from the main structure into a nearby cove.

The intriguing thing about this passage, aside from the description of a slab-roofed chamber, is the author's comment that the structure "appears to have claims to much greater interest than is usually attached to *that class of ruins.*"9 The statement presupposes an awareness of "ruins" and implies that these ruins were a part of accepted knowledge.

The same idea was suggested in Vermont, where MARC teams collected testimonies of retired farmers who told of horses falling into "field caves" and "stone-lined" pits. They recounted stories of their great-grandfathers' plows uncovering stone huts that "looked like they'd always been there." It appears that English settlers east of the Hudson River were more fortunate than their Dutch counterparts. Many of their "root cellars," "animal shelters," and "tool sheds," it seems, were already standing in the wilderness upon their arrival!

New England Antiquities Research Association (NEARA) investigator Elizabeth Sincerbeaux uncovered an intriguing account of the "man-works" of the Charles River Valley of eastern Massachusetts in a privately published pamphlet of 1895 entitled *An Inscribed Stone*, by Cornelia Norton Horsford. During the summer of 1894 Ms. Horsford invited Dr. Franz Boaz and Mr. David Boyle of the Canadian Institute at Toronto to visit her sites in and around Norfolk, Massachusetts. For a number of years Ms. Horsford had been compiling data on the mysterious slab-roofed chambers so abundant in that region. As a result of their investigation both men "declared that these works were neither the work of the Eskimo nor of the Canadian Indians."[10] Subsequently a Mr. Gerald Fawke and Mr. W. J. McGee, then in charge of the Bureau of Ethnology at the Smithsonian Institution, spent about five weeks examining the structures. Both of these gentlemen said that "collectively and with but one or two exceptions individually, these works differed more or less, but always distinctly, from anything they had previously studied, and that they could not be classed with the works of any race known to them."[11]

The account is remarkable for two reasons. Firstly, Franz Boaz, an early investigator of the American ethnographic scene, always let the data speak for itself. His method involved collecting as much material as possible about a particular problem before concluding anything. If these curious "man-works" were of colonial origin, then surely the inquisitive Boaz would have found out. Secondly, it is highly unlikely that Mr. McGee of the Smithsonian was unaware of that institution's own Thomas Report on America's stone enigmas, published in 1894. Scholars all over the country had been anxiously awaiting its delayed publication for years as Thomas struggled to amass all the mound data. Mr. McGee's implied statement that the stone structures of Massachusetts were not the work of the American Indians is indicative of the differing scholarly opinions within the Smithsonian. Not everyone was as convinced as Cyrus Thomas and his superiors that the Indians had something to do with all of the stone ruins in the United States.

Several years ago the possibility was raised that the northeastern stone chambers were the work of an abortive American native culture which for an undetermined, but nonetheless finite, period of time, developed considerable skill working and carving in stone. This is sheer speculation, for nothing in the historical or archeological record of the region testifies to this. Furthermore, aboriginal homes were made of bark and animal hides, not stone. Two types of Indian dwelling units prevailed throughout the northeast: the wigwam and the longhouse. The more common wigwam was formed by a framework of curved trees bent over and tied together with bark rope. Strips of bark and grass covered the saplings. Mud closed up air cracks. A hole in the top of the hut was left open to emit smoke from a centrally burning fire. Instead of a round framework, the longhouse consisted of a rectangular skeleton of arched poles. As in the wigwam, bark and grass also covered the frame, which sometimes extended up to 100 feet. Excellent firsthand descriptions of these dwellings by such early explorers as Verrazano and Henry Hudson, combined with our previous documentation, make it clear that the Indians who greeted the pioneers were in no way responsible for the slab-roofed stone chambers spread through the Northeast.

As for the claim that the chambers were vegetable storage areas, an understanding of colonial techniques of putting food by undermines it. In colonial times proper food storage was of great importance, as it still is in some of the colder, rural areas of the United States today. Our ancestors stored their produce in basements, cellars, outbuildings, and pits. This was the easiest and least expensive method for preserving the summer and fall harvest. But more than that, it was important for their winter survival.

Proper root cellaring required a cool, moist, enclosed area. Into the face of a hill or bank the colonist would dig a 2-by-4-foot-deep space, extending upwards at a slight incline. The open end of the cellar, where a wooden door or leather hide was attached, slanted downwards so rainwater would not enter the space. Any large stones within the pit had to be removed so that frost could not be conducted into the storage area. Cellars constructed below the ground were better than aboveground outbuildings because they maintained a desirable temperature longer and more uniformly than aboveground structures. In both cases a system of ventilation to control temperature and humidity had to be devised. The walls of the underground cellar had to be strong enough to support the weight of the insulative earthen roof. In many cases mortar not only reinforced the crude cellar, but it also helped insulate it by sealing up any damaging air drafts. Aboveground storage buildings were built of masonry or lumber. In either case they had to be well insulated with sand, straw, or hay.

Lime kilns, from which mortar was produced by the burning of limestone, were one of the earliest structures constructed by the pioneers. The kilns were easy to build, and their product made foundation work much easier—it takes less work to place and set several small stones with mortar than it does to quarry, move, and set 2-ton boulders. Thus it is not uncommon throughout the Northeast to see mortar-covered root cellars, which, incidentally, look nothing like slab-roofed chambers.

Slab-roofed chambers were not built by the colonists as root cellars. Many are located deep in the woods away from the nearest farm or barn site; and, as we have already seen, some of the early site reports speak of their existence upon the arrival of the first settlers. The placement angle of many chambers also precludes their use as root cellars. Many of them slant *downwards* into the banks of hillsides, which increases the chances of water seepage. Further, we know that rocks, marvelous conductors of frost, had to be taken out of the storage space, because frost can destroy a season's harvest. Yet all of the remote chambers recorded by MARC had no trace of mortar or any other insulative material. The walls were bare, cold stone—better to preserve dead bodies than to preserve delicate produce.

There has been some speculation that the slab-roofed chambers were colonial winter tombs—storage areas for corpses that had to wait for the ground to thaw before they could be buried. This is an exciting hypothesis, but unfortunately one which does not fit the known distribution patterns of the structures. It was just as cold west of the Hudson River as it was to the east, and, presumably, just as many people died on both sides of the river. Why, then, does the highest frequency of chambers occur in the New England region? If they were temporary crypts, then why were they built so close together? It is not uncommon to find clusters of eight to ten chambers along a three-quarter mile walk. Furthermore, MARC researchers have found only one nineteenth-century document which *may* be referring to chambers as tombs.

The size of most chambers reveals some interesting data. In Putnam County, southern New York, there are ten corbelled, long-barrowed structures scattered on both sides of a 1½-mile stretch of rural byway. One of the chambers on the road is typical of the structures found there. Its average width is 10 feet, its height is 6.5 feet, and its length is 27 feet, giving an approximate "storage" area of 1755 cubic feet. According to the United States Department of Agriculture, approximately 6 cubic feet of food-storage space is needed to keep the average urban dweller alive for one year. For a farmer, because of the greater expenditure of energy involved in performing chores, approximately 10 cubic feet of space is needed. If we assume the ten chambers were originally built as colonial root cellars, then we can calculate the maximum amount of cubic storage space available and then estimate the maximum number of people who could have been supported by the stored food:

> 1755 cubic feet per chamber x 10 chambers = 17,550 cubic feet (the maximum food storage area along 1½ miles of road)

Since 10 cubic feet of food space is needed per rural person, we can estimate the maximum number of people who could have utilized the stored food:

> 17550 cubic feet ÷ 10 = 1755 people

That's a lot of people for a small farm to feed, considering the fact that during revolutionary times the level of farm technology was such that one farmer could only hope to feed four people. Were there ever 1,755 people living along this particular Putnam County road before the present day? Extensive census research shows this hypothetical figure to be ridiculously high. The total population of the region surrounding the chambers was only 1,598 in 1845, and before that it was considerably less. Are we to assume that the highest density of the valley's potential population was situated along a 1½-mile road?

The doubtful status of the root cellar hypothesis becomes even more evident when we travel just 5-7 miles northeast of the road. In the area around Mahopac, New York, we find a similar situation. Scattered in the forest are scores of corbelled, long-barrowed chambers (see figure 2.7). In fact, in Putnam County we have defined at least forty similarly designed structures. If all these chambers served as root cellars, then who was using the roots? The figures make these so-called storage bins seem like colonial supermarkets! On the basis of the census data, we can be reasonably sure that the local population did not originally construct the chambers as root cellars. Storage and shipment of produce to other parts of the state can be ruled out as a possibility because the poorly laid, dirt-mud roads of the eighteenth and nineteenth centuries made travel difficult and oftentimes impossible. There was also no merchant tradition of long distance "trucking" of food in colonial America.

To assume that the chambers were constructed as icehouses, as some scholars believe, also does not make sense. If we apply our cubic area calculations to ice storage, we come up with enough ice in southern New England to create a glacier.

Some new thought has been given to the slab-roofed chamber enigma by Alfred M. Bingham, an attorney and former member of the Connecticut State Senate. Mr. Bingham has written a well-researched article suggesting that the chambers were merely the dwelling units erected by freed New England slaves. In isolated examples, the idea is attractive, but it doesn't necessarily explain the wide distribution of similarly styled chambers throughout *all* of New England.

It is shocking for many Americans to realize how extensive was the slave population of the North. In the eighteenth century the slave trade was New England's greatest and most lucrative industry. New England rum was shipped to Africa, where it was exchanged for slaves who were shipped to the West Indies. There they were exchanged for molasses which in turn was shipped to New England distilleries and made into rum for export to Africa. As a by-product of this triangular trade route, slaves were used on many New England farms. By 1750 black slavery was firmly established in many northern states. But soon afterwards, due to changing economic conditions, poor crop yields from soil-exhausted farms, and changing sympathies, many slaves were simply set free by their white owners. While many of the poorly equipped blacks died of hunger and exposure, some survived long enough to build small houses out of wood, not stone.

Bingham believes otherwise. He has freed slaves, with nothing more than their bare hands and the will to survive, erecting slab-roofed chambers as temporary or permanent squatter dwellings. What Mr. Bingham overlooks is that barehanded slaves didn't just pick up 1,000-pound, 7-by-1-foot granular quartz slabs and cart them off with no tools. The slabs had to be quarried out of bedding planes. Oxen (or a suitable number of men), rope, bars, levers, and an assortment of other gadgetry must have been needed to move the stones. It is highly improbable that the slaves' former masters supplied them with these expensive items before they were freed. It would have been far easier for the men to build simple lean-to's or wooden frame huts than to build with stone.

A few of these slab-roofed chambers have been partially excavated. A corbelled, long-barrowed chamber from Newton, New Hampshire, reportedly had a radio carbon date of 850 years B.P. (plus or minus 140 years),[12] while a test run on another nearby chamber placed it well within the colonial period.[13] The vastly different dates undoubtedly reflect the competence and quality of the excavators and excavations. A beehive structure from Vermont produced no precolonial artifacts after an initial test-trench excavation was begun by New England archeologist James Whittall during the summer of 1976. However, Whittall was only able to excavate the chamber's entranceway and not its interior.

There is good reason to suspect that detailed archeological evidence for the great antiquity of some of the chambers will be found once a full-scale excavation is carried out. We believe this is so because Byron Dix's remarkable calculations from central Vermont have revealed the hidden and esoteric meaning of several slab-roofed chambers. Two years of work at a New England site convinced Dix and his colleague, Elizabeth Sincer-beaux, that they were onto something important. Near the town of Woodstock, Vermont, the engineer set up an equatorial mount telescope and began to record the sun's path across the sky. The beauty of this instrument is that, once a few simple measurements are taken, the sun's position in the heavens for any time of day, twelve months of the year, can be calculated. Dix discovered that the declination angle of the long axis of the chamber was -23½ degrees. Putting this simply, he found that the slab-roofed chamber near Woodstock was built so that a person sitting inside the rear end of the structure could observe the sun rise on the shortest day of the year from a "notch" on the eastern horizon (see Plates 14 and 15). The shortest day of the year is December 21, the winter solstice.

Further investigation in other parts of the countryside led to the discovery of more than thirty similarly aligned stone chambers. At many sites surrounding the slab-roofed structures were carefully placed standing stones which, in turn, were lined up with specific horizon features to mark the sunrise and sunset during the four major yearly positions of the sun—approximately, the twenty-first of March, June, September, and December. Dix amassed impressive data which suggested that the early builders of the chambers had also utilized the moon's pathway across the night sky in choosing the locations and dimensions of their buildings. The length of the chamber and the width of the entranceway were a function of the amount of moonlight entering it over an 18.61-year cycle. Multiples of the megalithic yard cropped up again and seemed to have been used in erecting certain stone structures. Some of the slab-roofed chambers from southern New York and western Connecticut appear to conform to Byron Dix's calculations. The possibility that in both locales they were oriented along similar axes purely by chance is very unlikely.

In 1975 Dr. Barry Fell visited the slab-roofed chambers of central Vermont and added his own analysis as to the identity of the builders. At a site where Dix had plotted out the winter solstice, Fell looked at some nearby markings on a rock outcropping and exclaimed, "That's Celtic Ogam!" Within a few minutes the Harvard professor made a preliminary, but nonetheless startling, translation: "winter observation pillar." This was quite surprising, for Dix had told no one about his exciting calculations. In fact, he was still preparing the results of his study for a scientific paper. On a nearby standing stone which Dix believed marked out the equinox sunset, Dr. Fell translated some etchings cut across the stone as "the eye of Bel." This was shocking, for Bel was the Celtic sun god.

What was the purpose of these slab-roofed chambers?

Inscriptions

Throughout the millennia various cultural, ecological, and geographical factors have tended to channel human thought and expression into many different types of writing schemes. The first writing systems seem to have been designed to meet the specific needs of their creators— Babylonian laundry lists abound. But in time, simple expressions took on broader, more provocative meanings. Within certain bounds, people having a written language could silently communicate with others sharing the same mode of expression. Societies were able to record their doings and pass them on to later generations. Secrets learned from the trials and errors of one age could be transmitted through time to the next. During the Bronze Age in the Mediterranean, there existed hundreds of forms of script. Some continued to be used by peripheral cultures on the fringes of the Middle East, northwestern Spain and Ireland, while others passed into disuse and oblivion. The only one to survive the centuries has been our own.

Interest in ancient languages began with the explorations of the fifteenth, sixteenth, and seventeenth centuries, which fostered a new sense of antiquity throughout the Old World. Travelers came home with fantastic stories about strange inscriptions from such countries as Egypt, Greece, and the Americas. Speculations about these exotic markings were at first fanciful and then mystical. But these "explanations" had no place in late eighteenth-century Europe when scholars began to codify and classify the mass of curios collected from diverse regions of the globe. A critical, comparative sense was emerging. It was during this time period that the so-called great age of decipherment had its beginnings.

Epigraphy, or the study of inscriptions (particularly ancient ones), is a sociological pheonomenon specific to the modern world. As Oxford Professor Maurice Pope has noted, only in the last two or three centuries have men set out to recover the key to writing systems.

As one might suspect, there are a host of technical terms and definitions specific to epigraphic analysis. For our purposes it is unnecessary to detail all of these items, but there are a few which should be clarified. The term *script* refers to a total writing system, complete with its punctuation, special symbols, and different phonetic values. A script is usually made up of an *alphabet*, which is a set of letters each having a particular way of being pronounced. A *language*, in contrast, is the method of communication used between people.

To *decipher* means to explain the individual signs of a script. It does not mean understanding the message expressed by it. In the words of Professor Pope, "Decipherment opens the gate, interpretation passes into the field beyond."[14]

The people with whose inscriptions we are most familiar range from those who settled Europe to those who settled North Africa. The fate of the lands in the western Mediterranean was essentially determined by these settlers who came from the sea. As early as five thousand years ago Neolithic tribes sailed along the Atlantic seacoast and built massive stone monuments.[15] The Iberian Peninsula (modern Portugal and Spain) was subject to several waves of immigrant peoples. The peninsula natives, appropriately known as Iberians, suffered the onslaught of Celtic tribes that swept through the Pyrenees from the east. Under the brutal discipline of these hordes, a new form of culture took root. A curious blending of Celtic and Iberian art and stonework known as Celt-Iberian developed and flourished. Powerful trading outposts, such as the Kingdom of Tartessos in the southwestern part of the peninsula, maintained strong economic ties through gold and copper with the merchant Phoenicians. About the same time, groups of Libyans from the North African coast sailed to Iberia's fertile Andalusian plains and began to lay the foundations of an intensive agricultural system in southern Spain.

Thus by the late Bronze Age a variety of "foreign peoples" were mingling with the native Iberians—the Celts, the Libyans, and finally, the Phoenician-Carthaginians. According to epigrapher Barry Fell, the writing systems these groups supposedly brought with them underwent dialectic changes when they came in contact with the native Iberian language.

Mediterranean scholars have long puzzled over Iberic script (see figure 2.8). Although it was deciphered over fifty years ago, no one could read the language until 1975 when Dr. Fell first claimed he had worked out the script—curiously enough, from American examples on Susquehanna field stones—by reading it as Basque.[16] Fell then examined inscriptions from Spain and argued that he was able to differentiate between native Iberic script and script that had been written by the Libyans living there. Moreover, this writing system was found to be a Libyan dialect of the Carthaginian Punic language. It appeared further that some ancient scribes wrote this Iberian Punic, as he called it, with the alphabet of the early Basques (Iberic script), while others wrote it in the more familiar Semitic alphabet of the early Greeks.

But Fell didn't stop there. He also said that the many Celt-Iberian inscriptions, which had also baffled Spanish scholars for centuries, were in fact Iberian versions of what would later become known as Goidelic Celtic, the language of the Celtic peoples of Ireland and the Scottish Highlands (to be distinguished from the pre-Saxon Brythonic Celts of Brittany, Wales, and England, who spoke a different tongue).[17] The Celt-Iberian research also suggested a totally revolutionary theory—that the Celtic alphabet, known as Ogam, originated in Iberia around 800 B.C. and then spread north to Ireland (see figure 2.9). The orthodox view is that the Irish in the fourth century A.D. invented it and used it for simple mnemonics or gravestone inscriptions.

With only one exception, letters of the Ogam alphabet were represented by straight lines that derived their significance from their position on a continuous horizontal or vertical line. The Celt-Iberian alphabet differed from the British Ogam in that it was vowelless but other than a few consonantal differences, the alphabet, according to Fell, appeared on stones in stylistically the same manner as the Irish Ogam of the fourth century. In summary, Fell now feels (1) that he has partially "cracked the code" of Iberic inscriptions from northern Portugal and Spain on the basis of Iberic inscriptions found in America; (2) that in ancient Iberia the Punic language was written with native Iberic letters like those used in inscriptions presently being uncovered in America; and (3) that a hitherto unrecognized form of alphabet called Celt-Iberian Ogam has simultaneously come to light in the western Mediterranean and North America.

The discovery of inscribed stones in the United States

has had a long and embittered history marred by forgeries, professional tirades, blind ambition, cover-ups, and
academic tiptoeing. Hundreds of tablets with various
types of markings have been reported since colonial days
(see figure 2.10) but for one reason or another—the conditions under which the inscriptions were found or their
inaccessibility after discovery—most were simply ignored.
Scholars accepting the established scenario of an isolated
American continent could consider only two possibilities
for stones etched with an ancient European script: they
were forgeries, or they were authentic but had been
brought to America and planted in modern times. The
framework of scientific thought under which these academicians worked allowed no other conclusions. The pa-
rameters of logic could not be extended to include a third
alternative: that the stones were authentic and had been
deposited in pre-Columbian times by visiting people.

In recent years a craftier explanation has been offered to
account for the hundreds of marked stones found in the
eastern section of the country. Archeologists with no
background in ancient script analysis have routinely
dismissed the stone markings as by-products of such
accidents as natural erosion, impressions of growing tree
roots winding across a stone's surface, or scratches from
eighteenth-century field plows. On these grounds many
potential inscriptions have been overlooked.

That a few inscribed stones have in the past been faked
is undeniable. The motivations of the forgers were many:
some sought to confuse the historical record and subsequently ruin the careers of their naive colleagues, while
others deceived early museums and universities merely
for profit or fun. Bad publicity associated with bogus
stones has tended to enhance the doubts of the ultracon-
servative academic community. But most of these fake
stones are unique in quality, and this singularity is the
key element which makes them suspect. Furthermore, as
the noted Semiticist Dr. Cyrus Gordon acidly remarked in
his *Riddles in History*, to doubt the authenticity of the
multitude of inscriptions brought to light in the Western

Hemisphere, "it has become necessary to demonstrate a plot stretching at least from 1872 to 1971 [and now to 1978]. A ring of forgers or pranksters must be shown to have operated in Brazil, Minnesota, Maine, and Europe."[18]

One might still ask, have there ever been any ancient inscriptions found *in situ* with an archeological assemblage present? An engraving of an inscribed tablet excavated from a burial mound at Bat Creek, Tennessee, by Cyrus Thomas was published in the 1894 volume of the *Twelfth Annual Report to the Secretary of the Smithsonian*. The circumstances of the find suggested that there was no intrusion after burial. That is, once the mound was sealed, it wasn't opened up again until Thomas arrived on the scene (see Plate 16). The symbols on the stone were abruptly dismissed in the report as "beyond question, letters of the Cherokee alphabet." Cherokee was a syllabary devised in 1821 by an Indian chief after his return from England. The characters consisted of eighty-five inverted and transformed Roman letters combined with some European numerals and a few arbitrary characters.

The matter rested there until 1964, when, seventy years after the report was published, Henriette Mertz pointed out that the Smithsonian Institution had mistakenly published the engraving of the stone upside down. When Ms. Mertz simply turned the illustration around, the Semitic characters etched onto the artifact became strikingly obvious (see Plate 17). Cyrus Gordon, who later investigated the stone, concluded that the inscription had been carved in a style of Hebraic script that was used in the Middle East around 100 A.D.[19] Professor Gordon has done more than any other scholar to prove the authenticity of this one inscribed tablet. His writings on the matter express more than scholarly insight. They shadow the painful risks he has taken by publishing nonorthodox views. A number of academicians have reprimanded him for expressing the following views about the Tennessee stone excavated by Thomas.

The Bat Creek inscription . . . is not a souvenir imported from the Old World after 1492 to gratify some Cherokee Chief's love of East Mediterranean archeology—a love so great that he took the inscribed stone with him for eternity in the next life. The script was not even deciphered until the nineteenth century. Trying to explain away the Bat Creek evidence as anything other than American contact with Palestine around the second century A.D. can only amount to obscurantism. . . . The significance of the excavations at Bat Creek is that they attest inscriptionally and archeologically to a migration in early Christian times from Judea to our southeast.[20]

At Grave Creek, West Virginia, in 1838, another inscribed tablet was found at the bottom of a 60-foot mound. Henry Schoolcraft, a distinguished nineteenth-century historian, mentioned it in his voluminous work on the American Indian. "This curious relic . . . appears to reveal, in the unknown past, evidences of European intrusion into the continent."[21] Copies of the inscription were sent to several European scholars. Most of them dismissed it as nonsense. Professor Rafn of Copenhagen, however, declared quite confidently that the markings were Celt-Iberic. This is extremely interesting, for, in 1976, Barry Fell looked at the inscription and independently proclaimed it to be a form of script used by the Celts in Spain more than three thousand years ago.

In the New World, as in the Old, there are countless markings on rocks that tell a story spanning millennia. If handled properly, they could reveal the keys to the diffusion of culture from the Stone Age to Columbus (see Plate 18).

What do they say? And who wrote them?

3

Stone Mysteries: Northeastern Pennsylvania, Northern New Jersey, Southern New York

Table 3 and figure 3.1 indicate generally the distribution and kinds of artifacts and structures which are discussed in this chapter.

A. Susquehanna River Valley

The Susquehanna River is the longest river in the eastern United States that flows into the Atlantic Ocean. Its two main tributaries, the West and East branches, cut through the Appalachian Plateau of northeastern Pennsylvania. The West Branch rises in the western slopes of the Alleghenies before looping east-southeast for about 200 miles, the East Branch originates in New York State before flowing southward for 250 miles. The Susquehanna is formed by the joining of both branches at Northumberland, Pennsylvania. The united stream flows south and southeast for about 150 miles before emptying into the northern end of Chesapeake Bay.

Early settlers moved north from the bay to farm the

67

TABLE 3
Summary of Stone Structures and Artifacts

A. Susquehanna River Valley	B. Delaware River Valley	C. Hudson River Valley
1. Inscribed stones Mechanicsburg, Pennsylvania	1. Inscribed axe, Pemberton, New Jersey	1. Stone walls, Lower Manhattan, New York
2. Metal urn, Binghamton, New York; confluence of Susquehanna and Chenango Rivers	2. Inscribed amulets, Delaware Water Gap, New Jersey	2. Inscribed stone, upper Manhattan, New York
	3. Lifting Rocks, Deerpark, New York	3. Prehistoric walls, Ramapo, New York
	4. Lackawaxen River stones: a) Hawley Stone, Lackawaxen, Pennsylvania	4. Perched rock and semicircle, Greenwood Lake, New York
	b) Engraved pebbles, Lackawaxen, Pennsylvania	5. Inscribed stone, Bellvale, New York
	c) Conical stone piles, Barryville, New York	6. Perched rocks, Ladentown, New York
	d) Knapp Stone, Pleasant Mount, Pennsylvania	7. Indian dam, Plattekill, New York
	5. Old Mine Road, copper mines, New Jersey and New York	8. Standing stone, Poughkeepsie, New York; inscription, Wappingers Falls, New York
	6. Pick and wedge mines, Kittatinny-Shawangunk Mountain Range, New Jersey and New York	
	7. Stone piles, mines, Wurtsboro and Ellenville, New York	

mineral-rich soil in the lower Susquehanna Valley. By the late eighteenth century they had pushed into the upper valley, crossing the northeastern folds of the Appalachian Ridge by following the long inland route cut by the river and its tributaries. Rock outcroppings and rapids have always prevented long distance navigation on the river.

1. Inscribed Stones, Mechanicsburg, Pennsylvania

In the 1940s the late Dr. William Walker Strong, a professor of physics, collected a number of cubical blocks of stone from a plowed field in the vicinity of Dillsburg, Pennsylvania. The stones bore several kinds of grooves and markings which for years went unexplained, save for Dr. Strong's insistence that some of the obscure patterns resembled Phoenician letters. He had originally thought the markings were ancient script because many of the stone blocks bore grooves which were deep and appeared to be alphabetic in design. To test some of the rocks, the Department of Geology at Franklin and Marshall College sent samples to the Pennsylvania Geological Survey and to the National Bureau of Standards for two independent studies. But when the laboratories cut thin sections of the marks and subsequently showed that they followed the natural "veins" of the rock, "Dr. Strong immediately abandoned any faith in the V-shaped grooves, and agreed that they were a result of differential erosion."[1]

A remaining group of rocks contained broad, shallow etchings which Dr. Strong maintained were alphabetic. He was sure these were script and not weather markings. He never lived to hear the disappointing news, for he died before the report was issued. At both laboratories it was found that ". . . the grooves had been cut into the fully weathered outer zones of the diabase blocks, and that there was no reflection of the countour of the grooves in the distribution of the weathering zones."[2] In other words, the stones had not been exposed to the elements since the time of the groove cuts; otherwise the pattern of weathering would appear inside the cuts. Furthermore, the laboratories reported that they had found fresh steel dust impacted in the surfaces of the inscriptions. It was therefore concluded that the remaining stones were forgeries that "were foisted upon Dr. Strong by some of his associates who searched for Phoenician inscriptions with him."[3]

It would seem, then, that no further investigation need be made today. However, a number of things must be pointed out concerning the past report. Although it was concluded that the inscriptions on the broad, shallow-grooved stones were fraudulent, it is interesting to note that the authorities *originally* interpreted these modern-day alphabetic etchings "as chance cuts from agricultural machinery."[4] The very fact that scholars associated with the Pennsylvania State Museum and Franklin and Marshall Colleges could not recognize script makes one pause and wonder about some of the other hundreds of untested inscribed stones found by Dr. Strong, not to mention inscriptions found by other people in different parts of the country—stones that have been routinely dismissed as meaningless or cast aside as spurious.

The Mechanicsburg stones lay untouched in a local museum until NEARA bought up most of them for safekeeping. This was a wise decision, for close inspection of the stones later revealed that two distinct types of rock were present in the collection.[5] About thirty of the stones were of a natural claylike consistency. The scratches on these clay concretions were what the laboratories rightly determined to be the result of weathering. However, about three hundred stones were altogether different, being quite thick and heavy in consistency. These were the ones reputed to be modern forgeries.

The stones again lay untouched in a New Hampshire barn until 1975, when Barry Fell saw them and claimed they were inscribed with an Iberic script that was related to an ancient language of Portugal. According to Fell, they appeared to be primarily burial slabs of the members of an Iberian colony on the Susquehanna. Based on writing style, Fell hypothesized a date of 800-600 B.C. for the tombstones. The form and content of the deep-grooved stones were determined to be identical with those of similar slabs of that period found in the little-known Tras-os-Montes region of northern Portugal. A few months later stones found on Shelter Island at the eastern end of Long Island were brought to his attention. He translated them and found they were related to a similar context of coastal voyages.

It is highly unlikely that *all* of the 400 Pennsylvania field stones were meticulously etched and carefully buried by a misguided colleague of Dr. Strong. The vast amount of labor and scholarship needed to carry out such a task would preclude someone from performing it without getting caught or without a rumor being spread. Also, the farmer on whose land the stones were found would have been bound to notice sections of his field plowed up every morning, if we assume the forger worked by night. No such accounts were ever reported. Furthermore, stones with the same type of grooves and scratches have been found all over New England. Unless a vigilant team of forgers thought it important to scatter their goods throughout the Northeast, what we have is a mixture of authentically and naturally inscribed stones that have been overlooked for decades by professional archeologists who know nothing about script identification. In this context, it is intriguing to recall that west of Mechanicsburg, just beyond Huntington, an ancient stone marker once stood for years at the confluence of a river. The stone reputedly had undecipherable letters believed to have been Egyptian hieroglyphics. The markings of Celt-Iberian and/or Basque could easily have been mistaken for hieroglyphics by unknowing pioneers.

2. METAL URN, BINGHAMTON, NEW YORK

Further up the Susquehanna near its confluence with the Chenango River close to Binghamton, New York, a small metal urn was accidentally unearthed in the summer of 1973. After a heavy rainstorm washed away a good portion of his front yard, a young boy noticed a peculiar object partially exposed between muck and stones. After the boy called his father, they both spent the next few hours carefully removing the cone-shaped piece. Much to their surprise, the object turned out to be a metallic urn. But the biggest surprise was yet to come, for after washing off the mud and dirt covering the surface of the artifact, several Egyptian-looking figures came into view. In fact, when all of the grime was removed, it was clear to the father and son that they had a mystery on their hands. Perplexed by the unusual weight of the urn for its size—it weighs about a pound—they eventually forwarded it to a MARC field worker, who in turn sent it to our main office.

The urn is a hollow, cast-bronzelike piece that measures approximately 5 inches in height by 3 inches in width. Various images appear on the vessel's surface in bas-relief, including the palm leaf, sphinx, anka, and jaguar. The design is the same on both sides of the artifact. The urn appears to be a metal representation of an ancient Mediterranean pottery type known as *terra sigillata*. The motifs have a striking visual similarity with Tartessian designs found in Spain, which imitate both Punic and Egyptian styles (see Plates 10 and 20). The upper panel of the vessel depicts a typical south Iberian head of the Carthaginian goddess Tanit. Tanit, in Phoenician-Carthaginian cosmology, was the wife of Baal, the Semitic sun god. The lower, Egyptian-style panel depicts a prayer for rain. On the neck and base of the urn is the palmette design, a characteristically Phoenician feature.

Since the Phoenicians were in contact with so many other peoples, it is not surprising that their art usually exhibits a mixture of foreign elements. For instance, near the Phoenician-Carthaginian city of Gades we find many implements which show a combination of styles. Furthermore the Phoenician and foreign works continued to be imitated long after the decline of the Punic Empire.

If the Susquehanna urn is genuine and is Punic in origin it could date to the last quarter of the first millennium B.C. Unfortunately the land where the urn was found was once a swamp. Extensive landfill and construction over the past fifteen years have since covered over the marshes. If any other artifacts exist, they are more than likely buried beneath hundreds of feet of sand and concrete. An initial ground survey team sent out by MARC failed to expose any other debris. Nevertheless, seen in the context of other in situ artifacts from northeastern Pennsylvania, southern New York, and New Jersey, the urn, if original, may very well be one of the most valuable contributions to our discovery of America's prehistoric past.

B. Delaware River Valley

The Delaware River flows nearly 300 miles from its New York State source to below the city of Wilmington, where it empties into Delaware Bay. It is one of the more ancient rivers of North America in that it travels the same route today that it did some two hundred million years ago. Its course runs between deeply folded hills of resistant sandstone and conglomerate rock, which are actually the eroded bases of a once mighty range of mountains.[6]

The last Ice Age left its greatest impact upon the Delaware River Valley. All of the region was covered by frozen water sheets. Large boulders, clay, and gravel imbedded within the ice gouged their way south hollowing out some areas while filling in other regions with soil. Material that had been pushed along in front of the advancing glacier remained in place after the ice melted. Unsorted mixtures of stones, rounded from rolling along the bottom of the glaciers and bumping into each other, were deposited in many places along a folded layer of limestone and shale known as the Kittatinny-Shawangunk Range. Eons of weathering broke down the glacially transported material, eventually making for a deep, well-drained soil. Seventeenth-century Dutch, English, and Swedish settlers made use of the lush flatlands along the narrow valley of the Delaware River, where the land rises up to the Kittatinny-Shawangunk Range in New Jersey on the east and folds into the foothills of Pennsylvania's Pocono Mountains on the west.

The settlers traded with the Delaware Indians, cleared the land of loose stones, and widened the frontier road along the east bank of the river. There was fighting as the Indians were forced from their ancestral villages on the many islands within the Delaware. But after 1800, major roadways bypassed the area, and the impact of events, except for a brief resort boom in the late nineteenth and early twentieth centuries, was slight. Succeeding generations have peacefully tilled the soil to this day, leaving miniature landscapes of the past quite unaltered by modern design. The area's relatively low population density apparently has preserved many of the intriguing stone structures of the valley.

What is generally not realized is that before the Delaware and a number of other rivers were sucked dry by New York City's municipal water needs, they were much deeper and more navigable. Given a seagoing people knowledgeable about shoals, reefs, and breakers, it is not too difficult to imagine them building small craft capable of sailing partway along this inland waterway. If the colonists who settled the land flanking the Delaware River Valley had been somewhat more curious about the territory they stole from the Indians, we would not now be describing the many enigmatic stone mysteries they apparently found in their fields and valleys and simply shrugged off (see Plate 21).

1. Inscribed Axe, Pemberton, New Jersey

Pemberton is about fifteen miles east of the Delaware River. Access to the river is not difficult, for a natural water path has been formed by the Rancocas Creek. In 1859 Dr. J. W. C. Evans addressed a letter to the officers and members of the American Ethnological Society stating that his neighbor in Pemberton had found a 6-by-4-inch sandstone axe with ten characters incribed on it (see Plate 22). Dr. Evan's letter and an illustration of the stone were published in the *American Ethnological Proceedings*[7] which appeared in 1861. The report went unnoticed until James Whittall II, archeologist for the Early Sites Research Society of New England, came across it in a Boston library. Whittall subsequently published part of the report and Barry Fell's interpretation of the markings in the Society's *Bulletin.*[8]

Dr. Fell interpreted the markings as follows:

> The script is TARTESSIAN.
>
> The language is IBERIC.

b --- l

laba

z - k   s - l $\bar{a}$ - bh - d   h

ka - za   lasa   da - bha - $\bar{a}$ ha

"STAND FIRM, ON GUARD, PARRY, CLOSE IN AND STRIKE."

For the vocabulary he went to a standard Arabic dictionary. His analysis is shown below.

—stand firm; be alert

—look out! be on guard

—parry a blow

—come close, cleave together

—strike a blow

The incisions on the Pemberton Stone Axe cannot be scoffed at, for further up the Delaware River we have evidence of other stones inscribed with markings also believed to be Iberic Script.

2. INSCRIBED AMULETS, DELAWARE WATER GAP, NEW JERSEY

There have been other inscribed stones found in abundance in the Delaware River Valley. As usual, regional archeologists, unable to explain the meaning of the etched symbols, have simply put the artifacts aside. The most impressive item yet recorded by MARC was found by F. Dayton Staats of Oxford, New Jersey, while surface hunting on a site near the Delaware Water Gap, New Jersey. Edward Lenik, a New Jersey archeologist who has done extensive work in the Delaware Valley, was the first scientist to examine the stone. He described it as an elongated "pebble tool dating to the late Woodland period."[9] Many similarly polished, etched stones have been recovered from excavations in the upper Delaware area, but only recently have they been studied from an epigraphic viewpoint.

Lenik believes the stone's markings are capital letters of the English language:

> On the reverse side of the pebble tool there are several randomly incised lines which do not appear to have any pattern or design. However, in the center are three incised letters, . . . namely "ThE." It is interesting to note that the "T" is in caps, the "h" in lower case lettering and the "E" also in caps.[10]

The artifact was thought to have been of aboriginal origin and to have been either thrown away or lost by an Indian, only to be later picked up by a white traveler, who carved an English word on it and subsequently lost it. Lenik concluded that the stone's function and the aboriginal etched markings were unknown.

The drawing accompanying Lenik's paper was sent to the Epigraphic Society in Arlington, Massachusetts, for analysis. Dr. Fell's interpretation of the petroglyph differed strikingly from Lenik's. Fell noted that the illustration had been inadvertently published upside down, just like the Bat Creek inscription as printed by the Smithsonian in its 1894 report. Turning the stone right side up immediately destroyed any resemblance the markings might have borne to English. According to Fell, the faint etchings could not have been the wanton scribblings of English settlers because they were examples of Iberic script, written in the Andalusian language. The Harvard professor said the stone was a man's amulet for good luck in love, with a text that could be interpreted as "to arouse desire, to pick." Equivalent Andalusian sexual amulets from southern Spain date back circa 200 B.C. to 100 A.D. After the first century A.D. the texts change from Iberic to Latin. Thus, if the polished pebble stone is actually an Andalusian amulet, it most likely dates to somewhere between 200 B.C. and 100 A.D. (See fig. 3.2.) Another inscribed stone was found along the banks of the river, not far from the first one. Again, the markings were interpreted to be in an Iberic script dating from approximately the same centuries.

3. LIFTING ROCKS, DEERPARK, NEW YORK

High above the Delaware River, near the New York, New Jersey, and Pennsylvania borders, on top of a glacially scarred knoll once home to predatory birds and wandering deer, lie the mysterious Lifting Rocks. Almost 1000 feet above sea level, at the peak of Hawks Nest Mountain, three boulders several feet in circumference, each propped up by smaller 12-inch stones, rest several yards from each other, forming a huge triangle. For years the Lifting Rocks lay practically unnoticed by most of the twenty thousand people in the nearby city of Port Jervis. The occasional hunter or backpacker usually passed by the stones quite content with vague childhood stories of Indian powwow rites being performed there.

A local newspaper reporter changed all that in 1975. Journalist Doug Hay pieced together an article from an old reference he had inadvertently stumbled upon. The reporter found that James M. Allerton, a noted historian, surveyor, and lawyer of the late 1800s had described the Lifting Rocks in a fanciful melodrama entitled, *The Hawks Nest, or The Last of the Cahoonshees: A Tale of the Delaware Valley and Historical Romance of 1690:*

> In looking upon these, you gaze upon one of the wonders of the world. Here are three large rocks, but a few hundred feet apart, weighing from 30 to 100 tons, elevated above the

ground about five feet and resting on three stone pillars. These pillars are equal distance apart—as much so as if they had been placed there on geometrical principles.

Where did those huge rocks come from? When were they placed there, and by what power were they raised and placed on these triangular pillars?[11]

Hay climbed the mountain only to discover that the size of the stones was greatly exaggerated by Allerton. He noticed that the rocks were actually irregularly shaped boulders, roughly 6 feet long by 3 feet high, which had been lifted on one end. The pillars consisted of smaller rocks placed beneath the lifted ends of the boulders. Two of the three rocks were readily identifiable from Allerton's description, despite his amplification. The third was not so easily picked out from the other sizeable boulders on top of the mountain—perhaps, the reporter thought, because the pillars had fallen due to natural or human causes in the eighty-three years since the book was written.

Allerton claimed that many of the traditions upon which his book was based came from persons who were either dead or very old in 1892. Some of the sites he wrote about were pointed out to him as a youngster in 1839. However, his primary information source was Jacob C. Wilson, "a man of limited education, but of an inquiring mind and retentive memory . . . well read in history, both ancient and modern, especially English, French, Holland, Roman and Egyptian . . . and especially that part that related to the North American Indians."[12]

When I read Doug Hay's article I found the idea of a "miniature Stonehenge" on top of a peak in New York State, as Hay's piece purported the Lifting Rocks to be, too amusing to pass by. I climbed Hawks Nest Mountain one wintery day for a good laugh. It wasn't funny. Although not as awe-inspiring as the book and article, the Lifting Rocks were intriguing, along with the mystery to which they stood in mute testimony. A survey of the site performed a few months later revealed features interesting enough to warrant aerial photography and further surface exploration.

During the summer of 1976, a MARC ground crew set out to define the immediate area surrounding the I-stone (see figure 3.3). We carefully cleared all of the turf within a 2-foot radius of the stone, checking for the presence of charcoal and ceramics. After we removed about 6 inches of sod and soil from the northern sector of the I-stone, a crescent-shaped marking came to light. At first we thought the marking was simply a "memory" of the last Ice Age—as glaciers crept southwards they very often pressured underlying bedrock into crescentric fractures. It is not uncommon to find these thin curves on the summits of mountaintops which were once covered over with moving ice.

There are many such parabolic fractures at the Lifting Rocks site. However, the marking first uncovered by MARC researcher Robert Miller is clearly different from the other glacial 'chattermarks.' It is a single indentation that has been deeply incised into the bedrock. At an undetermined time in the past, someone with a sharp instrument cut out a lunar-shaped groove directly in front of a triangular perched boulder. A thorough examination of the I-stone has since revealed that it has been worked into its present form. The placement of the perched rocks and the indentation may have astronomical significance.

Viewed from the air and as depicted on the survey sheet, the Lifting Rocks form an impressive triangular configuration. A few feet from the "triangle" is a hollowed depression of about 2 feet in diameter. The hole is just large enough for a man to sit comfortably in. By sitting within the hollow, a line of sight could be drawn with side DB of the triangle. Our preliminary survey showed that this sight line is approximately aligned on the horizon where the moon's major setting occurs every 18.61 years. Future work is planned at this site to determine if the sight line is spurious. For now, however, we are speculating on the possible uses of the Lifting Rocks with respect to what we know of other societies that utilized such arrangements of stone.

In the western Mediterranean, the Phoenician mother and fertility goddess, Astarte, was known as Tanit. Tanit

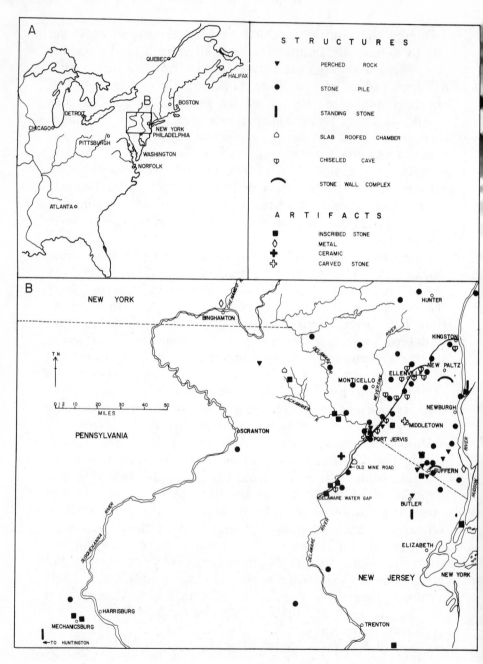

Fig. 3.1. Distribution of stone structures in the Susquehanna, Delaware, and west Hudson River Valleys (Map by Kalpana R. Shah)

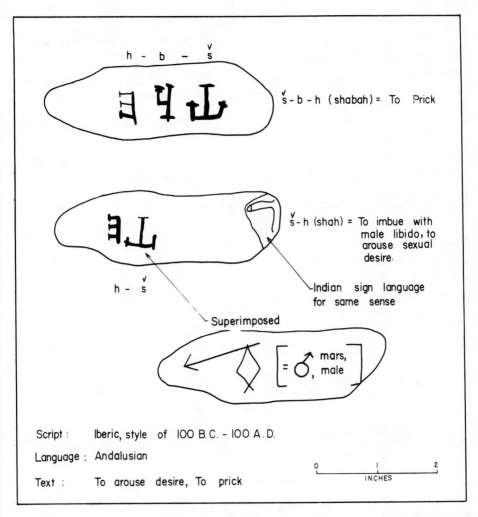

Fig. 3.2. Phallic amulet, Delaware Water Gap, New Jersey (Drawing by Kalpana R. Shah)

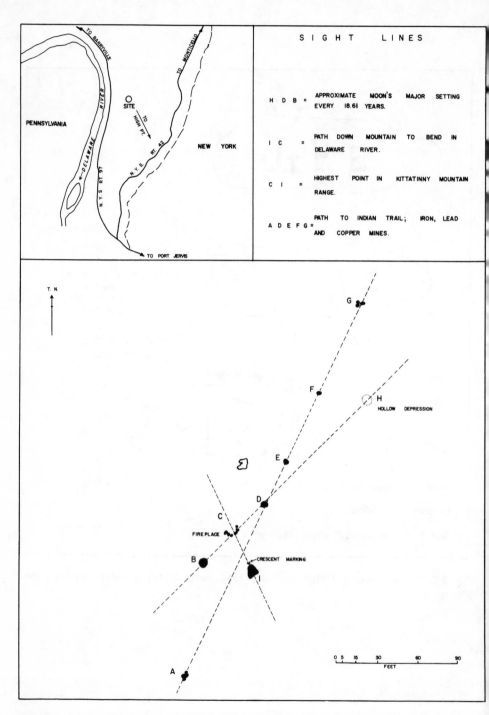

Fig. 3.3. Lifting Rocks, Hawks Nest Mountain, Deer Park, New York (Drawing by Kalpana R. Shah, after plans by T. F. Brennan)

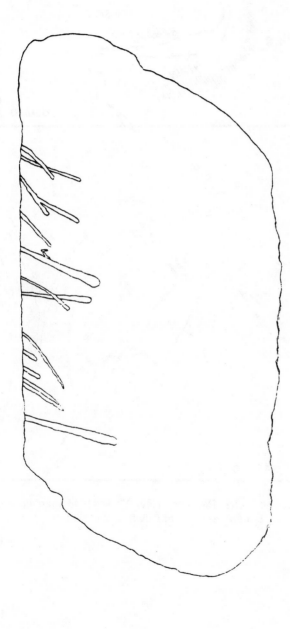

Fig. 3.4. Stone found at Inwood, a wooded section of northwest Manhattan, in 1894. The stone, measuring 3 feet in length by 2 feet in width and breadth, is etched with markings that may be a vowelless form of Ogam, an alphabet which may have been used by Iberian Celts as early as 800 B.C. (Horsford, *An Inscribed Stone*)

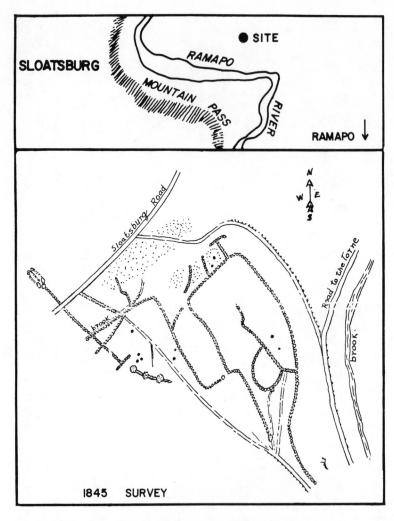

Fig. 3.5. Prehistoric walls, Ramapo, New York (1845 map courtesy of Pierson Mapes, 1975 map courtesy of Edward J. Lenik)

FEATURES EXCAVATED:

1. STONE FIREPLACE

2. ROCK FILLED DEPRESSION

3. STONE MOUND

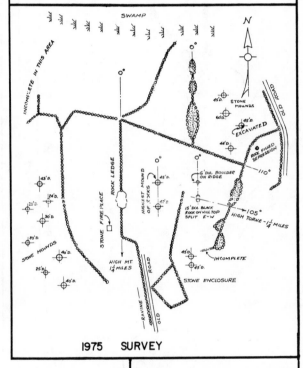

1975 SURVEY

0   290   580   870
FEET
Applies Only To 1975
Survey

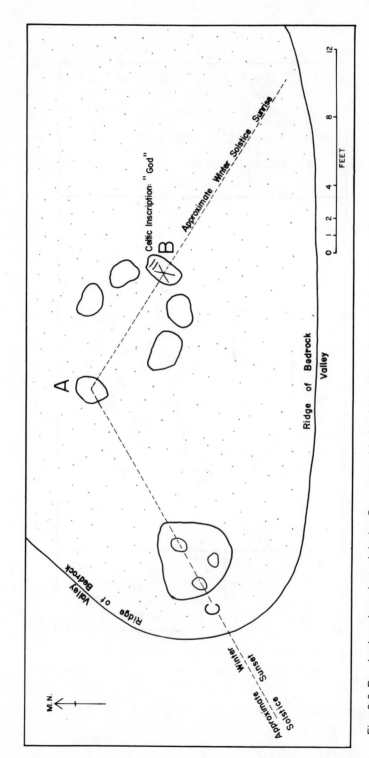

Fig. 3.6. Perched rock and semicircle, Greenwood Lake, New York (Drawing by Kalpana R. Shah)

Fig. 3.7. Hypothetical reconstruction of winter solstice sunset at perched rocks, Ladentown, New York (Drawing by Kalpana R. Shah)

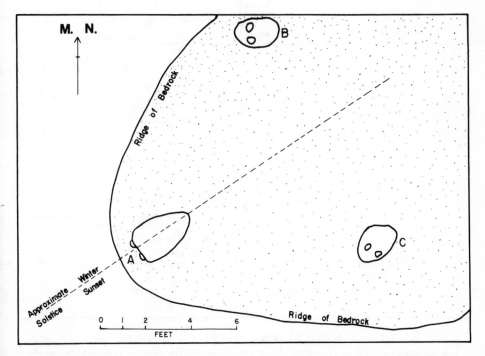

Fig. 3.8. Perched rocks, Ladentown, New York (Drawing by Kalpana R. Shah)

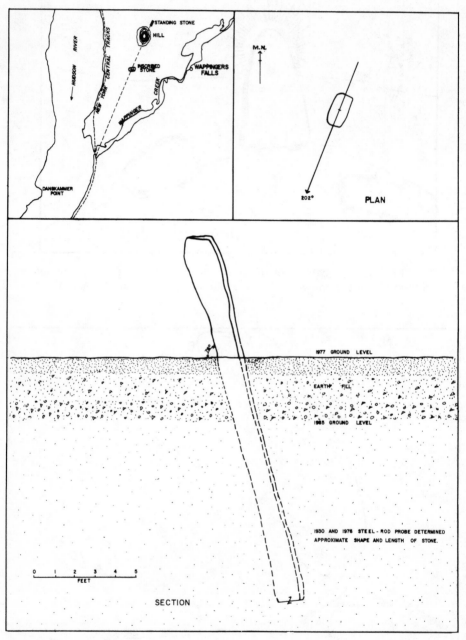

Fig. 3.9. Standing stone, Poughkeepsie, New York (Drawing by Kalpana R. Shah)

Fig. 3.10. Celtic sanctuary at Buchenberg, Starnberg, Bavaria, Germany, circa 300 B.C. In Europe these rectangular entrenchments occur only in certain parts of southern Germany and Normandy. The regularity of the ground plan indicates that strict specifications were used to lay out the sacred structures. They always were built near water, and tiny bronze statuettes of animals have been discovered in nearby cairnfields. Photo by K. Schwarz, Munich.

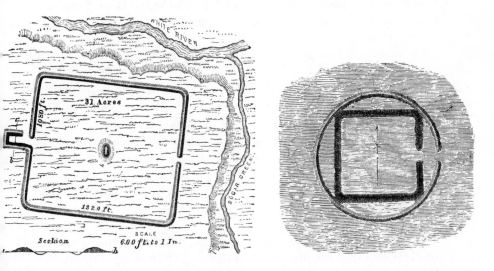

Fig. 3.11. Geometric works found in Ohio and Indiana during the nineteenth century by early settlers. American archaeologists believe these works to be American Indian in origin. From Baldwin, *Ancient America*.

was the celestial goddess of the moon. Her sign consisted of a triangle, a disc, and a crescent. The symbol is believed to be a stylized human figure with the lunar crescent representing the goddess Tanit's consort, the Phoenician sun god Baal, who is represented by the disk. The triangle is believed to be the body incarnate of Baal and Tanit, the sun and moon, the collective whole which soars through the heavens in perpetual harmony with the universe. These two symbols are found throughout the Western Mediterranean on burial stelae and on hilltop sanctuaries.

On Hawks Nest Mountain we have the crescent and the triangle in direct association with a possible lunar alignment. It appears that by arranging the boulders in the form of a triangle, various lines of sight were created which probably had astronomical and ritualistic importance to the people who moved the stones. It is possible that the relationship between these sight lines and the moon (and possibly the sun) showed seasonal changes which helped the people to know the right time of year to plant crops. The mother goddess of the Old World had long been associated with farming. Man in times past had to set up open air temples to please the fickle goddess. On the Hawks Nest we have an interesting assortment of altarlike stones which may have been used to call attention to important astronomical bodies.

The ritual use of fire often accompanied Tanit worship. Our survey teams found ample evidence of high-intensity fires around the I-stone, in the form of five-cracked base rock.

Within the many crevices, we found a phenomenal amount of tiny ground-up pieces of ceramics. It proved impossible however, to reconstruct any of the pottery bits, as most of them were little more than dust. Apparently, for whatever reason, sometime long ago a people lit their fires and smashed their pottery on the Lifting Rocks. It was perplexing. Nothing more could be defined from our test-trench work. We again looked at our survey charts and rethought the site, keeping in mind the image of a blazing inferno high atop a mountain peak.

The Lifting Rocks are situated on a knoll that is quite visible from the Delaware some 1000 feet below. An acute bend in the river occurs just a half-mile northwest of the site. To someone sailing downriver, a fire on top of the Hawks Nest would be the most noticeable sight around. We wondered whether such a spectacle could have served as a boundary marker of sorts—a ceremonial station that pointed the way to both secular and sacred ground. We took a compass bearing from the tip of the triangular I-stone and followed a straight path through a semicircular stone fireplace. Much to our delight, the bearing led directly to the bend in the river. The I-stone pointed towards a trail that meandered down the mountain. Nearby we spotted many stone piles constructed upon base boulders.

Going off in the other direction, we found that the souheast axis of the I-stone led directly to a site known as the High Point Monument. The spot is the highest mountain peak in the Kittatiny-Shawangunk range. In the 1930s a retired Army colonel erected an obelisk-type structure as a memorial to soldiers of past wars. If ever there was a stone monument that preceded the twentieth-century one, it was surely destroyed by modern work crews. There is every indication that there was some type of structure on this spot, for from the peak a compelling 360-degree horizon view can be seen. On clear, moonlit nights the reflection of the Delaware River in the bend just beyond Hawks Nest Mountain glistens like a white ribbon. On moonless nights the stars appear to be within hand's reach as they journey across the sky. And at dawn, the glorious sun peers through the purple of early morning mists, unobstructed by trees or earth.

The Lifting Rocks site is situated only a few miles from the Kittatinny-Shawangunk Range. Along the western side of the ridge, a narrow valley extends northeastward to the Hudson River. Local legend has it that in the early 1600s Dutch entrepreneurs constructed a 104-mile road within the valley to ship copper and lead to the Hudson River city of Kingston, New York. MARC has collected data that suggest a much more ancient origin for the copper road. For now it can be said that the sight line created by stones A,D,E,F,G in figure 3.3 points toward the locale of a historical Indian village, Cahoozie, and beyond. Following the sight line from the village will eventually place one on the copper pathway known as the Old Mine Road. Along the way are stone cairns that appear to guide the sojourner in a northeasterly direction. Indeed, every 8.9 miles along the Shawangunk Ridge one comes across mountain slopes containing hundreds of conical stone piles, all constructed on base boulders.

Our initial analysis indicated that the triangular configuration of stones atop Hawks Nest Mountain pointed up the Delaware River and along the Shawangunk Valley. If we actually had stumbled across a crude astro-signal-ceremonial station, then surely we should find other corroborative evidence of a people skilled in such affairs. It was a good assumption, because once the exploratory teams knew what they were looking for they started to find an incredible assortment of artifacts—beer cans, Coke bottles, iron yokes, flintlocks, arrowheads, tomahawks, amulets, and inscribed stones. They were exposing the cultural debris of an area that probably had seen over three thousand years of New and Old World traffic.

4. LACKAWAXEN RIVER STONES

a. HAWLEY STONE, LACKAWAXEN, PENNSYLVANIA

In 1969, while trucking water to fight a forest blaze, a fireman spotted an inscribed block on an island at the confluence of the Lackawaxen and Delaware Rivers, an area some 20 miles upriver from Hawks Nest Mountain. After removing the stone from the riverbed, the fireman contacted Dr. Vernon Leslie, a former editor of the *Canadian Journal of Anthropology*. Dr. Leslie in turn issued a report to the New England Antiquities Research Association. The provenance of the find was misleadingly listed as Hawley, Pennsylvania, in the *NEARA Newsletter*,[13] for fear that publication of the exact location would attract curiosity seekers who might steal or destroy other possi-

Plate 1. The Great Mound, near Miamisburg, Ohio, is typical of the mysteries encountered by the early settlers of America. (Baldwin, *Ancient America*)

Plate 2. Inexplicable earthworks at Hopeton, Ohio. Combinations of the square and circle are common in these ancient works. So perfect were the figures that an early team of investigators, Squier and Davis, remarked that "the builders possessed a standard of measurement, and had a means of determining angles." (Baldwin, *Ancient America*)

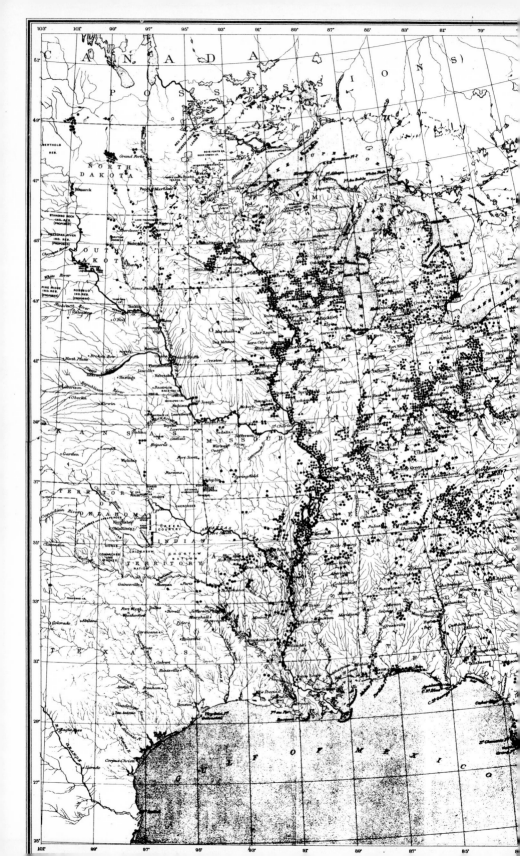

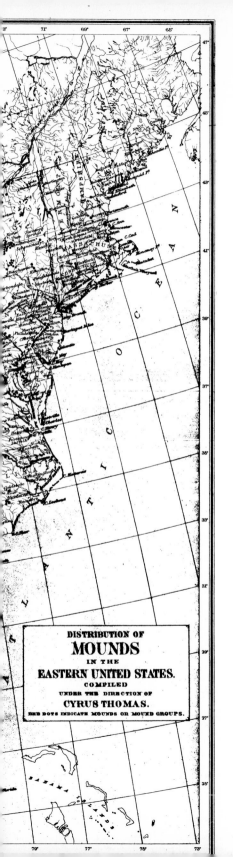

Plate 3. Map showing the distribution of mounds gutted by Cyrus Thomas on behalf of the Smithsonian Institution in the late 1890s (Smithsonian Institution, *Twelfth Annual Report,* 1894)

Plate 4. Female terra cotta figurine from a deposit cache, Isla Plana, Ibiza, Balearics, Spain, circa seventh century B.C. (Courtesy of Museo Arqueologio, Ibiza)

Plate 5. A kneeling female (drinking vessel) from a burial mound near Idlewilde (Obion County), Tennessee, previously believed to be American Indian in origin (Smithsonian Institution, *Twelfth Annual Report*)

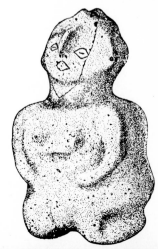

Plate 6. MARC research assistant Jamie Simpson at stone pile complex near Ellenville, New York. There are over 300 conical heaps at this site. (Photo by S. M. Trento)

Plate 7. Cairns from Jabal Agabih, southern Arabia. Those shown are part of a northwest-southeast ridgetop alignment believed to have formed an ancient route system. Nearby cairns have been found with base openings. (Photo courtesy Thames and Hudson)

Plate 8. Conical cairns discovered underneath a mound near Patterson, North Carolina, by the Thomas expedition (Smithsonian Institution, *Twelfth Annual Report*)

Plate 9. Perched rock, Greenwood Lake, New York. Roger Riley poses near rock found at the edge of a cliff. (Photo by S. M. Trento)

Plate 10. Perched rock, Hawks Nest Lifting Rock, Deer Park, New York (Photo by S. M. Trento)

Plate 11. Menhir at Cagliari, Sardinia (Courtesy of H. H. Hofstädtter, Baden-Baden)

Plate 12. Standing stone, Poughkeepsie, New York (Photo by S. M. Trento)

Plate 13. Chamber aligned towards the equinox sunrise, near North Salem, New York. A walled entranceway leads to an oval room situated about 2 feet below ground level. One hundred yards to the rear an inscribed stone has been incorporated into a colonial field wall. (Photo by S. M. Trento)

Plate 14. Corbelled, long-barrowed, slab-roofed chamber near Kent Cliffs, New York. Research assistant Jamie Simpson standing at chamber's entrance gives an idea of the scale of the cut stones. Chambers such as this one are frequently aligned towards the winter solstice sunrise or sunset. (Photo by S. M. Trento)

Plate 15. Inside the South Woodstock, Vermont, slab-roofed chamber shortly before the winter solstice. The sun can be seen in line with the center of the structure's entranceway about one hour after sunrise. Byron Dix has determined that the chamber's orientation is, in fact, aligned exactly towards sunrise on December 21. It has been suggested that this structure was used by the early inhabitants of central Vermont as a ritual edifice. (Photo by S. M. Trento)

Plate 16. Horizontal section of the Bat Creek Mound No. 3, Loudon County, Tennessee. The inscribed stone was found under the head of skeleton No. 1 after it was struck by a steel rod used in probing. (Smithsonian Institution, *Twelfth Annual Report*)

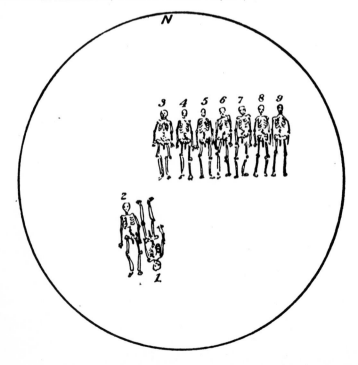

Plate 17. The inscribed stone found in the Bat Creek Mound, Loudon County, Tennessee, as published by the Smithsonian Institution. The chief excavator, Cyrus Thomas, reported that "the engraved characters on it are beyond question letters of the Cherokee alphabet," invented about 1821. It has since been determined that the symbols are Hebraic script from the second century A.D. (Smithsonian Institution, *Twelfth Annual Report*)

Plate 18. The Hawley Stone. The inscribed block was actually found near the Lackawaxen-Delaware River confluence. The inscription (chalked for photo) has not yet been deciphered. (Photo by Dr. Vernon Leslie)

Plate 19. Metal urn found near the confluence of the Chenango and Susquehanna Rivers, Binghamton, New York. Punic and Egyptian style; may date to 1000–500 B.C. (Photo by S. M. Trento)

Plate 20. Tanit (Astarte) plaques from the Mediterranean, circa sixth or fifth centuries B.C. Note similarity of headdress. (*Left,* courtesy of Donald B. Harden; *center and right,* courtesy of William F. Albright)

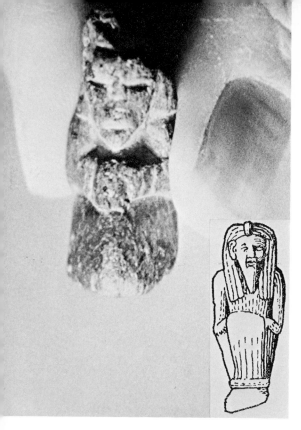

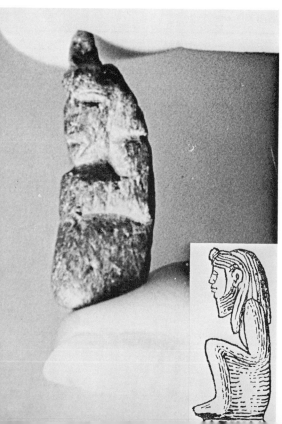

Plate 21. Seated-person pendant carved from obsidian, found along the banks of the Delaware River not far from Hawks Nest Mountain by Antonia Ryder. Inset illustration is a small bronze figurine cast in Egyptian style that was uncovered in Carthage. It dates to the sixth century B.C. The resemblance between the Delaware find and the Carthaginian artifact is striking. (Photos by S. M. Trento, inset courtesy of Donald B. Harden)

Plate 22. Inscribed stone axe, Pemberton, New Jersey. Currier and Ives print. The script is Tartessian and the language is Iberic.

Plate 23. Knapp Stone found on the West Branch of the Lackawaxen River, Pleasant Mount, Pennsylvania. Iberic inscription circa 300 B.C. (Photos by S. M. Trento)

Plate 24. Physiographic diagram of New York region. (Courtesy of Hammond Incorporated, Maplewood, New Jersey)

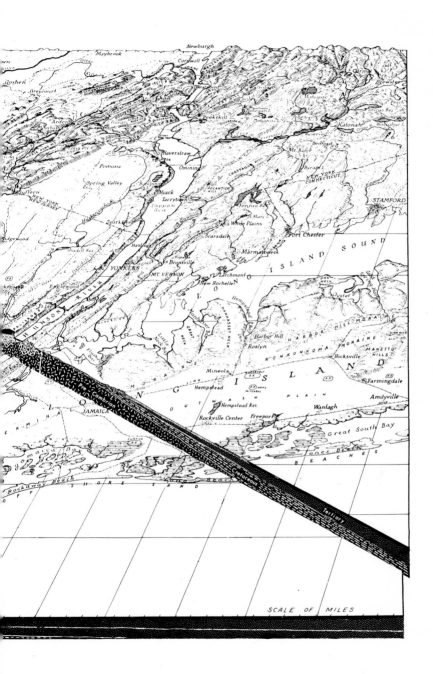

SCALE OF MILES

Plate 25. Nineteenth-century illustration of stone heap with two cavities, Mount Carbon, West Virginia. The Smithsonian's field team under Professor Cyrus Thomas' direction located similar heaps on the summit of nearly all the prominent bluffs, spurs, and high spots in the region. Several "ancient walls" nearby stretched across the countryside for miles.

Plate 26. Claire Lofrese rests on the side of a circular cavity found within the "prehistoric wall" complex, Ramapo, New York. In the foreground, another depression can clearly be seen. Cavities have been discovered at wall sites near the towns of Plattekill, Putnam Valley, and Kent Cliffs, New York State. (Photo by S. M. Trento)

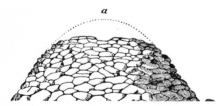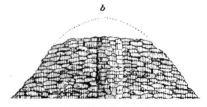

Plate 27. Nineteenth-century engraving of stone heap, with 3-foot-wide vertical shaft, from Fayette County, West Virginia. These were called "well-holes" by early pioneers. The Smithsonian reported in 1894 that decayed bones were often found within the layers of the heap, with the skull pointing towards the shaft.

ble artifacts before a full-scale investigation could be mounted. According to Dr. Leslie, the markings on the stone were very faint and shallow, as if years of flowing water had removed the sharpness of the symbols. There was, however, a definite pattern to them. The stone was eventually taken to Florida after its owner decided to move south.

MARC at first learned that the inscription on the stone might be in Ibero-Libyan script. Although this preliminary identification and interpretation by Dr. Fell was later to prove incorrect—he was basing his analysis upon a very poor photograph of the stone—MARC conducted an aerial survey which revealed some surprising traces of very old ground disturbances along the riverbanks. Color aerial photographs exposed many peculiarly associated settlement features running the length of the Delaware from the Hawks Nest to the confluence. A few months later, air surveys carried out near Danbury, Connecticut, later exposed similar "ringlike" impressions which ran counter to the colonial landscapes (see Chapter 5).

b. ENGRAVED PEBBLES, LACKAWAXEN, PENNSYLVANIA

Ground exploratory teams sent into fields along the riverbanks recorded further conical stone piles and balanced rocks. One of the teams hauled a 500-pound granite block from a river island near where the Hawley Stone was found. The cut stone contained many parallel grooves and striations along its surface. As yet, the markings on this stone as well as those cut into the Hawley Stone remain uninterpreted. But it is important to note that similar stones with grooves and slashes have been found throughout New England and Europe.

Based on these preliminary findings—ground disturbance patterns and possibly two inscribed stones—a test-trench excavation was performed at a potential occupation site some 100 yards from the Lackawaxen-Delaware confluence. At a depth of about 3 feet, a small inscribed pebble was found associated with tiny flakes of chipped stone.

No further artifacts were found. An investigation of the area showed that many community people living near the rivers over the years had found similarly inscribed "pebbles." Jodie Lynn Kuhn, a student at Delaware Valley Community College, brought such an inscribed stone to this center's attention. The stone is indeed interesting, for it seems to belong to the same series as the similarly 3- and 4-holed rough engraved pebbles found in the Tras-os-Montes dolmens and other funeral sites in northern Portugal. These objects were either tied to the body of the deceased by the threaded holes, or else they served as charms attached to the clothing or necklace of a living person. Although the Tras-os-Montes examples have been previously read as Basque, it has been difficult to determine whether the ones we found near the Lackawaxen were indeed Basque or Celt-Iberian. They were, however, likely to be one or the other, as the culture was the same. The date, if it had been a European find, would be around 800 B.C.

It is unlikely that the stones found by MARC and other people along the two rivers were forgeries, because the full implications of Celt-Iberian script were only recognized as recently as 1975. Furthermore, its reportage in past years has been infrequent and limited to professional epigraphic journals.

Thus the combined results of our field work brought to light a cache of marked stones and an interesting deposition site near the confluence of the Lackawaxen and Delaware Rivers. The stones were inscribed with symbols unknown to the American Indians which have been interpreted as a variety of script that was used in ancient Europe.

c. CONICAL STONE PILES, BARRYVILLE, NEW YORK

Five miles downriver from the Lackawaxen confluence a field team spotted a conical pile towering 7 feet above a base boulder. The pile lies hidden in a forest thicket about 100 yards from the banks of the Delaware River. Behind the beautifully preserved structure are the toppled remains of two similarly erected piles. The field team followed the axis running through all three piles to see if anything further could be detected. Across the river, not far from the sighting axis, the crew found a flat table rock. They later learned that residents in the nearby community of Shohola speak of the granite slab as the Universe Stone.

Set beside the swiftly running Shohola Creek in a forest opening, the Universe Stone offers hikers a peaceful resting spot. The 10-by 7-foot cut stone block was thought by the Shohola Indians to be the eye of the universe. Local legend has it that the Indians used to travel from miles around to sit in quiet meditation on the stone, for it was the center of all creation. From this spot, life spread out to the world. The sacredness of this region of northeastern Pennsylvania and its undertones of procreation were not immediately apparent to us. It wasn't until other inscribed stones were uncovered and brought to the attention of epigraphers that the full implications of the many sites in the valley were realized.

The Center of the World, or Navel, is a tradition found among many peoples from India to Peru. The center can be a pillar, a tree, a mountain, or even a fire altar. It was usually a sacred place where the collective spirit of a community gathered to celebrate the glories of past ages. In much this fashion, the Shohola stone, seen in association with the inscribed sexual amulets and the possible alignment-direction configuration of the Hawks Nest Lifting Rocks, seems to project a certain holiness or sacredness onto the Delaware River Valley. Just why this spot may have been chosen years ago is unknown. Perhaps it was an area rich in game and fish. Perhaps it was simply the overwhelming beauty of the valley.

Whatever the reason, we do know that this "sacredness" idea has been expressed elsewhere. Thirty miles up the Lackawaxen, another inscribed slab was pulled out of the riverbank. This time the markings were readily decipherable. They spoke of the sanctity of the setting sun.

d. KNAPP STONE, PLEASANT MOUNT, PENNSYLVANIA

During the summer of 1974, a high school student from a rural community in northeastern Pennsylvania found a 40-pound stone in an outcrop of rocks along the west branch of the Lackawaxen near the town of Pleasant Mount. It wasn't just an ordinary stone. The 12-inch-long-by-8-inch-thick sandstone slab had a sketch of mountains, the sun, and trees carved on it; and most intriguingly, in the upper left-hand corner of the slab was a series of unusual markings which appeared to be some form of script (see Plate 23).

The stone was first reported in a rural newspaper[14] and was brought to my attention by Jo Ann James, then a student at Delaware Valley Community College. James Knapp, the young man who found the stone, was contacted to learn why he had waited close to three years before releasing information about it. He said that at the time there was no one in his small community who was knowledgeable about such matters. He soon forgot about the stone. It lay on his family's living room floor until he read an article about stone mysteries in America. Only then did Knapp suspect that he had something important.

James Knapp's failure to immediately report the inscribed stone is typical of present and past cases from around the country. For the layperson living in rural America, there is really no one to go to for help in explaining an inscribed stone. There is simply no access to scientists. For someone outside the university structure to saunter into an archeology department with inscribed stone in hand, the chances of meeting an acquiescent epigraphic specialist are less than nil.

The markings on Knapp's stone have been interpreted as Iberic script in a style which dates to around 300-200 B.C. A rough reading of the script yields the following: "On the appointed day, the sun sets in the notch opposite the House of Worship."[15] Given this interpretation, the scene etched on the stone takes on much more meaning, for such a place actually exists in the vicinity of Pleasant Mount, Pennsylvania. It is a westerly view of a mountain river valley. Based on the translation, we hypothesized that the inscribed stone may have had something to do with the setting winter solstice. We then searched the area and found a spot where the view of the notch as depicted on the stone came into view. After plotting out our assumed "observation point," we calculated where the sun would set during the winter solstice. We weren't too far off in our calculations, for from our eyeballed vantage point the sun would indeed set approximately within the mountain pass on December 21.

The translation also suggested that the "observation point" was some type of structure (House of Worship). We were standing on ground soil at the base of a sloping hill, and several exploratory teams scoured the area in all directions. It was well worth the effort. Near the top of the hill there may be the ruined vestige of a large, corbelled, slab-roofed chamber.

It is a peculiar sensation to be standing within a massive stone structure that in all likelihood was used over two thousand years ago to mark the sun on a particular day. It takes but little effort to imagine dancing hordes of people waiting in revelous expectation for the sun, their god, to enter their domain. It would have been natural for a scribe to have carved out the locale of such a god-house. Perhaps this edifice was used by travelers going from the Susquehanna River to the Delaware via the Lackawaxen River Valley. Perhaps it was used by groups of Iberian work gangs who were searching for copper and other ores in northeastern Pennsylvania. We will never know the identity of all of the people who may have used the chamber.

5. OLD MINE ROAD, COPPER MINES, NEW JERSEY, NEW YORK

If the material we've been discussing is indeed of Old World origin, then we must offer some tangible reasons as to why ancient people from the Mediterranean or Western Europe would risk their necks crossing an ocean to trek along a New World river valley and presumably leave pebble amulets, cut stone blocks, perched rocks, stone cairns, and sun chambers in their wake. A possible answer deals with random exploration for valuable mineral ores.

In modern times the first recorded exploration that could have carried reports of the New World's riches back to Europe was that of Henry Hudson in 1609. Within a few days after Hudson entered New York Harbor he reported that the Indians of the country had "yellow copper." A subsequent expedition brought a group of settlers up the Delaware River in quest of trading posts. Reports filed in the *History of the Dutch West Indian Company, 1621-1675*, attest to the rich ores of the area. In 1644 a letter from the Director of the New Netherlands Company to the States General in Holland stated that various minerals including copper, iron, and lead were being found in the Delaware Valley. In 1659 a letter written by the directors of the Dutch West Indian Company was sent to their American representative, John Aldrich, vice-director of the lower Delaware. In it they stated that they had indirectly heard of great quantities of copper being found in the countryside to the far northwest of Manhattan Island.

Along the east bank of the Delaware River, starting approximately where the Delaware Water Gap inscribed amulets were found, continuing northwards along the Kittatinny-Shawangunk Ridge, and ending at the Hudson River port city of Kingson, New York, there once existed a 104-mile dirt path known as the Old Mine Road. The road, long since asphalted and rerouted, is still a major artery of transportation in northwestern New Jersey and now goes by the name Route 209.

The fame bestowed upon the Old Mine Road stemmed from the dubious fact that it was the oldest trade highway in the nation. Local legend has it that sometime before 1650 the road was hewn out of primeval woodlands by a hardy gang of displaced Dutchmen to transport heavy loads of copper ore from mines in Pahaquarry Township, New Jersey, northward along the river to Kingston (or

Esopus, as it was then known). From there the ore was shipped down the Hudson River for eventual transport to Holland. Reasons for not simply hauling the ore due east over New Jersey to reach New Amsterdam presumably included the rough terrain, mountain ridges, heavy forest cover and uncooperative Indians.

For years it was assumed on very tenuous grounds that the Dutch, soon after laboriously completing the road, gave up their mining activity when they realized that the amount of time, effort, and cost involved in transporting the ore precluded any profits. Given what we know about the enterprising Dutch West India Company, it is amazing to think that this tale could have gone unquestioned by local historians for such a long period of time. The shrewd burghers would have foreseen the future practical difficulties. The Directors of the Company would never have invested the money to construct such a nonprofitable road.

Dr. Vernon Leslie, a local scholar from northeastern Pennsylvania, has recently compiled the most definitive argument against any Dutch road building or mining efforts along the banks of the upper Delaware Valley. Among his many points, Dr. Leslie notes that copper at Pahaquarry occurs in a mineral known as chalcolite. To get the copper, the chalcolite ore must first be crushed and then blasted in a furnace to reduce the mineral to an oxide. Further heating of the oxide eventually results in elemental copper. As Leslie astutely comments,

. . . if the Dutch worked the Pahaquarry Mine in the middle 1600s, there had to be a proper installation for crushing, charcoal production, and smelting. This entailed the presence of an adequate work force and the consumption of great amounts of fuel. The only alternative was the transportation of quantities of low-grade ore containing a small percentage of copper through a hundred miles of primitive forest to Kingston.[16]

No surviving Dutch records exist in either Kingston or Holland which speak of the smelting of copper by the Dutch West India Company. If a clandestine work force was used, then one would expect to find mid-seventeenth-century Dutch debris—"broken bottles, broken dishes, lost buttons, broken clay pipes, lost coins, broken tools, etc."[17] We find no Dutch rubbish. But we do find the debris of an ancient Old World people—inscribed amulets, engraved pebbles similar to those found in the tombs of Northern Portugal, and aligned rocks.

6. PICK AND WEDGE MINES, NEW JERSEY AND NEW YORK

Today few scholars accept any Dutch mining activity in the Delaware River Valley much before 1650. But we are nonetheless still faced with the evidence that digging at Pahaquarry has existed for a long time, and that "the so-called Old Mine Road is indeed old."[18] Perhaps the most impressive evidence for an early nonaboriginal people coming into the Delaware Valley to search for copper veins are the mines themselves. Along the entire ridge of the Kittatinny and Shawangunk there are numerous cuts and tunnels carved into the base of the mountains. MARC has recorded that at least seven of these "mines" were worked entirely by hand tools. That is, some people in the dim past simply walked up to the mountain face, took up their hammers, and pounded picks and wedges into base rock. Some of these tunnels measure 6 feet wide, 4 feet high, and 500 feet deep. The amount of effort and time needed to pry open rock in this manner has been estimated by one local stonemason to be at least ten months for each mine. The skill and finish bestowed upon these exploratory tunnels is unique by comparison with Dutch mineral excavation. The Dutch, and practically everyone who searched for and mined ore during colonial days, used gunpowder to blast away stone. It was much cheaper and usually the only way for exploratory teams to test the mineral wealth of an area—they couldn't very well spend almost a year hacking away in one place. No trace of gunpowder or the subsequent blasts has been found in the tunnels along the Kittatinny-Shawangunk Ridge.

The Lake Superior mining region in northern Michigan

is only a few hundred miles from the Pahaquarry copper mines. For years archeologists have puzzled over who mined the vast quantity of copper from the peninsula (see Chapter 1). The ancient, mysterious people who hunted metal in that area could have very easily traveled over the Blue Ridge Mountains to prospect for more minerals. When. we take all of the stone items in the Delaware Valley together we see more than enough evidence to lend support to this theory.

We don't suppose the prehistoric miners found the New Jersey-New York veins adequate, for as previously mentioned, the quality of the copper ore was quite poor. They in all probability were simply exploring northeastern Pennsylvania and northern New Jersey for richer layers of ore. That a long-term occupation of the Susquehanna and Delaware River Valley by many peoples took place appears evident from the many styles of script identified on stones recovered from the region. The script undergoes a known style change in accordance with the passage of time. Similar character deviations have been observed in Iberian inscribed stones.

7. STONE PILES, MINES, WURTSBORO AND ELLENVILLE, NEW YORK

This lush flatland near the confluence of the Delaware and Neversink Rivers once supported a thriving Algonquin Indian population. The juncture of these rivers provided an excellent means of travel and trade—the Neversink runs north-south for 35 miles before meeting the eastward flowing Delaware at a junction where they veer sharply south and eventually flow into Delaware Bay, 150 miles downriver. Three miles east of the confluence, not far from an old Indian burial ground, the first white men in the area made mention of the Willehoosa, which is Dutch for "Indian house." The early Dutch settlers described it as a cavern dug out of a rock on the side of the Shawangunk Mountains. The cave was said to contain three separate compartments each about the size of an ordinary room.

Although the Willehoosa no longer exists (it is believed
to have been destroyed in the last century when a railroad
bed was expanded), MARC has investigated other so-
called Indian houses along the ridge. In every case we
found evidence of pick and wedge mining. And furthermore, we found that near every one of these "exploratory"
tunnels there were radial lines of stone piles.

At a cairn site near Ellenville, New York, an exploratory trench sunk beneath a tiny opening at the base of a
stone pile revealed a 6-inch layer of charcoal at a depth of
about 1½ feet. Although no bones or artifacts were recovered, the fine consistency of blackened ash suggested that
a fire had once burned there for quite some time. A future
full-scale excavation is planned to obtain testable charcoal
samples.

As our investigation spread to other parts of the Northeast, we amassed data suggesting that some of the conical
piles acted as sites where fires were burned. It was very
possible, then, that the cairns we were plotting out along
the hills of New Jersey and New York had served as
"directional beacons."

Stone piles and mines seem to zigzag across the Shawangunk Ridge. But we also found that the mines and piles
continue past Kingston and into central Vermont. In fact,
detailed site reports showed that in central Vermont,
around Woodstock and South Reading, similar copper
shafts apparently had been quarried in antiquity, and
similar legends of mining roads had been handed down
through the years. The Old Mine Road appears to have
been an ancient pathway that led into central New England from the Delaware River Valley.

If the above scenario holds any degree of truth to it,
then we should find corroborative material elsewhere
which suggests that a long-gone people wandered through
the North Jersey forests. Although hardly useful as evidence, the following account does stir the imagination.

Colonel Joseph Brant was a Dartmouth-educated Mohawk sachem (chief) whose biography was written by
William Stone in 1838. In the book Stone cites a lengthy

and informative conversation between Brant and a questioning scholar:

> "Among other things relating to the western country," says Mr. Woodruff, "I was curious to learn in the course of my conversations with Captain Brant, what information he could give me respecting the *tumuli* [mounds] which are found on and near the margin rivers and lakes, from the St. Lawrence to the Mississippi. He stated, in reply, that the subject had been handed down time immemorial, that in an age long gone by, there came white men from a foreign country, and by consent of the Indians established trading-houses and settlements where these *tumuli* are found. A friendly intercourse was continued for several years; many of the white men brought their wives, and had children born to them; and additions to their numbers were made yearly from their own country. These circumstances at length gave rise to jealousies among the Indians, and fears began to be entertained in regard to the increasing numbers, wealth, and ulterior views of the new comers; apprehending that, becoming strong, they might one day seize upon the country as their own. A secret council, composed of the chiefs of all the different nations from the St. Lawrence to the Mississippi, was therefore convoked; the result of which, after long deliberation, was a resolution that on a certain night designated for that purpose, all their white neighbors, men, women, and children, should be exterminated. The most profound secrecy was essential to the execution of such a purpose; and such was the fidelity with which the fatal determination was kept, that the conspiracy was successful, and the device carried completely into effect. Not a soul was left to tell the tale."[19]

Perhaps there is more than a splinter of truth to this provocative oral legend.

C. Hudson River Valley

From a Coney Island co-op it is possible to see the New York Narrows, the water divide between the boroughs of Brooklyn and Staten Island, where the Atlantic Ocean meets the Upper Bay of New York Harbor (see Plate 24). Here in 1524, the Italian explorer Giovanni da Verrazano sailed past the Canarsie Indians to discover New York. Eighty-five years later, Henry Hudson entered the "great river" and sailed as far as Albany. During the journey he frequently commented to his ship's diarist about the beautiful scenery, bountiful lands, and pleasant water in and around the river that would eventually take his name. Future travelers were also to remark about the numerous springs, wells, and other attributes of the lower Hudson Valley. Much later in time New York Harbor became known throughout the shipping industry as one of the world's best natural water inlets.

The Hudson begins as a trout stream in the Adirondack Mountains of New York State. Below the Mohawk River, one of the largest tributaries feeding the Hudson, the river flows southward, widening and deepening its channel. For much of its course, the Hudson is actually a great estuary in which fresh mountain waters mix with the salt tides of the Atlantic.

If, as the accumulating evidence strongly suggests, there was trans-Atlantic communication with North America in ancient times, then we would expect to find evidence in and around the greater New York area, because the entranceway to a major northern water route, the Hudson River, is found there. Unfortunately, most of the islands and land masses in New York Harbor have long been covered over with asphalt and concrete. If ever there was a major outpost of prehistoric European colonists in lower Manhattan Island, it has either been long since destroyed or hidden beneath layers of modern cultural refuse. Occasionally, however, tantalizing tidbits can be uncovered in early documents.

1. STONE WALLS, LOWER MANHATTAN, NEW YORK

In 1751 the *New York Gazette* ran the following item:

> STONE WALL: Last week as some workmen were digging down the bank of the North River [the Hudson River], just

to the back of the English Church [Trinity Church on Broadway] in order to build a still house [distillery], a stone wall was discovered between four and five feet thick, near eight feet underground, and is supposed to have been the breast work of a battery, though we can't learn that the oldest men living amongst us know anything of such a battery being there, which affords some matter of speculation to the curious here.[20]

Trinity Church in lower Manhattan was constructed in 1697 as the city's first Protestant Episcopal Church. (The notorious pirate Captain William Kidd is said to have donated the block and tackle with which the church was first built). If the wall uncovered in 1751 was part of a Dutch construction, then we should see some evidence of stonework in seventeenth-century sketches of New Amsterdam. After examining several original plans in the map rooms of New York's numerous libraries, we found that the Castello Map, drawn around 1660, best illustrated the area in question.

An enclosed Dutch garden where Trinity Church was eventually built can readily be seen in a reproduction of the map. Adjacent to the garden was the wall which protected the fledgling colony of New Amsterdam. The Wall Street of today takes its name directly from the battery wall which spanned the width of Manhattan. It seems that in 1652 Dutch Governor Peter Stuyvesant ordered a palisade built around the colony of New Amsterdam to protect the town from feared invasions by the English. In September 1664 the worst of the Dutch fears were confirmed: the fleet of the Duke of York seized the town as part of the English-Dutch war in Europe.

At first we assumed that the stone wall mentioned in the *New York Gazette* was either the battery wall or the garden enclosure. The garden wall was quickly dismissed after further investigation, because our research revealed that in the eighteenth century Trinity Church was backed up to the water. The article specifically states that digging was carried out down the *bank* of the Hudson, "just to the back of" the church. Thus, we had to rule out the garden wall because it did not extend to the riverbank. Also, judging from the relative scale on numerous maps, we discovered that the garden enclosure was not 4-5 feet thick.

The possibility does exist that the wall excavated in 1751 was indeed part of the Dutch battery wall, but there are several factors which cast just a shadow of doubt upon this explanation. When the English finally gained control over New Amsterdam they did not immediately tear down the battery wall. In fact, things went on as usual in the town, save for a change of rulers. In time, however, the English overseers saw no reason to maintain the fortification wall, so they eventually removed it. The last of the wall was torn down in 1699 to make way for a growing city.

How could 8 feet of dirt have been deposited on a battery wall over a maximum time period of eighty-seven years (1664-1751) in colonial America? It is prudent to recall that in the seventeenth and eighteenth centuries there were no construction crews with diesel powered cranes, bulldozers, and other earth movers. Even for the quickly expanding city of New York, in the late 1600s it is highly unlikely that such an accumulation of soil could have been dropped by the rise and fall of new buildings. There is also the "memory lapse" brought up in the news article. If the wall was an old section of the battery, then certainly someone should have remembered it. Yet no one did. The wall appears to have been in place long before the Dutch set foot on Manhattan Island; and, tantalizingly, the Indians living in this part of America were never known to work in stone.

In the early 1900s as the city began its subway mass transit system, other stone walls were unearthed at very low depths. Even today it is not unusual for Manhattan building contractors to run across unexpected, subterranean, man-made objects. The island has seen the cultural imprint of many nations. It has been home to millions of people for thousands of years.

2. Inscribed Stone, Upper Manhattan, New York

An inscribed stone was uncovered by Alexander Cheno-weth in the fall of 1894, while he was digging in a high knoll near his home at Inwood, a wooded spot on the northwestern tip of Manhattan Island (see figure 3.4). Chenoweth, a civil engineer for the City of New York, found the stone lying about a foot below ground level. It had apparently been quarried and shaped, for it was described as being split across the top and bottom, with the top having a hammered or pitted surface.

For a while, the markings on the stone caused much debate in the academic community. Cornelia Horsford, a scholar from Cambridge, Massachusetts, believed the etchings were the Runic scrawlings of a band of Roman Catholic Norsemen (Vikings) who traveled to America in the thirteenth century either to tax or number the congregation supposedly living along the Hudson River. The stone, which according to her translation read, "Sons of the Church tax, or take a census,"[21] was inscribed and buried to commemorate the event—a kind of medieval time capsule. Archeologists for the American Museum of Natural History in New York felt differently. When Chenoweth donated his discovery to the Museum's anthropology department, it was classified as a "giant grooved sinker," a stone used by the Indians to weight down their fish nets. The staff then filed an identification card, moved the stone to the basement, and forgot about it for the next eighty-two years.

It is not uncommon to find these net sinkers (grooved stones) along the coastal region of many Atlantic states. Their size was apparently dependent upon the type and amount of fish to be caught, as well as the speed of the water current. But in general, Atlantic net sinkers tended to be small, portable stones. The Inwood Stone is a boulder, however, measuring approximately 3 feet in length by 2 feet in height and thickness. As no other giant sinker with such peculiar markings was ever found in the vicinity of Inwood, it is unlikely that this single stone was used to weight down nets. Outside Inwood, innumerable slabs have been found in the greater New York area that have grooves and slashes equivalent in style and spacing to the Chenoweth find. These etchings, formerly thought to be an Indian method for keeping track of time, are being reexamined. Renewed epigraphic interest in America's past has prompted museum officials to take another look at their collection of net sinkers and tally markers.

Stones recently discovered in Maine, New Hampshire, Vermont, Massachusetts, Connecticut, New York, Oklahoma, Texas, Arkansas, and the Caribbean have incisions that are almost identical with those found on the museum artifacts. The markings on these slabs, including the Inwood stone, are now believed to be a vowelless form of Ogam, an alphabet which may have been used by Iberian Celts as early as 800 B.C.

3. "Prehistoric Walls," Ramapo, New York

Northwest of Manhattan Island is a range of mountains that begins in Pennsylvania and continues through northern New Jersey and southern New York State. In the Hudson River region they're known as the Highlands. Between the Highlands and the Kittatinny-Shawangunk Ridge is a fertile, well-drained land that is part of the longest valley in the eastern United States; it runs over a thousand miles from Alabama to Montreal. Since the earliest times the Great Valley, as it is called, has always been an important agricultural zone. In modern times, due to its general remoteness, the area has never supported great numbers of people. Similarly, it supported no major colonial town and was crossed only with great difficulty by the railroads of the last century.

If not for several prominent passageways that breach the mountains, the Highlands would cut off the seaboard from the rich valleys to the west. In the northern part of the range, known locally as the Ramapo Mountains, a winding path cut eons ago by the Ramapo River provides a natural river highway for people traveling into the Great Valley and beyond. Along a hilltop overlooking the Ramapo Pass, a massive complex of stone walls meanders over some 200 acres of ground. The strange stonework, consisting of gigantic elliptical-mounds and circular stone piles, as well as an assortment of haphazardly placed walls, has defied explanation ever since a fascinating map of the site was drawn by an anonymous surveyor in 1845. The map, rediscovered in modern times, is entitled, "Supposed Prehistoric Walls in the Wrightman Fields, Ramapo, New York."

The hilltop where the site is located is heavily wooded; fresh water and swamps are an ever present feature. Aside from the rambling walls, there are several stone piles. Field teams have recorded eight mounds varying in diameter from 43-45 feet and in height from 3-4 feet. Eight other mounds were found to be generally smaller, varying in diameter from 20-43 feet and in height from 3-4 feet. One intriguing mound measured a spectacular 60 feet in diameter, while another measured a remarkable 8 feet in height. Several of the larger piles were found to contain rectangular and circular cavities, or carefully laid-out depressions. These gaping vertical openings were usually no deeper than 2-3 feet.

The 1845 map of the walls prompted an extended archeological investigation by the North Jersey Highlands Historical Society and the New England Antiquities Research Association (see figure 3.5). A report of their work filed by archeologist Edward J. Lenik in the *New York State Archeological Association Bulletin*[22] summarizes several interesting theories that have developed over the years concerning the origin of the walls. Lenik and crew evidently went to some pains to examine the following speculations about the prehistoric wall site.

1. Indians built the stone walls and mounds.

2. The site is a fortification built by a colonial militia stationed at Fort Sidman (a Revolutionary War fort under Colonel Hawthorn's regiment, whose responsibility it was to guard the Ramapo Pass to prevent the British from

taking the ironworks at the mid-Hudson Valley).

3. The walls and mounds were built by farmers in the process of clearing the land.

4. The walls are property lines, animal enclosures, or corrals.

5. The stone walls and mounds were built by an early race of non-Indians as a religious-ceremonial complex.[23]

Four years of documentary analysis, site survey, and archeological excavation turned up no evidence for any of the above speculations, although based on the meager data accumulated, Lenik favored the hypothesis that the walls and mounds were built by land-clearing farmers who sought to make the area more suitable for pasturage. However, the number of piles found in association with low lying walls—3 feet in height—seems to preclude any type of farming activity at the site, for why would colonial farmers go to such tremendous trouble to carefully pile stones if they were merely clearing a field for crops and/or pasture? (See Plates 25, 26, and 27.) The same arrangement would also appear to preclude any hypothesis about a defensive fortification, for the walls are too low and the mounds are too small. What, then, are the mysterious walls and mounds of the Ramapo Mountains?

The site occupies a distinct position on a hilltop overlooking not only the Ramapo Valley but also the Eastern Great Valley as well. The fact that several elliptical stone piles and stone walls lie on an axis of zero degrees due north (see figure 3.5) indicates that some type of astronomical observation may have taken place there. Also, the numerous old roads leading to the site, according to the 1845 map and recent surveys, were carefully lined with stones giving the general impression of an important processional pathway. Could the wall site on top of a mountain in southern New York State have served as a ceremonial center for all those who entered the Ramapo Pass? The conspicuous lack of artifacts at the excavations indicates that whoever built the structures took a lot of care not to deface or despoil the site with debris. The proximity of the other perched rocks, circles, and cairns believed to be ancient in origin strongly suggests that the prehistoric Ramapo walls served some ritualistic hilltop function for a long-gone people.

4. PERCHED ROCK AND SEMICIRCLE, GREENWOOD LAKE, NEW YORK

About 8 miles northwest of the Ramapo Walls along a natural valley pass, a 6-by-5-by-3-foot boulder rests upon rounded stones near the edge of an exposed limestone ridge. Ten feet from the perched boulders are six cubical blocks of limestone that have been arranged in a semicircle. The stones went unnoticed and unrecorded until a local hiker contacted MARC and led us to the site.

The arrangement of the stones is significant in that it conforms to certain fixed angles measured from the astronomical north-south axis. Stone A (see figure 3.6 and Plate 28) appears to have been used as an observation point to sight along sight lines AB and AC. An observer standing at stone A on December 21 would notice the sun rising directly over stone B. At day's end he would notice the sun setting over stone C, the perched boulder. The Greenwood Lake site could have been used to observe the rising and setting of the sun during the winter solstice.

But who could have arranged the stones in such a fashion, and why? The first clue emerged when we examined stone B of the semicircle. It was marked with deep engravings of vertical slashes flanked by a symbol which resembled a flattened X. Comparing our symbols with those found on a stone near Danbury. Connecticut, by John Williams of the Epigraphic Society, we realized that both markings were of the same design. The Danbury inscription occurs near a slab-roofed chamber and is believed to represent a qualifying epithet to Bel, the ancient Celtic sun god. The fact that the stones are placed in such a way as to allow for a visual record of the rising and setting sun on a particular day of the year, plus the fact that a hitherto unrecognized script used three thousand years ago in Europe is carved on one of the stones, suggests that the perched rock and semicircle are the handiwork of a band of Old World explorers who sailed across the Atlantic sometime before Columbus.

We searched the surrounding mountains for evidence of similar perched rocks and inscriptions. We didn't have far to go.

5. INSCRIBED STONE, BELLVALE, NEW YORK

A few miles northwest of Greenwood Lake, MARC field worker Richard Grando found a 200-pound inscribed boulder lying in the midst of a forest thicket on the top of the western slope of Bellvale mountain (see Plates 29 and 30). Three sides of the stone had been worked smooth. On one of the corners several deep U-shaped grooves had been cut in an orderly fashion. The incisions conform to others found throughout America. Similar markings on stones from Vermont and Maine have been classified as a script used by the ancient Iberian Celts. Close to where the stone was found is a colonial iron forge. It is very possible that the high-grade ore deposit was mined long before English settlers wandered into the Warwick Valley of southern New York State.

6. PERCHED ROCKS, LADENTOWN, NEW YORK

An extensive search of the surrounding hilltops led to another configuration of perched rocks. Near the hamlet of Ladentown, New York, at the top of a peak known as Circle Mountain, three rocks are perched on bedrock at the edge of a cliff. When viewed from above, the glacially transported boulders appear to form a triangle. Measurements taken by MARC show that a triangle with equal sides (10.4 feet), has been constructed at the cliff's edge. Further work indicated that stone A (see figures 3.7 and 3.8) at one time was perched on top of three smaller stones. Stone A is at least two times the length of the other boulders. When it was perched, it must have offered an imposing sight to passersby. Orientations indicated that during the winter solstice, an observer standing between stones B and C would notice the sun directly over vertical stone A.

The stone alignments presented here are only a small sampling of many similarly arranged sites in Pennsylvania, New York, and New Jersey. Such an abundance is indicative of a great need for them. We do know that elsewhere in the world various ancient people who worked in stone, like the Celts and Iberians, kept track of the seasons by marking out the solstices. An annual calendar was imperative for a seasonal economy of agriculture. But marking out celestial events requires a great deal of time and a system of record keeping. A priestly caste emerged whose function it was to keep records to regulate the routine of planting and harvesting. The association of prayer with different celestial events inevitably led to a wealthy and powerful caste who seemingly communed with the sky gods through stone temples on hilltops.

The New World astronomical alignments could have been used to regulate small-scale agricultural operations, but their unique situation—atop isolated knolls overlooking *key mountain passes*—suggests another explanation as well: the scheduling or signaling of travelers through the mountain routes. Perhaps tiny settlements of Old World peoples and/or astronomer priests needed a calendar to indicate when bands of pilgrims searching for god, or groups of miners searching for ore, might be passing through. Based on the type of engraved pebbles and inscribed slabs found west of the Hudson River in northeastern Pennsylvania near river confluences and in west-central New York near copper mines, this may very well have been the case. With a calendar it was possible to date the migrations and to predict the most opportune season to commence them.

7. INDIAN DAM, PLATTEKILL, NEW YORK

If the Ramapo "prehistoric wall" site were the only example of unusually large and inexplicable stone walls and pilings in he mid-Hudson Valley, then it would be easy to pass it off as spurious. It is not possible to do this, however, because 30 miles almost due north of the "prehistoric walls" there exists a "bit of ancient masonry in the town of Plattekill known as the 'Indian Dam.'" In a delightful 1887 book entitled *Legends of the Shawangunk,* author Philip H. Smith described "one of the greatest curiosities, in point of the mysteriousness of its origins in the county of Ulster," New York.

> The dam in question consists of two stone walls joined at an obtuse angle, and is about one hundred and fifty yards in length, eight or ten feet in height at the highest part, and four feet in width at the top. It is built across a stream at the outlet of a heavily timbered swamp, and would submerge about one hundred acres. As there is scarcely any perceptible fall, the dam could hardly have been built to furnish water power, hence the question as to the purpose of its construction has never been satisfactorily answered. What is stranger still, when the first settlers came into the vicinity, more than a century ago, the dam was there in the same condition in which it is now found; nor could they ascertain when, by whom, or for what purpose it was built.
>
> Though called the Indian Dam, it is not probable the Indians had anything to do with its construction, as they were not given to wall building. Its origin may have been coeval with that of the ancient roads in the vicinity of the Shawangunk mountain, called the "Mine Roads" [Old Mine Road], indications of which may yet be seen at various points at the foot of the declivities on either side, of which neither history nor tradition can give a satisfactory account.[24]

In August 1976 MARC associate Neil Novesky and I set out to locate the stonework described more than ninety years earlier. We found that, south of the town of Plattekill in the midst of a heavily wooded forest, an enormous stone wall, its top pitted with rectangular openings, stretched 150 yards in a long parabolic arc near the periphery of a decaying swamp. The wall measured 16 feet in width at its base and 4 feet at the top, just as

Smith noted. Other measurements tallied with Smith's description. The techniques of stone placement and the intriguing depressions along the wall's top were just like the stone features noted at the Ramapo site.

The function of the "Indian Dam" remains unclear. Although the depressions are large enough for a man to sit in, it is highly unlikely that the wall was used for defense. It simply does not enclose anything; there are no other walls in the vicinity that could have served as sides to a "fort." A stream originating from the swamp lying just north of the structure flows in a southerly direction, undercutting it in one section. At first glance the wall does give the general impression of a dam. Upon further observation, however, the parabolic shape of the stonework, as well as the width of the swamp and surrounding flat-lands, makes any interpretation of the site as a dam absurd. The wall was simply not designed to contain water.

An extensive documentary search failed to produce an adequate explanation for the strange stonework. The "Indian Dam" is but another enigma of the mid-Hudson Valley. It stands alone, massive, laboriously constructed for some purpose forgotten with the passage of centuries. One cannot help but recall our earlier description of a stone wall found about 75 miles to the south along the Hudson River in lower Manhattan.

Aerial photography later revealed an obscure path extending eastward from the so-called Indian Dam for approximately 6 miles. The trail appeared to lead towards a piece of land projecting into the Hudson River. It was here in the early 1600s that Dutch skippers sailing up the river observed the Wappinger Indians perform their religious ceremonies on a flat-rock promontory which stood a few miles north of the present city of Newburgh, New York. "De Duyfel's Danskammer" (the Devil's Dance Chamber), as it was called by the Calvinist Dutchmen, was the spot where the Indians worshipped their sun god, Bachtamo, by screaming and cavorting around a blazing fire. To the first Europeans such obscene antics were quickly assumed to be a form of devil worship—hence the name given to the locale.

By 1720 Bachtamo worship had been stopped by European suppression. This not only interfered with the socio-religious customs of the Wappinger Indians, thereby contributing to the ultimate disintegration of aboriginal culture, but it also may have destroyed some of the last cosmological remnants of an earlier non-Indian community, for not more than 3 miles away, a crude stone monument stands alone, silently reflecting the dim presence of a mysterious people.

8. Standing Stone, Poughkeepsie, New York, and Inscriptions, Wappingers Falls, New York

Across the Hudson River from the Danskammer Point, which has now been almost entirely obliterated by a modern power plant, a navigable inlet known as the Wappinger Creek cuts deeply into the Highland Mountains. Here, the enigmatic Wappinger Indians inhabited the eastern shore of the river up through the arrival of the first Dutch settlers. For reasons known only to the Wappinger tribes, the land surrounding the creek was the capital of their confederacy. A thorough documentary and site-survey investigation conducted by MARC has shown that not only was the region the political capital of the confederacy, but it was the religious capital as well.

At the northeastern base of an 80-foot hill, equidistant from the Hudson River and Wappinger Creek, about a mile south from Poughkeepsie, a rectangular slab of limestone protrudes from the property of a local resident. According to the landowner, who has lived in the region for nearly forty-six years, the land around the stone was once an extensive farm owned by his family. The stone presently measures approximately 5.8 feet in height and a foot in width. It once stood several feet higher, but in 1965, 3-4 feet of earth fill was put in around its base to level off the property. Thus, before 1965, the standing height of the slab was close to 9 feet. In the 1930s the resident's grandfather, concerned that the stone would topple over from the weight of his grandchildren, who used to climb all over it, probed below the stone with steel rods to determine its socket length. His concern quickly faded when he discovered the stone to be as deep underground as it was above, thereby giving it a total length of about .18 feet!

Local legend has it that an Indian chief and/or a Revolutionary War general is buried beneath the stone, but there is no direct evidence to support this. The stone is definitely not the by-product of natural weathering, for it has been shaped, as can clearly be seen at its base. According to several accounts in the neighboring town of Wappingers Falls, the stone was already standing in place when the first Dutchman wandered across the creek.

A striking characteristic of the Poughkeepsie stone is its visual similarity to the isolated standing stones (menhirs) found all over Europe. In the Old World what they signify varies considerably according to period, region, and with whom you talk. In Ireland, for example, certain menhirs were believed by villagers to be related to sexuality. It was not uncommon to find, up to the nineteenth century, sterile women rubbing their bodies against the menhir in hopes of becoming imbued with the stone's fertility. The phallic overtones associated with standing stones are thought to be related to pre-Christian fertility rituals. In parts of the Mediterranean menhirs are believed to be connected with various cosmic-religious rites and/or with the cult of ancestor worship. Perhaps the folklore of the Indian chief has some substance to it, although it is highly unlikely that an *Indian* chief is buried beneath the soil.

In parts of Britain and Northern Portugal, individual standing stones are believed to have been territorial markers or directional indicators. In those countries, the functional explanation transforms certain menhirs into prehistoric road signs. The idea is not as silly as it sounds, for some type of marker must have been used thousands of years ago to guide prehistoric man through dense forest growth toward his home or religious center.

This does not necessarily mean that a stone's mundane, practical role superceded a possible ceremonial one. Indeed, the stones may have been used for a variety of purposes, such as scheduling agricultural operations in accordance with knowledge of the sun's seasonal positions on the horizon. At the same time the stones could have been used on another level, one with more aesthetic overtones. Perhaps they were the dwelling places of gods; perhaps they were merely monuments. The great size of these structures surely impressed megalithic man as much as it does the urban dweller of today. Clearly, menhirs in both the Old and New World remain mysterious structures that lack definite interpretations.

The Poughkeepsie standing stone leans over, making an angle of about 76 degrees with the ground (see figure 3.9). The longitudinal axis of the stone's vertical plane is tilted towards a direction of about 202 degrees southwest. That is, the stone appears to be tipped in such a way as to be pointing towards the southwest at a compass bearing of 202 degrees. If the "direction" of the stone is followed, one discovers that it leads to the top of the highest hill in the nearby area.

During the summer of 1976 a MARC ground team decided to follow the general direction of the stone as best they could. The implications of the hike are far-reaching. About a half-mile from the slab, an inscribed stone was found incorporated within a colonial field wall. The markings are deeply cut onto a block of sandstone. Thus far, no interpretation has been made. But it is evident that the markings are in the same style as those found at the Greenwood Lake site, Bellvale Mountain, and at Danbury, Connecticut (see Chapter 4).

Continuing the search, the field crew discovered that the 2-mile walk had led them to the mouth of the Wappinger Creek, where the Danskammer Point could be clearly and easily seen. It appeared that the standing stone could have been used as a sighting marker that pointed in the general direction of the navigable Wappinger Creek inlet. The fact that a stone inscribed with an alphabet (Iberic Ogam) believed to be of ancient European origin was found in a field wall close by a directional "pathway" leads one to assume that the same people who left the inscription had something to do with erecting the standing stone. There is no archeological evidence in the northeast which suggests that American Indians either knew the Iberic Ogam alphabet or quarried, transported, and implanted standing stones.

Although no artifactual debris in the vicinity of the Danskammer has yet come to light which would tie the standing stone and inscription in with the worship of Bachtamo, it would not be surprising to one day learn that the Algonquins dancing around the fires at the Danskammer were actually evoking the image of a deity known to tribes on the other side of the Atlantic Ocean.

An early reference to Hudson River Indian "priests" ministering at their altars may have more truth to it than previously realized, for 20 miles southeast of the Poughkeepsie standing stone a good number of strange stone rooms lie scattered throughout meadows and cliffsides. Half-buried within the eastern and western slopes of hillsides, enormous slab-roofed chambers peer out from thick sod coverings and patiently wait for the first rays of the rising midwinter sun to penetrate their dark hollows. Stones found nearby, etched with the markings of a dead people, tell of forgotten deities and unknown men. A perched rock, perhaps raised thousands of years ago as a burial tomb for a special king or priest, overwhelms us today with its sheer massiveness.

Not far from the rock, a small chamber, oriented to capture the morning sunlight during the equinox, when day equals night, rests in a meadow near an overgrown swamp. A few yards away a squat, cube-shaped stone lends its permanence to a farm wall. But this is no ordinary stone: it is inscribed with symbols that speak of worship. Sometime in the past, before colonial settlers cleared the fields of decaying trees and loose boulders, the stone was probably resting upright, proclaiming to all who passed by that the chamber was the house of a god.

4
Stone Mysteries: Southeastern New York, Southwestern Connecticut

Table 4 and figure 4.1 indicate generally the distribution and kinds of structures which are discussed in this chapter.

A. Southwest Coast of Connecticut

To the settlers living along the Quinnipiac River in southern Connecticut, the coastal prong of land stretching west from the Housatonic to the Hudson was a 3,000-square-mile tract of uncharted wilderness. Known as the western forest, the land was the terror of the white man, for along its way roamed the dreaded Mohawk Indians. In the early 1600s, few dared venture into this terrifying region. The first English pioneers were obliged to confine their farms to the well-traveled coastline bordering the Long Island Sound.

As the Indian threat was gradually and successfully eliminated, the colonists became more secure in their new homes. Setting out to systematically clear the land for

TABLE 4
Summary of Stone Structures

A. Southwest Coast of Connecticut	B. Upper Croton River Valley	C. Housatonic River Valley
1. Inscribed hearthstone, Riverside, Connecticut	1. Double chamber, stone wall complexes, Putnam Valley, New York	1. Standing stones and inscription, Washington, Connecticut
	2. Slab-roofed chambers, southeastern New York, southwestern Connecticut	2. Hebrew inscriptions, semicircle New Preston, Connecticut
	3. Balanced Rock, North Salem, New York	3. Inscribed rock, Kent, Connecticut
		4. Stone pile, stone circle, Washington, Massachusetts

pasturage and farming, they swept away age-old trees and rotting brush. But in doing so, they uncovered the half-obliterated remains of an ancient agricultural operation. Amid the clearings were dim traces left by unknown farmers whose skill surpassed anything practiced by the "savages" the settlers had recently subdued. In the seemingly virgin, uncultivated countryside north of the Sound, the white man was startled by the evidence of a thrifty industry harking back to some forgotten era when a busy population must have tilled the soil and constructed crude stone shelters far up into the hillsides. Along the fertile valleys, the settlers thankfully built their homes and outbuildings on the foundations of another age.

As the seasons wore on, the once fertile soil lost its nutrients. Low crop yields forced families to move westward into the Ohio and Mississippi Valleys. By the early 1800s, a good many eastern farms were abandoned. Generations passed by. Old surveys and land rights were misplaced or destroyed as successive waves of migrating

Europeans took over these lands. But this time the stone mysteries that had greeted the original pioneers were overlooked. Some of the structures were so intertwined within the colonial settlement that their uniqueness remained hidden to all but the most keen-eyed antiquarians. Other telltale signs of ancient doings lay buried beneath years of forest growth.

Occasionally, however, the past crept into the present.

1. INSCRIBED HEARTHSTONE, RIVERSIDE, CONNECTICUT

A stone with incisions similar to the Chenowith find was recently discovered a short distance from New York City. During the spring of 1977, Cece Kirkorian, then chairman of the Archeological Associates of Greenwich, Connecticut, informed MARC of an inscribed hearthstone flanking the basement fireplace of an eighteenth-century house in Riverside, a shoretown some 20 miles northeast of Manhattan. The estate, established around 1765, was once the center of a 250-acre farm. Situated but a stone's throw from Long Island Sound, the original grounds were graced by an apple orchard, a pond, and a meandering brook.

A young lawyer and his wife bought the huge house in 1937 and made it their home. For close to forty years, on cold New England evenings made even colder by the moist sea breeze peculiar to coastal towns, the couple often retired to the warmth of their downstairs den. Nothing unusual was ever noticed in the cozy, wood-paneled room. The brick fireplace on the north wall was a delightful reminder of a rustic past when families depended solely upon the heat of burning logs for their comfort and cooking. Blackened by the soot of over two hundred years, it was typical of many other traditional heating units, having, in the words of Shakespeare, "fires unrak'd and hearths unswept."

In 1973, the young son of a neighbor visiting the house was playing in the basement den. While sitting near the hearthstone, he accidentally brushed away years of charcoal dust and, as children often do, noticed the unusual.

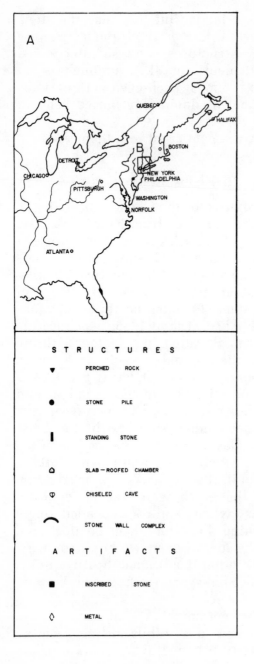

Fig. 4.1. Distribution of
stone structures in the
Hudson, Croton, and
Housatonic River Valleys
(Map by Kalpana R. Shah)

A

QUEBEC
HALIFAX
BOSTON
B
DETROIT
CHICAGO
NEW YORK
PITTSBURGH
PHILADELPHIA
WASHINGTON
NORFOLK
ATLANTA

S T R U C T U R E S

▼ PERCHED ROCK

● STONE PILE

❘ STANDING STONE

⌂ SLAB — ROOFED CHAMBER

Ⴔ CHISELED CAVE

⌒ STONE WALL COMPLEX

A R T I F A C T S

■ INSCRIBED STONE

◊ METAL

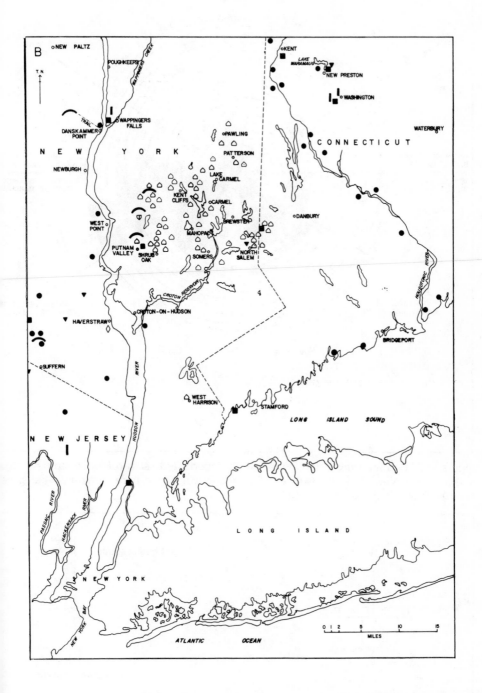

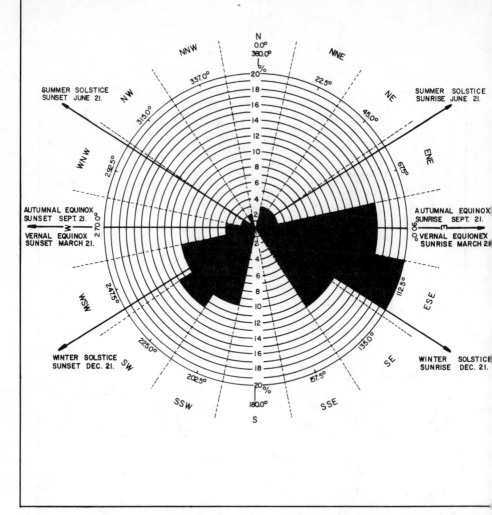

Figure 4.2. Entranceway orientations of fifty corbelled, slab-roofed chambers from southeastern New York and western Connecticut (latitude approximately 41 degrees north). (Drawing by Kalpana R. Shah)

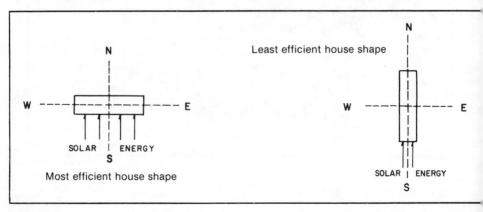

Fig. 4.3. Relationship of house shape to solar heating potential. (Drawing by Kalpana R. Shah)

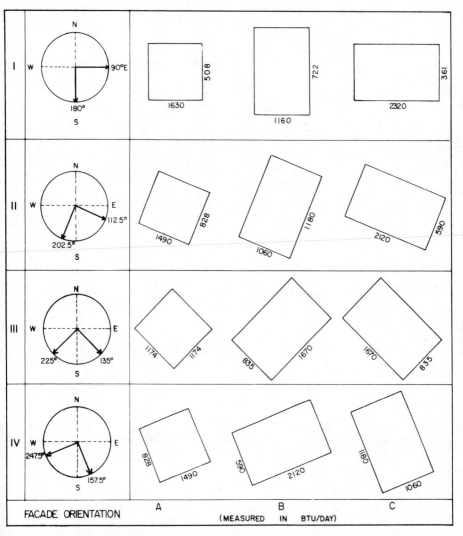

Fig. 4.4. Relative insolation of structures of different orientation and shape—January 21, latitude approximately 41 degrees north. Values represent relative insolation on a hypothetical structure with an area of one square foot. (Drawing by Kalpana R. Shah, after Bruce Anderson)

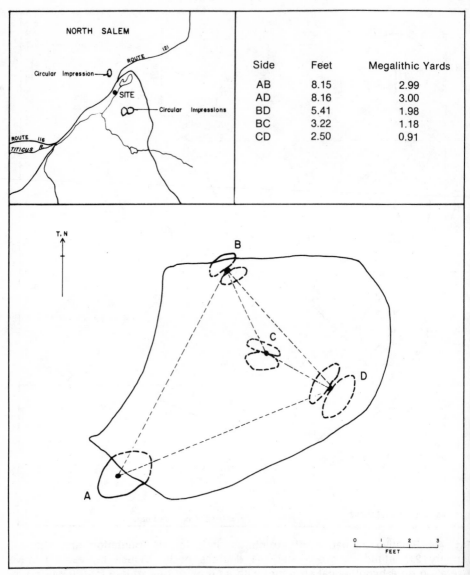

Side	Feet	Megalithic Yards
AB	8.15	2.99
AD	8.16	3.00
BD	5.41	1.98
BC	3.22	1.18
CD	2.50	0.91

Fig. 4.5. Balanced Rock, North Salem, New York. (Drawing by Kalpana R. Shah)

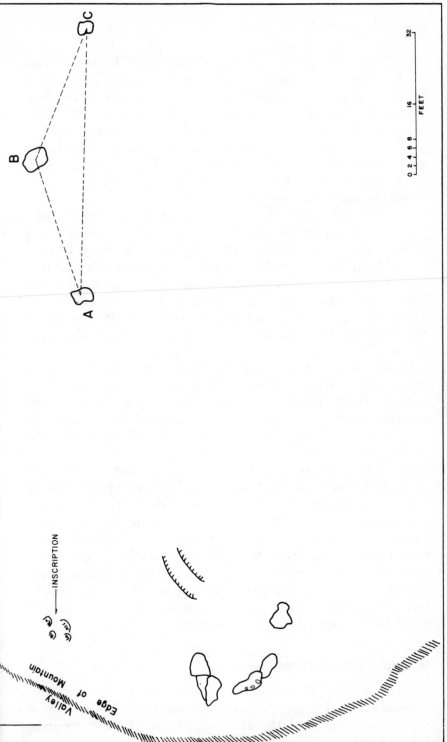

Fig. 4.6. Semicircle, Hebrew inscription, and perched rocks, New Preston, Connecticut. (Drawing by Kalpana R. Shah)

"What are these markings on the fireplace?" he asked. The markings were a complete puzzle to the owners (see Plates 31, 32, and 33). Throughout all the months and years they had relaxed in the room, they had never seen what this ten-year-old boy was now pointing to. No one in the community seemed to have any information about the hearthstone. It was never mentioned in previous sales of the house. Indeed, there was no reason to mention such a mundane feature . . . or so it seemed.

Hearthstones were slabs laid in front of fireplaces. They provided a convenient platform for cooking vessels while at the same time keeping the fire and ash away from a room. Instead of searching the countryside for a suitable slab, our ancestors sometimes simply extended the tile floor of a fireplace into the living quarters, thereby eliminating the need for a separating stone. Individual taste and availability of material usually determined the style of a hearth.

Years of heat have split the long Riverside stone into two sections. Along one side of the slab are two horizontal grooves that have been crossed by several vertical and slanting marks. The grooves are neither glacial chattermarks nor pot scratches. They have been systematically pecked out by some type of pointed instrument.

In all probability the stone was either standing upright or lying beneath the soil when the first settlers arrived in southern Connecticut. This must have been so, for the markings on the hearthstone are in the same style as those found in the Inwood Stone and others scattered throughout the Old and New Worlds. Inscriptions of the same type from northern Portugal and southern Spain, only recently identified, decoded, and translated, are thought to have been written by an adventurous seafaring people some twenty-five hundred years ago.

B. Upper Croton River Valley

Approximately 25 miles north of Manhattan, a narrow tongue of land known as Croton Point reaches out from the eastern bank of the Hudson River. The Kitchawong chieftaincy of the Algonquin Tribe once guarded the entrance to the Croton River from a fortified village situated on the neck of the peninsula.

The waterways feeding the Croton River Valley draw their life from the deep woods which cover the undulating mountain system known as the Hudson Highlands. Hidden streams pulsate through underground crevices formed eons ago by the constant ebbing of rainwater through limestone cracks. The streams drain the forested interior and eventually emerge from their subterranean channels to crash over steep, boulder-ridden alcoves before joining the Croton Reservoir System. At one time, the many branches of the river supplied sufficient waterpower for a cottage industry of lumber mills. The hardwood frames of many seventeenth-century Dutch homes overlooking the high Hudson banks were probably cut by these colonial saws.

During the Revolutionary War, the Highlands, which embrace an area of over 234 square miles east and west of the Croton River, were a key military stronghold for the struggling colonies. Considerable military activity took place there due to the important supply trails traversing the mountains and linking upper and lower New York. It was vital for the patriots to protect these routes from the encroaching army of King George. At the high point of the war, several walls and earth embankments were erected at a point near the Hudson where the river veers sharply in its course. The crude fortresses, later named West Point, blocked off the continent from further military advance. Crucial to the success of the garrison was an integral series of defense fortifications scattered along the Highland Mountains on both sides of the river. Today, the locations of these strongholds are easily identified from the original maps of the period now housed in the library of the United States Military Academy at West Point.

After the war several ironworks and tanneries were established along the Croton's tributaries. Large wooden dams were erected as a cheap source of waterpower. Blocks of quarried stone were laid flat against the earth in an effort to create retaining walls. Beyond the northern reaches of the Croton, farms were built. As most of this land is incapable of being plowed due to the rocky terrain and poor soil, it is not unusual that many of the farms are confined to the fertile hollows of the mountains. A great number of these ruined barn foundations, lumber mills, and lime kilns date back to the seventeenth and eighteenth centuries.

But scattered throughout the heavy wood cover of the Highlands, there are an equal number of drystone works which go unclassified and unexplained. Along the rugged sides of boulder-strewn knolls, MARC investigators have recorded many structures which are neither military redoubts nor English pigpens. They are constructed in a style quite different from the other well-known mortared remains. They appear to be the ruined vestiges of a people given to shaping, transporting and building with huge masses of stone.

After years of scholarly neglect and facile, armchair assumptions about our immediate ancestors' building habits, we are just beginning to recognize and understand key differences between, for example, a gristmill dam logically situated across a fast-flowing stream and a giant, slabbed, crescent-shaped wall illogically towing 20 feet above a marsh, miles from the beaten paths of both yesterday and today. Within a 10-mile radius of the upper Croton River our teams have reported the existence of over forty slab-roofed chambers, three stone wall complexes, and several mines, which, according to early documents, were worked long before seventeenth-century farmers cleared the land. Undoubtedly, more structures exist on mountain slopes not yet visited or perhaps overlooked by our researchers. Coupled with this are the many sites which must have been inundated by the Croton Reservoir Project of the last century.

1. Double Chamber, Stone Wall Complexes
Putnam Valley, New York

Located near the path of an old Indian trail is one of the most impressive wall complexes yet recorded by our crew.

Covering an area of over 500 square yards, an enormous rectangular enclosure of carefully laid boulders rests near a dense swamp. Adjacent to the heavy embankment, two slab-roofed chambers, side by side, yet of unequal size, seem to guard the western opening of the complex. It is difficult to imagine what purpose the site could have had in past ages. Throughout the years it has remained a mystery to local historians.

The northern section of the enclosure is covered by a graded earthway. Parallel to this side, across a rectangular enclave littered with the plastic trash of twentieth-century man, are two more drystone walls. The southern section stands alone, uncovered by earth and grass. Measuring more than 8 feet in width along the top and 14 feet at the base, the walls, standing 6 feet tall, gradually increase in height as they stretch along—one for 50 feet, the other for 67 feet—eventually converging to form the extreme southern corner of the enclosure. This is the most bizarre, inexplicable feature of the site (see Plates 34 and 35). Here, as the walls join in a squared corner, crudely hewn stones, some estimated to weigh more than 2000 pounds, have been piled 16 feet high, giving the distinct impression of a defense fortification. What may thus have been kept out of the enclosure is unknown. Today, only wild ivy, green weeds, and the occasional hiker dare to scale the stones.

Along the southern walls several collapsed cavities measuring 2-3 feet in diameter, 1-2 feet in depth were found. Although these depressions were only partially open at the time they were examined, there were enough stones still in place near the bottom for us to see that an extraordinary amount of care was taken to construct them. It will be recalled that an identical arrangement was seen west of the Hudson River at the Plattekill "Indian Dam" site and at the Ramapo "Prehistoric Walls" site. Furthermore, similar cavities in West Virginia excavated by the Smithsonian Institution in the 1890s revealed the cremated remains of several people. Beneath different layers of stone, several charred skeletons were found to have been laid out with the heads pointing towards the circular depression. The identity of the people buried was never definitely determined. Future investigation may very well expose the same finds at the Putnam Valley sites.

The two adjoining slab-roofed chambers are an integral part of the Putnam Valley walled complex. They are not the same size. One measures 25 by 8.5 by 6 feet, the other, 16 by 5.5 by 5 feet. They have been carefully laid with gigantic slabs of granite. We later found that chambers and walls are not isolated phenomena. They usually occur together and in groups.

About two and a half miles north of the double chamber site another complex of huge stone walls and heaps is strewn along the sides of a deep valley. Not far from a wet marsh a cluster of walls 6-8 feet wide and 2-3 feet in height winds across rocky ledges and a sunken bog. A number of circular cavities the same size as those in Putnam Valley can easily be spotted among the ruins. Nearby, there is evidence in the form of slag heaps of some long-neglected mining operation. Rusting nineteenth-century farm implements and shards of three-hundred-year-old Dutch pottery lie undisturbed, as if they had been left just yesterday.

Evidently some of the quarried stone walls were built during the postcolonial era to harness the swiftly flowing Canopus Creek. The iron mines probably represent expensive eighteenth-century attempts to tap the region's rich mineral sources. But other mining shafts, the cavitied walls, and a few equinox-facing slab-roofed chambers found further up the hillside seem to tell a different story. Although later incorporated within a colonial enterprise, they probably date back to a different time period. Indeed, a mid-nineteenth-century document tells of an obscure silver mine being worked in ancient times and containing "old tools with the handles rotted out."[1]

A few miles from the Canopus Creek walls, deep within Clarence Fahnestock Memorial State Park, is another rectangular stone wall complex of gigantic proportions. Several immense slab-roofed chambers, all facing the same direction, are a short distance away. Reaching a height of 20 feet, the four walls enclose empty space. No foundations or remains, save the occasional cigarette butt, can be seen within. Three stone-lined cavities 3 feet in diameter and just as many feet apart, grace one side of the enclosure. A swamp is close by. The incredible height of the enclosure presupposes a deep footing, probably reaching well below the frost level. It also represents a major undertaking in the way of clearing land, quarrying, transporting, and building with large stone blocks.

Up until 1976, when our teams first reported their existence and searched for common characteristics, the walled complexes in this part of the state had never been investigated. Our very preliminary work suggests several parallels with stoneworks found elsewhere in the United States and Europe. Cyrus Thomas, in the late 1890s, reported seeing many "ancient stone walls" 1-2 feet high and 6 feet wide winding their way across miles of eastern America. Near Manchester, Tennessee, at a site known as "The Old Stone Fort" several walls up to 18 feet thick at the base were scattered atop a high plateau. The stones for the enclosure were obtained from stratified cliffs up to a half-mile away. Some of them measured up to 6 feet in length and 3 feet in width, requiring, as Thomas put it, "2 to 4 stout men to carry them."

Several other stone wall sites were reported by the settlers of the Ohio and Mississippi Valleys. On top of high bluffs, farmers discovered walls, some of them 8 feet high and wide, surrounding several acres of cultivated soil. Stone-lined pits, stone circles, and conical cairns were always situated near the enclosures' entranceways. Very few trenches have been sunk at these Ohio and Illinois sites. Perhaps because of the few excavations that have been performed, very little was revealed, save some superficial burials probably from another time period. Today it still is not known who built these stoneworks.

When we try to explain massive wall complexes in terms of the Indian culture contemporaneous with the colonists, we are at a loss to do so. The stoneworks were as mystifying to the Indians as they were to the white man. And, as we have already seen, the archeological record to date gives us no indication that prior northeastern tribes were the lithic engineers. However, if we go back to the first recorded artifacts found among these ruins before they were trampled over by misguided antiquarians, we come up with some possible answers.

Many of the relics found in the last century among the New World ruins (stone axeheads, flint, bone arrow heads and lance heads) were described as "so precisely resembling those disinterred from early British barrows, that the most experienced eye could hardly tell the one from the other."[2] This alone should give us pause. When we look to the fifth-century B.C. Celtic Hill forts of Britain and Iberia with their guard chambers, defensive earth mounds with walls 12-14 feet thick and 14 feet high, with their segmented bastions and associated cairns, we are struck by the curious resemblance to the stone enclosures of eastern America. In the earliest Iberian strongholds it is not uncommon to find several drystone dwelling chambers buttressed against the enclosure—just like the Putnam Valley double-chamber site.

Celtic warriors of France and Scotland built special 1-2 foot wide cavities into their fortification walls to display the skulls of their defeated enemies. This gristly habit thoroughly disgusted Julius Caesar and other early chroniclers. Close to two hundred fifty Celtic forts have been defined in the foothills of the Bavarian Alps, and many more have been found in northern Portugal as well. An intriguing aspect of these structures is that they are always built near a body of water, be it a bog, swamp, lake, river, or stone-lined shaft. Human sacrifices were cast into the water and earth shafts in an effort to please the gods. Within walking distance of all the walled sites reported by MARC researchers, the remains of deep vertical "tunnels" were noted. As we expanded our inquiry into the rest of New England, we discovered several more unexplained shafts. These stone enclosures of southeastern New York are probably a result of the labor of men from across the Atlantic.

2. SLAB-ROOFED CHAMBERS, SOUTHEASTERN NEW YORK, SOUTHWESTERN CONNECTICUT

To many of the residents living in southeastern New York State, the vaulted chambers strewn along the upper crests of the Highland Mountains are nothing more than the dirt cellars which for years held their ancestors' winter supply of the autumn harvest. Roofed with immense, overlapping stones and covered by thick mounds of turf, the cellars present no mystery to their contemporary owners. "We used to store potatoes in 'em," said one old-timer. "Been here as long as I can remember," replied another.

Indeed. While there is no reason to doubt that the chambers were at one time or another used as root cellars, there is an accumulating body of data which suggests that they were not all built solely for that purpose. The number of chambers frequently found together, as well as their general shape and layout, appears inconsistent with the idea of their construction as mere granaries or animal shelters. When we add to this the quantity of inscribed slabs bearing the marks of Celtic and Semitic writing systems found during the last few centuries, and more recently by our coworkers, in close association with slab-roofed, chamber-wall complexes, it can only be concluded that we are dealing with the interrelated ruins of a people whose skill in moving cyclopean stone equalled that of the prehistoric tribes of Europe and the Mediterranean. The chambers of southeastern New York and most of New England appear to be the congregated structures of a social community; they are strangely different from any that have been built since colonial times.

When we compare these ruins with the wood-framed homes of the earliest settlers, it is impossible to overlook the remarkable differences presented by the two states of society, separated not only by time but by habits and ideas as well. How striking is the contrast between the tight compactness of the pioneer log cabin with its sodded seams and the megalithic grandeur of the mortarless, slab-roofed chamber. It is evident that no amount of manpower was spared in the completion of these chambers, some estimated to have capstones weighing up to 30 tons.

Individually, the chambers say very little. But when grouped together, they tell a story far more interesting and enigmatic than winterized potato cabins. The best way, then, to understand their meaning, is to diverge from the usual format of individually listing each stone structure and instead discuss them as an aggregate. In an area covering over 300 square miles of southeastern New York and southwestern Connecticut, fifty corbelled, slab-roofed chambers were examined by MARC teams. Some of the simpler measurements taken included interior base length, width, height, diagonal, and entranceway orientation. As the data accumulated an intriguing picture emerged.

Five clusters each consisting of nine to twelve chambers were found distributed approximately 3 miles from each other in the dense woods outside the towns of Putnam Valley, Kent Cliffs, Patterson, Mahopac, North Salem, and Danbury. Within each cluster the chambers tended to be approximately 2,500-3,000 feet apart. This may be a local peculiarity, for although some of our site reports from New England suggest a parallel situation, archeologist James Whittall, who is presently compiling a detailed grid system for predicting the whereabouts of buried stone chambers in the Northeast, tells us that in some parts of Massachusetts and New Hampshire the interchamber distance exceeds 1½ miles. Many of the chambers built into hillsides were found to command a magnificent view of the distant horizon during the winter months when the vegetation cover was gone. There were also some structures that differed in placement orientation. These tended to be located near the foot of hillsides.

Practically all of the chambers we surveyed were fashioned from massive chunks of stone which revealed no tool marks. The slabs had apparently been pried out of bedrock with devices that left no traces. One such quarrying technique that's been in use for at least six thousand years and which may have been used in southeastern and southwestern Connecticut involved the placement of dry

wooden wedges into the natural cracks of a stone. Once
the wedges were in place, water was poured over them.
As the wood swelled, the fracture in the stone eventually
widened, making it easier to whack off a chunk with a big
stick. Another method of quarrying without metal was to
build very hot fires on a stone surface and then douse it
with water or vinegar to produce cleavage. The Carthaginian general Hannibal supposedly blazed a rock trail
through the Alps when his engineers realized that vinegar
induced more rock fractures than water.

Because many of the chambers had dirt floors, it was
impossible to accurately measure interior height. We chose
not to probe into the soil for fear of disturbing any
possible strata that might lie beneath the surface. But
even with this restriction, the average interior height of a
sample of fifty chambers turned out to be 6.3 feet. The
remarkable consistency of this figure (with some heights
fluctuating by only a few inches above and below the
average) leads us to suspect that not much ground soil lies
beneath the surface.

Interior length was measured along the longitudinal axis
of each chamber at a height equal to the lowest row of
stone slabs before corbelling began. Length was determined to the outermost façade of the entranceway. Base
width was determined by bisecting the longitudinal axis
and measuring along the lowest row of stone slabs. The
base diagonals were also measured along the base stones
from the chamber's rear to forward corners. Some
chambers had rounded corners, making it impossible in
these cases to accurately determine the diagonal.

In order to determine how many chambers faced in
what direction, we first had to record each chamber's
entranceway orientation (measured along the interior longitudinal axis) and then plot the field data onto a simple
circle graph divided into sixteen equal parts of 22.5-degree
intervals. The rationale for the divisions was based on the
most common New England orientations for home positioning. Thus we have N, NNE, NE, ENE, E, ESE, SE, SSE,
S, SSW, SW, WSW, W, WNW, NW, NNW, where N =

North (zero degrees), E = East (90 degrees), S = South (180 degrees), W = West (270 degrees). From the illustration figure 4.2 we can see a general tendency for the sample of fifty chambers to fall more or less below the east-west line, with the following breakdown: 20 percent faced ESE, 16 percent faced E, 12 percent faced SE or SW, 10 percent faced SSW or WSW, 6 percent faced SSE, 4 percent faced W, and 2 percent faced NNE, NE, ENE, WNW, or NNW.

In its most general terms, the data represented in the graph fall into two categories: those chambers facing the eastern-southeastern sky, and those facing the southwestern sky. The chambers in both of these categories tended to be situated near the crests of mountain peaks in full view of the local horizon. They were always constructed of enormous drystone slabs of granite, some reaching 15 feet in length and 5 feet in width. Those structures facing the northwest and northeast tended to face mountain ridges and other natural features. They were usually constructed of small field stones. Building mortar was usually present.

The eastern-southeastern-oriented chambers tended to be smaller than the southwestern group. The former structures usually had an interior length measuring about 1½ times the width, in contrast to he latter group, whose interior length often measured between 2 and 2½ times the width. Both groups, however, had a general shape which resembled an elongated rectangle.

It is clear from the graph that some of the chambers appear to be aligned towards the equinox and winter solstice sunrises/sunsets. Even though the sample consisted of only fifty chambers, our field teams were able to find that these particular structures were evenly distributed among the five clusters of chambers over a 300-square-mile-area. In other words, it seemed as if each grouping of chambers had a few (one to three) stone buildings which were aligned towards specific solar events.

Alerted to the possibility that these "special" chambers may have served some type of ritualistic community function, our teams carefully searched the surrounding terrain for evidence of population gatherings. We found numerous ground disturbance patterns which were indicative of ancient settlements. Furthermore, we found several stone slabs marked with a script believed to be a variety of Celtic Ogam and Iberian Punic, both languages spoken in the Mediterranean region in the eighth century B.C. The possibility that we were working with buildings from an age when the sun meant something more to people than a source of tans seemed very real indeed.

During the course of a year, the sun seems to rise and set at a different point along the horizon. The reason for this, of course, is the tilting of the earth's axis as it spins around the sun. During the summer months, the Northern Hemisphere is tipped towards the sun. As a result, the sun seems to rise and set north of the east-west line. But during the winter months, the Northern Hemisphere is tilted away. The sun thereby seems to rise south of the east-west line.

Another consequence of this tilting effect is the altitude of the sun above the horizon in different seasons. In the summertime, the sun reaches its highest position in the sky at midday. Its rays strike the earth almost at a perpendicular. But during the winter months, when the Northern Hemisphere is tilted away, the sun is quite low in the sky; its rays are diffused across the earth. Two thousand years ago, Socrates realized the practical architectural beauty of this phenomenon.

> Now in houses with a south aspect, the sun's rays penetrate into the porticoes in winter, but in summer the path of the sun is right over our heads and above the roof, so that there is shade. If, then, this is the best arrangement, we should build the south side loftier to get the winter sun and the north side lower to keep out the cold winds.[3]

In light of the above comments, it appears that the chambers we examined from southeastern New York and southwestern Connecticut had entranceways oriented to make maximum visual use of the low-lying winter sun.

While it is well known that northeastern farmers routinely built their wooden homes and dirt outbuildings with entranceways facing the east and south to avoid the cold northwesterly winds and to absorb most of the limited, but nonetheless, potent heat radiation from a low winter sun (colonial New England homes always had the kitchen on the cold north side while the living and bedrooms basked in more comfortable southern exposure), the slab-roofed chambers, on the other hand, seem designed to take full dramatic advantage of the winter sun's diffused light at the expense of its heating potential.

Taking the local horizon and other natural features into account, the optimum orientation for a house in a temperate climate like New York is 162.5 degrees southeast. For the cooler climate of Vermont or New Hampshire, located at a higher latitude, the best entranceway orientation to get the greatest amount of solar heat is 168 degrees southeast. The ideal shape of a winter house (one that loses the least heat and gains the most solar radiation)[4] is one having a broad east-west direction and a narrow north-south axis. In this way the sun's rays reach a wider surface area of the house. The least efficient shape is one that has a narrow east-west axis and a long north-south axis. Thus a dwelling unit's solar heat retention depends upon different ratios of length to width (see figure 4.3).

Solar designers have combined the results of their experiments and have come up with a method for quantitatively comparing the amount of heat absorbed by houses of different orientation and shape. *Insolation* is the term used to describe the quantity of solar radiation striking an object. Clear-day insolation tables for different latitudes have been prepared to provide average hourly and daily insolation values.[5] When these tables are applied to house orientation and shape the relative amounts of solar radiation striking different surfaces can be easily compared. Higher insolation values mean that a wall is receiving more heat than one with a lower value.

In figure 4.4 insolation values measured in BTUs (British Thermal Units) have been listed for a hypothetical 1-by-1-foot structure at different orientations. The values represent the quantity of solar heat reaching the structure's walls during January, the coldest month of the year. Thus for a structure oriented towards the south, a square shape (I-A) receives 1630 BTUs per day; a rectangular shape with a long north-south, narrow east-west axis (I-B) receives 1160 BTUs per day; and a rectangular structure with a short north-south, broad east-west axis (I-C) receives 2320 BTUs per day. The optimum orientation and shape to receive the maximum amount of solar heat is clearly shape I-C.

When we apply the foregoing concepts to the slab-roofed chambers examined by MARC teams, we find that their combined orientation and shape make them the least likely candidates for a solar heating design award. Their cavernous rectangular form, narrow entranceway, and exposed interior stonework make them quite susceptible to chilling ground frost. Therefore, they were not constructed with the heating potential of the sun in mind, as so many people have seriously suggested. Their purpose seems rather to have been one of two things: to keep something very cold or to admit the horizon light from a winter sun.

If it weren't for most of the chambers' peculiar placement, it could be argued that they were icehouses. Perhaps some of the ones closer to the valley roads were used to store winter ice; their orientation would prevent the summer sun from entering them, making them admirably adapted to this. However, most of the ones we measured were well up the sides of hills. The rationale for hauling huge chunks of slippery ice to the crest of a hill is hard to come by. And the quantity of chambers also casts a serious doubt on this speculation (see Chapter 2).

It also cannot be argued that a fundamental limitation of available material or technique produced a basic chamber style. On innumerable occasions our teams have examined ceiling slabs whose width, if not partially covered by turf, would have exceeded the entire chamber's length. Constructing a wide chamber would have been as simple as moving the corbelling towards the outer reaches of the ceiling slabs. There must have been a very important reason for sticking to the long, rectangular style.

So what does all of this mean? It means that we can seriously put to rest the theory that all of the slab-roofed chambers of southeastern New York and southwestern Connecticut have been constructed since colonial times and that, when we consider the astronomical overtones suggested by our data, we can rigorously define the antiquity of the chambers. Could the rising sun at specific times of the year have been of particular importance to the well-being of Colonial animals (see Plate 36) or vegetable produce? Hardly. Many of the slab-roofed chambers found throughout the Northeast are the product of a society whose members had a keen interest in the winter solstices and equinoxes. There is absolutely no evidence that our immediate forefathers used or even cared about these solar events. We do know, however, that for many communities in prehistoric Europe these unique times were not only keys to their planting and harvesting success, but were also special religious moments when the deity of the sun entered their domain and made it sacred. In parts of northwestern France and Portugal, for instance, passage tombs dating to 4000 B.C. are all oriented in a direction lying between northeast and southwest. And megalithic structures from the Balearics, dating to the third century B.C., show a definite preference for the east-southeast—exactly the case we observed in our small sample of chambers (see Plates 37 and 38).

The slab-roofed chambers strewn along the ridgetops of the New York-Connecticut vicinity seem to have been placed so that early morning sunlight during the winter, early spring, and late autumn would penetrate their dark interiors for only a few moments, before a rising sun cast its rays elsewhere. The orientation data with respect to the local horizon is unmistakable. During the summer months when the sun is north of the east-west line, the chambers remain dark. Only a few chambers appeared to be aligned toward the winter solstice and equinox sunrise-

/sunset. Detailed surveys and extensive declination data will no doubt clarify this picture. It is important to note, however, that in central Vermont and southern New Hampshire other investigators have been finding similar .structures whose orientation with respect to key astronomical events was apparently well thought out before the first granite slabs were dragged into place.

Preliminary translations of inscribed posts built into the New York-Connecticut chambers suggest that some of them were used by early Celtic tribes as ceremonial "sun temples." It is doubtful that all of them were used for such esoteric purposes, for how many temples can there be in a small area? Most of them were probably used as burial crypts. There is good historic evidence for this from the Midwest.

In Minnesota, Iowa, and western Pennsylvania the Smithsonian, in the 1890s, reported finding great numbers of corbelled chambers filled with human skeletal debris (see Plates 39 and 40). The frequency of the finds naturally led the investigating officials to assume that the builders of the graves were Indians. Typically, after the chambers were opened and divested of all contextual material, no one thought of going back and checking the accuracy of the Institute's interpretation. Thus, from the halls of academia, we have a curious paradox: corbelled vaulted chambers found west of the Susquehanna River are American Indian in origin, while the very same chambers tucked away in the backwoods of New England are assumed by many eastern archeologists to be of early English origin (see Plates 41 and 42).

3. BALANCED ROCK, NORTH SALEM, NEW YORK

The terrain east of the upper Croton Reservoir is not as rocky or steep as the jagged Highlands to the immediate west. Consequently, the first farms were sprawling enterprises spreading across many acres of flat-topped rises. At one time, dairying and the growing of vegetable crops constituted the main livelihood of the families living there. Settled sometime prior to 1685, North Salem was built near a former Indian path which led south to Manhattan. English immigrants later widened the trail to accommodate oxen teams and coaches.

Today, not more than a few hundred yards from the post office, 30 feet from the main road, a 16-by-14-by-10-foot pink granite boulder rests in perfect equilibrium on several stone supports. Known as the Balanced Rock, it is located on Route 116 near Keeler Lane. As early as 1790, visiting European geologists were riding through North Salem commenting on the peculiar stone. Most of them believed the rock to be the result of natural decomposition, or as they put it, "of primeval diluvian torrents." A century later, the few American scholars who actually visited the site claimed that glaciers, grinding their way to the sea, brought the granite chunk from the White Mountains of New Hampshire, the nearest known pink granite deposit. As the ice melted, said the scientists, the encased boulder settled on top of a mass of rock debris. Over the next hundreds of thousands of years, erosion weathered off the lighter debris beneath the boulder, leaving the more resistant base rocks in place.

One of the first specialists to question the natural origin of the Balanced Rock was professor of mineralogy John Finch. In an 1824 issue of the *American Journal of Science* Finch explains how he accidentally stumbled upon a geological reference to the stone and was certain that the account spoke of a Celtic monument, "although the writer . . . is evidently not aware of the valuable relic of antiquity which he has described."[6] After citing two paragraphs from the article and mentioning how scholars attributed the phenomenon to nature, Professor Finch astutely notes that "primitive limestone never appears above the surface of the ground in the shape of small conical pillars, but in large massy blocks."[7] He was right. The supporting stones are crystalline limestone.

In Finch's day there were apparently some people who believed the Balanced Rock might have been a contemporary fake. "Others may suppose that some ardent admirer of Celtic antiquities erected this monument for his own amusement."[8] Interestingly, he dismisses this notion on the grounds that "the immense weight of the upper stone renders this improbable."[9] Based on the cubic density of pink granite, the upper boulder weighs approximately 90 tons. The professor was, in essence, expressing the utter amazement men have had when gazing upon megalithic monuments. That is, how did the ancients lift so much tonnage? Engineering skills in 1824, according to Finch's remark, were not even comparable to those which must have been used in the remote past. The 200,000-pound boulder was indeed transported 233 miles southwest from its New England source during the last glaciation. But as far as its being deposited by chance on top of seven limestone slabs, six of which are flush against each other, giving the erroneous impression of cleavage—that is another story.

Visually, the Balance Rock is remarkably similar to a class of tombs known as dolmens, or stone tables (see Plates 43 and 44). Found throughout the British Isles, the Continent, and Asia (everywhere except North America, say the archeologists), dolmens consist of a huge capstone supported by three, four, or more stone slabs, or by smaller stacks of untrimmed stones. The idea was to create a cist chamber in the space between the base stones. Depending on the size of the tomb, one or more bodies were placed within the grave in a contracted position. The cists were frequently placed in a northeast-southwest direction with the head of the corpse usually pointing towards the north. Occasionally, evidence of the megalithic yard was found in the distances between the support stones. In parts of Ireland, Mallorca and Malta, we find that the unit of length used to lay out the points where the base slabs touch the capstone was 2.72 feet. For reasons, as yet unknown (although probably pointing to a religious scenario), even multiples of this special number have been found to be expressed in many European and Mediterranean megalithic remains (see Plates 45, 46, and 47).

It is believed that most dolmens were covered with a mound of dirt. Throughout the centuries, however, the hands of both nature and man have removed the earth and exposed the inner stone coffins. Dolmen tombs were in vogue for an incredibly long period of time—from around 5000 B.C. to, in cases such as the Balearic Islands in the Western Mediterranean, 1200 B.C.

Rings of standing stones can sometimes be seen surrounding the dolmen. In other cases, circular ditches partially filled in with the refuse of thousands of years, but nonetheless still visible as slight depressions, are nearby. Over the centuries many circles of stone were toppled by zealous priests or industrious farmers. In the absence of the actual stones, the space they once occupied can still be seen by flying overhead in an airplane; and since this discovery in the 1920s, British archeologists have relied increasingly on aerial photography to help explain these curious circular ground impressions, which are now believed to be former ritual centers where the megalithic builders kindled fires and practised sociomagical ceremonies involving sun worship and the observation of other heavenly bodies. (see Plates 48 and 49.)

Because many of the world's dolmens occur along coastal lands, some authorities believe that megalithic fever— the insatiable craze to build with inexplicably huge stone—was spread by a seafaring, merchant society. The associated cultural debris scattered along the western coast of Europe from Iberia to Ireland, for example, makes it difficult to dispute this theory as some have tried to do. The archeological and linguistic links between these regions are indeed impressive. When we add to this the research data of the physical anthropologist, we find that similarities in the frequencies of certain genetic markers, like blood type, indicate that at some distant time populations of Mediterranean origin did inhabit Ireland and Scotland, leaving their genetic legacy with people living there today.[10]

At the North Salem site, MARC workers measured the distances between the contact points of the supporting stones. Overall, the results were very suggestive of the megalithic yard. From figure 4.5 it can be seen that the granite boulder rests on top of a triangular formation of standing slabs. Sides AB and AD are, for all practical purposes, of equal lengths (AB=8.15 feet, AD=8.16 feet). Side BD is 5.41 feet, BC is 3.22 feet, and CD is 2.50 feet. In other words, the foundation is an isosceles triangle (one having two equal sides). When we converted our measurements into intervals of the megalithic yard (distance in feet ÷ 2.72), we began to understand the nature of the force that balanced the North Salem rock.

Unless glaciers were prone to unload their rocks at intervals of 2.72 feet, the units expressed at this site are the very units of measure which were used to set up some of the megalithic monuments of prehistoric Europe and the Mediterranean.

Unlike the other perched rocks we have seen, the North Salem stone does have a layer of ground soil present. Today, we merely see the necks of deeply sunk base stones. Over the years surplus soil from a nearby barn foundation and a widened road has been banked against the limestone supports. This can clearly be seen from early nineteenth-century illustrations of the stone. If the ground beneath the capstone were removed, we would more than likely see a triangular cist chamber whose orientation, as measured from points A to C on the exposed base slabs, runs northeast-southwest—just like the dolmen tombs of the Old World. Encouraged by these exciting discoveries, a film crew shot aerial photos of the Balanced Rock. In one photograph a large circular pattern unexpectedly appeared. About 600 feet northwest of the Balanced Rock, a ringlike impression lay on top of a flat, grassless meadow. Enlargements of other exposures of the spot showed the same thing. A team sent into the field reported that without the print in hand it was impossible to make out the entire form. However, using the aerial photograph as a guide, they were able to map out a band of slightly discolored soil 10 feet in width, visibly depressed, stretching along the ground surface in the shape of a circle, and having a diameter of 90 feet.

Another crew sent up for detailed work came back with some staggering shots. Southeast of the Balanced Rock, in a recently harvested field, were two more circular, ground disturbance rings (see Plate 59). But these were adjacent to one another and four times as large as the other circle—between 290 and 330 feet in diameter, the band of each ring averaging about 50 feet in width! The circular impressions ran contrary to the field's recently plowed paths, suggesting that whatever left the soil stains was there long before seventeenth-century English immigrants cleared the Westchester forests and planted the seeds of modern agriculture.

We have since determined that the impressions are, in fact, the remains of circular earthworks, with ditches completely filled in and obliterated except, of course, when viewed from the air, where the roots of plants and ground water can be seen following the ditch outlines, revealing subtle shading differences in soil colorations. Further, upon searching the numerous field walls surrounding the adjacent rings we found not a few flat-faced stones bearing the same style of markings discovered elsewhere in the Northeast, leading us to conclude that colonial farmers, in their time-consuming efforts to clear meadows of stone for the planting of crops, must have dragged the inscribed slabs to one side and later unknowingly used them to build their property walls.

One such inscription was located in a field wall 2½ miles northeast of the Balanced Rock, just off Turner Road in Danbury, Connecticut. There, a 1½-by-1-by-1-foot slab sits within a stone property divide. Across its flat face, two different but chronologically related scripts have been etched one above the other. The top expression is believed to be a form of ancient Ogam, while the lower markings have been deciphered as Iberian Punic. Both inscriptions appear to refer to "god"; the stone is thought to be a votive symbol to the Celtic sun god, Bel, and the Phoenician sun god, Baal.

A few yards from the inscription, the long axis of a slab-roofed chamber has been positioned to catch the first rays of the morning sunrise during the equinoxes. Off to the side, a large slab has been laid across the deep shaft of a stone-lined water well. Further down the road, four more chambers peer out of the sides of small earthen knolls. A swamp separates the so-called equinox chamber from these other impressive constructions.

It is evident that the chambers, inscription, circles, and Balanced Rock form an associated lithic complex. The pattern is unquestionably similar to, if not the same as, that in many European megalithic sites. In northern Scotland and parts of England, Wales, and Ireland, vast numbers of partially buried slab-roofed chambers, known locally as weems, earth houses, and Picts' houses, are often found near dolmens, standing stones, and cairns. Some of the European chambers, which presumably were the homes and/or tombs of the megalith builders, date to 3000 B.C.

In other parts of America there are many sites, whose features parallel those surrounding the North Salem stone. Of particular interest is a double circular embankment in the Kanawha Valley of West Virginia. Excavated in the late 1800s by the Smithsonian Institution, the embankment consisted of two concentric walls, the outer being 295 feet in diameter, the inner reaching 213 feet. Between them a narrow ditch had been filled in with dirt. They were known simply as "sacred enclosures," and nothing was ever found within them to explain their puzzling structure. It was noted, however, that over the years many stone graves had been discovered in nearby fields.

American scholars in the 1800s were surprised to find Indians buried within box-shaped slab tombs (see Plates 51, 52, and 53). The stone graves, often covered over by a mound of earth, were widespread, being found along the Mississippi, Ohio, Tennessee, Susquehanna, and Delaware River Valleys. The cists titillated the imagination of America's savants, who saw within them a definite link to Old World burials. Dr Joseph Jones, a respected nineteenth-century antiquarian for the Smithsonian, wrote:

> In looking at the rude, stone coffins of Tennessee, I have again and again been impressed with the idea that in former ages this ancient race [the builders of America's mysterious

earthworks] must have come in contact with Europeans and derived this mode of burial from them.[11]

Cyrus Thomas, in his 1894 report to the Smithsonian, criticized the stone-grave-equals-ancient-European-contact theory, arguing that during historic times, Indians buried their dead in stone cists. He therefore concluded "that those graves found in the mounds are attributable to the same people (or allied tribes) found using them at a later date."[12]

This line of reasoning, however, in no way proves that stone graves developed independently in the Americas. There still remains the equally valid possibility that early Indian tribes learned the *general idea* of cist-mound burial from other peoples rather than inventing and implementing it themselves. There is just enough building technique variation in America's known Indian tombs to suggest this.

The first hunters were quick to realize that a rotting hunk of flesh draws the attention of unwelcome beasts. Rather than risk their necks burying grandpa in some far-off place, these men simply dug a pit in their cave floor and dumped the old boy in, covering him over with kitchen rubbish. A few millennia later, cemeteries and living space were rigorously defined. But by then, bands of men had spread across the globe searching for food, fun, and probably better weather. In the process, a wide variety of burial methods evolved, some specific to the demands of the socioecological environment, others peculiar in and of themselves: Egyptian pharaohs fancied mummification and pyramids; prehistoric Mallorcans cremated their loved ones in quicklime; Germanic tribes, according to Caesar, heaped stones over the dead; Viking tribes sent their kings off on burning ships; and the Apache strapped their relatives high atop wooden platforms, leaving the corpse to the sun, wind, and birds.

Although the general idea was the same—the removal of the dead from the presence of the living—over the past several thousand years an incredible diversity of burial customs has arisen. To believe, as Cyrus Thomas did and

contemporary archeologists still do, that the many similarities in burial traditions of the Algonquins and the
tribes of prehistoric Europe (like the cist burial with
northeast-southwest orientation) were merely the results
of a chance, independent innovation, is patently absurd.
That two widely different—according to the academic
community—cultures should simultaneously develop fun-
erary traditions that are equivalent without some form of
intermingling may seem like a highly unlikely situation to
the layperson, who is probably right in believing so.

C. Housatonic River Valley

The Housatonic River originates near Pittsfield, Massachusetts, flowing southerly for about 150 miles through
Connecticut to the Long Island Sound. Gneiss, schist, and
crystalline limestone make up the majority of weatherworn rocks embedded in the region's thin topsoil. Occasional marshes and overgrown swamps give the area a
decidedly primitive look. This is odd considering the fact
that New York City is not more than an hour's drive to
the south. To European settlers who followed the early
explorers, this region was a vast primeval forest of fir and
hardwood. Giant oak and chestnut trees abounded where
today the barren meadow and the moist soil cover the
land. Wild animals like the timber wolf and black bear
plagued the immigrants for generations.

In the late 1950s several large stone piles were first
reported by Connecticut archeologist Frank Glynn. As one
travels the length of the Housatonic, many conical stone
cairns can be found within a mile or two inland of the
riverbank.

1. STANDING STONES AND INSCRIPTION, WASHINGTON, CONNECTICUT

Eight miles east of the central Housatonic near the town
of Washington, in western Connecticut, a cluster of five
long stones standing within 2000 feet of each other has

been reported. Although they are similar in style and placement to other standing stones scattered throughout New England and the world, an extensive documentary search of the Washington region failed to reveal a historical origin for them. They remain as baffling as the clusters of standing stones recently discovered off the Thames river in southeastern Connecticut, in the Massachusetts Berkshires and the Green Mountains of Vermont, and along the Merrimack River in New Hampshire.

The Washington standing stones have obviously outlived the traditions of their erectors. But we can still glean some information from the locale. A few hundred feet from two adjacent menhirs, a chunk of granite has been laid into a courtyard patio. The stone has been shaped on the edges to fit a stonemason's design. On the face of the block several deep grooves have been cut which bear an incredible resemblance to those on other inscribed stones uncovered in Connecticut and New York.

Why would a stonemason have chosen an inscribed block to build with? It is unlikely that he wouldn't have noticed it. Perhaps the mason as a master craftsman of stone, the oldest, most secure building material of man, sensed something special about the block. Perhaps by using the stone, by giving it a home, the mason felt he was preserving what another man, obviously skilled in stone scribing, had done to the rock he now held in his hands. We will never know if this was the reasoning, for the inscribed block was laid over one hundred years ago. What we do know is that the stone has a definite Semitic-style inscription carved across its surface.

2. HEBREW INSCRIPTIONS, SEMICIRCLE, PERCHED ROCKS, NEW PRESTON, CONNECTICUT

Almost two hundred years ago Dr. Ezra Stiles, president of Yale College from 1778 to 1795, traveled 7 miles north of Washington to New Preston, Connecticut, and recorded in his *Itineraries and Memoirs*[13] a "Hebrew Inscription" engraved on the summit of a nearby mountain peak above Lake Waramaug. On 8 October 1789, the energetic New England scholar scurried up a weatherworn hilltop to measure and sketch the mysterious carvings. On the northwestern side of the mountain peak, Stiles found four separate inscriptions each enclosed within a semicircle. Two of the enclosed engravings formed a northerly set, while the other two formed a southerly set. The carved semicircles opened at approximately 325 degrees NW.

The report, among other New England curiosities collected by Dr. Stiles, eventually found its way into the manuscript collection at Yale University library. It lay there until the early 1970s, when New Jersey archeologist Edward J. Lenik happened upon an obscure book reference which mentioned Ezra Stiles's survey. The archeologist made several fruitless attempts to locate the inscription before he traveled to Yale to investigate Dr. Stiles's original documentation.

By the winter of 1976 Mary Browne, an avid hiker from Washingon, Connecticut, had guided Lenik to the inscription, just as she had done about a month earlier for a MARC exploratory team. Although severely damaged by modern graffiti, the inscriptions described by Stiles more than one hundred eighty-seven years ago are still plainly visible. The sketches, photographs, rubbings, and measurements made in November 1976 by MARC field artist Claire Lofrese and myself were repeated six months later in the springtime when the coloration of the lichen covering the carvings changed to a lighter hue, thereby allowing much better visibility.

The letters of the inscriptions are not ancient. They are in a style of Hebrew that is readily understandable to modern students of the script. Severe weather erosion, however, has worn away the nuances of the carvings, thereby making an exact translation next to impossible. Based on actual casts made at the site, the northern set of carvings has been interpreted as "Abram" and "Isaac," while the southerly pair translates as "Moses" and

"Adam." Edward Lenik interpreted Stiles's drawing of the southerly pair of words to read *Sarah* and *Adam* respectively.[14] The difference in names can be attributed to Stiles's accidental misreading of one Hebrew symbol.

What do these names mean? Lenik has reported that Stiles reputedly attributed the inscriptions to Jewish miners who inhabited the Cornwall, Kent, and New Milford, Connecticut, vicinity in the mid-eighteenth century and who were thought to be searching for precious metals. The semicircles surrounding each word give us a clue as to the inscriptions' purpose—they were probably memorial carvings to four Jews who died in the region sometime before 1789. Male chauvinism aside, the exclusion of a woman's name from the interpretation increases the likelihood that an exploratory band of men was indeed searching for something in the rugged wilderness of Western Connecticut. It is nonetheless still puzzling that such an inaccessible spot on a particular mountaintop should warrant the names of four individuals. An extraordinary degree of care went into the placement and execution of the carvings. Furthermore, a nearby grouping of man-made lithic features has ritualistic overtones.

A few yards southwest of the inscriptions are six glacial erratics that have been positioned into a 20-foot wide semicircle. Ranging in size from 2-3 feet high, 4-8 feet wide, and 3-4 feet broad, the boulders are arranged in a shape reminiscent of the Perched Rock semicircle site near Greenwood Lake, New York. In front of the boulders are two shallow troughs that have been cracked by burning fires. This part of the mountainside commands a magnificent view of the distant southern horizon. The stone semicircle opens to the northeast, where, 100 feet away on the summit of the bare peak, three boulders have been placed a set distance apart (see figure 4.6). One of the stones, measuring 4 by 8 by 6 feet, has been lifted about 1½ feet on its side by a smaller stone. Data collected by the first MARC team showed that the three boulders were situated in the shape of an isosceles triangle, with sides AB and BC having equal lengths. Based on the field sketch, it appears that the apex of the triangle faces due north in a pattern suggesting an orientation on the celestial North Pole.

The arrangement of stones into a triangular configuration has been a fairly repetitious pattern. At the Delaware cliff site in Deerpark, New York, we saw a similar arrangement of stones. At Ladentown, New York, another group of rocks had been positioned in this way. The support stones beneath the North Salem, New York, boulder also form an isosceles triangle. Several other sites from southern Connecticut, central Vermont, and New Hampshire, all conform to this interesting pattern. The resemblance among all of these sites is indicative of a common system being used to lay out the stones. As for the questions of who placed them and what they were used for, we can at best offer only speculations based on the combined array of data.

All of the stone configuration sites recorded by our teams were found on top of mountain peaks, in full view of the heavens. The fractured areas immediately surrounding the boulders all appeared to have been subjected to intense and sustained heat stress—the kind that a roaring bonfire would produce. Within the general vicinity of the sites, some type of inscription had always been found: near the Delaware cliffs, Iberic pebble stones; near Ladentown, Celtic Ogam; near North Salem, again an Ogam stone.

At the New Preston, Connecticut, site a semicircle of boulders in full view of the southwestern sky and an isosceles triangle of boulders apparently oriented due north are both associated with several Hebrew inscriptions that we know are not nineteenth- or twentieth-century forgeries. The possibility that the boulder configurations and inscriptions are in some way related cannot be ruled out, for we do know that in certain regions of the Middle East various Semitic cultures, up to recent times, carved memorials or sacred words on cliffsides and arranged stones in circles.

It seems, then, that the eighteenth-century Hebrew

inscription at the Connecticut site was placed, perhaps by happenstance, at an ancient mountain of worship. Of course it is quite possible that the men who carved the names were familiar with the Old Testament and therefore recognized the semicircle as a sacred place and felt justified in honoring their dead nearby. Until MARC teams have completed a comprehensive survey of the New Preston site as well as the surrounding area, we must refrain from any definite conclusions. For now we can only point this out as but another piece of a neglected American stone puzzle.

3. INSCRIBED ROCK, KENT, CONNECTICUT

One month after visiting the Hebrew inscriptions, Dr. Stiles trekked through 10 miles of dense Connecticut forest to reach the township of Kent where, at a place called Scaticook, he found an inscribed stone.

> Over against Scaticook and about 100 rods (1600 feet) East of Housatonic River, is an eminence or elevation which is called Cobble Hill. On the top of this stands the rock charged with antique unknown characters. This rock is by itself and not a portion of the mountains; it is of white flint; ranges north and south; is from 12 to 14 feet long and from 8 to 10 feet wide at base and top; and of an uneven surface. On the top I did not perceive any characters; but the sides all around are irregularly charged with unknown characters, made not indeed with the incision of a chisel, yet most certainly with an iron tool, and that by pecks or picking, after the manner of a Dighten Rock. The lacunae or excavations are from a quarter to an inch wide; and from one tenth to two tenths of an inch deep. The engraving did not appear to be recent or new, but very old.[15]

The rock has not been seen since the late eighteenth century. Several attempts to rediscover it have all failed. One recent expedition, however, turned up a different inscription.

During the winter of 1976, archeologist Edward Lenik and a survey team scouted South Kent in search of the stone described by Stiles. Instead of finding the "pecked" white flint" mentioned in the report, the team came across a 5-foot-high by 10-foot-wide by 13.5-foot-long sandstone boulder with an inscription cut along its vertical north-eastern face. It was known to the local inhabitants as "Molly Fisher Rock." Lenik believed the linear cluster of markings did not represent aboriginal symbols, but rather a "Semitic script."[16] They are, however, very different in style from the New Preston symbols. Thus far a positive identification of the inscription is still to be determined. But the markings do appear to resemble several others found in southern New York and central Vermont.

4. STONE PILE, STONE CIRCLE, WASHINGTON, MASSACHUSETTS

Tucked away in the Berkshire Mountains of western Massachusetts a couple of miles from Route 8 off an old country road, a well-built, conical stone pile rests in a remote section of the town of Washington. Measuring 7 feet in height and in base width, the pile tapers up to a width of about 3 feet before being capped with a white quartz stone. A protected alcove at the base opens due north.

Known locally as Washington Mystery Monument, the pile has baffled residents for years (see Plate 54). Several historians have visited the site in search of answers but have found none. In the late 1960s freelance writer Wadsworth Pierce compiled a collection of interesting observations about the stone, noting that "it is . . . not mentioned in any early records of the town or in the nearby community."[17] He tracked down an elderly woman who was born on the property where the pile now stands and asked her about it. She said "that her father told her that it was there when he bought the land. Beyond that the previous owner had told the woman's father that it was there when he settled the land."[18]

The stone pile is interesting in that it has a base opening which is about 2 feet high and wide and 1 foot deep. Although different, this feature is not unknown. At the conical pile site near Ellenville, New York, three cairns out of several hundred were found to have similar openings. A test trench dug in front of an opening near the base rock exposed a 6-inch layer of charcoal at a depth of 1½ feet. It was evident that something had been burning there for a very long time. Interestingly, to Wadsworth Pierce, the opening in the Washington cairn resembled a huge hearth.

About a quarter-mile away are two concentric stone circles. The diameter of the outer ring is about 4 feet, while that of the inner ring is about 3 feet. Within the center of the inner circle is a large quartz rock. Many of the 2-by-2-by-2 foot stones making up the circles are overgrown with moss. They appear to be deeply planted. In the nearby community of Ashfield, several other conical piles with base cavities facing due north have been found. The Washington Monument is merely one example of a cluster of similarly constructed piles.

Evidently, a great deal of effort went into building the Washington cairn. The careful placement of stones, some of which weigh several hundred pounds, makes it clear that this structure is not a memorial heap where passing Indians tossed a stone either out of respect for long-gone relations or because it was customary. It meets all the conditions of a conical stone pile site.

Early New England travelers believed these carefully placed piles were in some way related to the altars of stone used by the ancient Israelites who burned fires atop them. The visual resemblance between many American cairns and those found in the Middle East, particularly Arabia, is indeed striking. Stone circles have occasionally been found in rough proximity to Arabian cairns. When we recall that 60 miles to the south along the Housatonic watershed at New Preston, Connecticut, several Hebraic inscriptions were found on a cliffside in close proximity to a semicircle of stones and a triangular arrangement of perched rocks aligned due north, then perhaps we ought to reconsider the Israeli connection proposed by America's first savants.

5

Stone Mysteries: Southern New England

$\mathbf{T}$able 5 and figure 5.1 indicate generally the types and distribution of structures discussed in this chapter.

A. Lower Connecticut River Valley

Cascading from a bog "in a trout hatchery near Canada," as New England poet Robert Frost once said, the headwaters of the Connecticut River flow 410 miles southward through forest and meadow, forming the state boundary between New Hampshire and Vermont, then weaving across western Massachusetts and central Connecticut before emptying into Long Island Sound. Pioneer settlement along the Connecticut River Valley (see figure 5.2) goes back more than three hundred years. Dutch entrepreneurs set up trading posts along the marshes and salt flats of the lower reaches in order to buy beaver pelts from the Indians. Fur was a hot item in the seventeenth cenury. It graced the hats and clothes of many Europeans. But encroaching English immigrants, more interested in set-

TABLE 5
Summary of Stone Structures

A. Lower Connecticut River Valley	B. Thames River Valley and Northern Tributary	C. Charles River Valley, Massachusetts Bay
1. Stone tunnels, Goshen, Massachusetts	1. Stone wall complex, slab-roofed chambers, alignments, stone circles, Groton, Connecticut	1. Inscribed stone, Weston, Massachusetts
	2. Stone piles, slab-roofed chambers, Thompson, Connecticut	2. Inscribed stone, Weymouth, Massachusetts
	3. Standing stones, Thompson, Connecticut	

tling what would become one of the most productive farm valleys in the east, eventually expelled the Dutch traders.

The Puritans made their way from Massachusetts through a dense forest of giant white cathedral pines described by one of the travelers as "a boundless contiguity of shade." Compared to the rocky soil of the eastern coast, the valley was indeed paradise. Multitudes of river shad, salmon, and an abundant wildlife along the broad, fertile floodplain, only confirmed this Puritan belief. Shifting sandbars near the Connecticut's mouth at Old Saybrook have prevented large, deep-draft vessels from entering the waterway. As a result, heavy shipping industry never developed in the valley. Many stretches of the riverbank have retained their wild, unspoiled beauty.

The lower Connecticut Valley is host to a variety of lithic structures. Among the most common are large stone piles. As early as 1705, at a spot 3 miles upriver from Old Saybrook, a map was drawn up depicting "a heap of stones"[1] as a boundary marker. The English assumed the pile separated the territory of two chiefs; but this was never confirmed by the Indians. In the 1950s archeologist Frank Glynn excavated two large heaps along the Connecticut shoreline and found that they were constructed between three thousand and four thousand years ago by the mysterious Woodland Indians (see Chapter 2).

About 5 miles northeast of Old Saybrook, covering an area of over 10 acres, is a group of meandering stone walls, several slab-roofed chambers, a few three-sided enclosures standing 5 feet high, some stone-lined cavities, and other lithic structures. The lack of adequate ground soil coupled with the extreme rockiness of the site makes it difficult to imagine how an early settlement of English pioneers could have coaxed their cattle to graze or convinced their plants to grow. Yet the local interpretation for these dilapidated stone structures is that they are a colonial settlement. There is, however, no evidence for this. The site has neither been properly surveyed nor excavated. Furthermore, the general layout of the buildings as well as the spot chosen to erect the structures—a high ridge of barren rock near a swamp—conforms to the pattern of other sites we have investigated in New England, such as Andover, Massachusetts, where a similar configuration of slab-roofed chambers was used as an ancient burial place. Another site of the same design lies but 10 miles to the east, across the Thames River at Groton, Connecticut. Thus, at the entranceway to one of the longest river valleys in New England—one that could be used to travel 500 miles north to the Saint Lawrence River by following the headwater tributaries—a sophisticated array of stone chambers and enclosures was built at some time in the past. No colonial records of this or any other similar site have ever been found by MARC teams. There is no official indication that they were constructed by seventeenth-century English settlers.

Farther up the valley, near Leverett and Shutesbury, Massachusetts, a cluster of slab-roofed chambers has been found and measured by the New England Antiquities

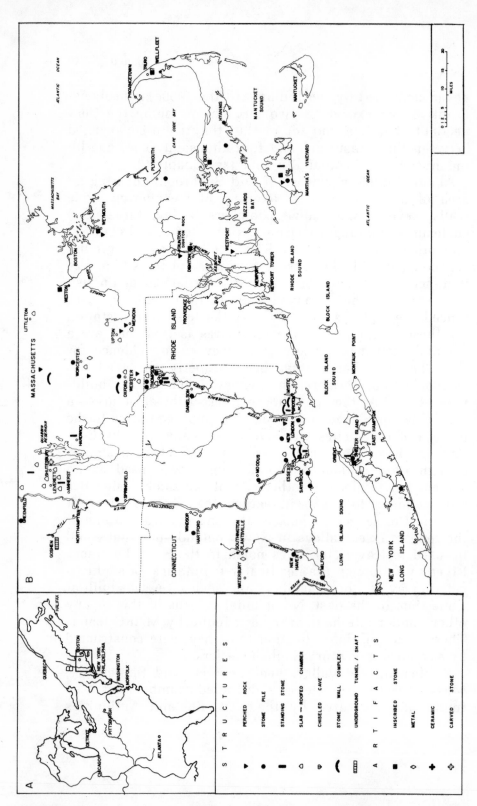

Fig. 5.1. Distribution of stone structures in southern New England (Map by Kalpana R. Shah)

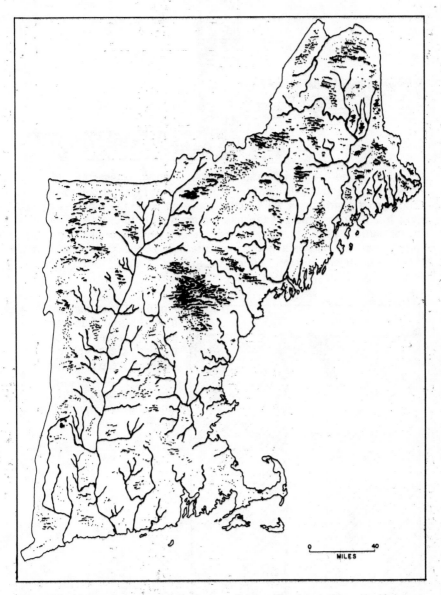

Fig. 5.2. Major rivers and tributaries of New England (Map by Kalpana R. Shah)

Fig. 5.3. Stone-lined shaft and tunnels, Goshen, Massachusetts. Built into a clay hardpan hillside, one of the densest types of soil to dig, the underground structures were first discovered when the pioneers moved into the Goshen region in the mid-eighteenth century. The absence of water surrounding the tunnels, both today and in prehistoric times, precludes their use as a well. It is tentatively suggested that they may have been used to store grains or to hide people during times of warfare. (Courtesy of Yankee, Inc.)

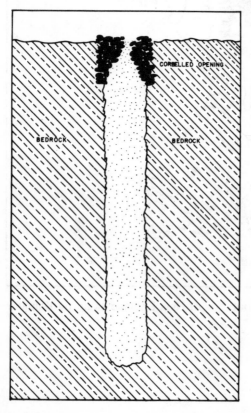

Fig. 5.4. Cross-section of a ritual burial shaft from central France, used by the early Celts. Votive offerings were thrown into long pit in an effort to please the earth spirits. (Drawing by Kalpana R. Shah)

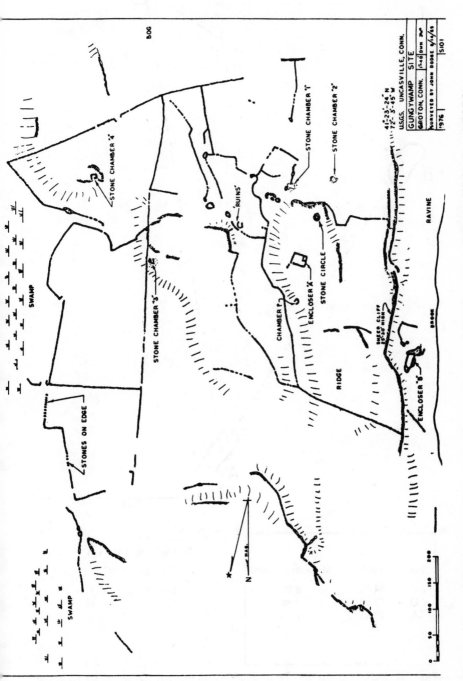

Fig. 5.5 Gungywamp stone wall complex, Groton, Connecticut. (Courtesy of James Whittall and ESRS)

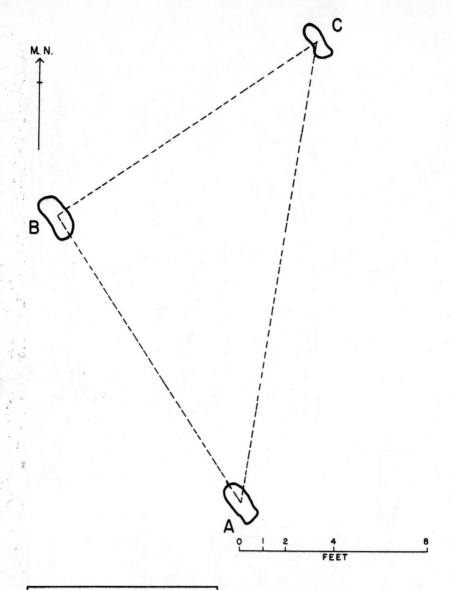

M. N.

C

B

A

0 I 2   4   8
       FEET

Side	Feet	Megalithic Yards
AB	14.16	5.20
BC	13.29	4.88
CA	19.41	7.13

Pythagorian Theorum

$AB^2 + BC^2 = AC^2$

$377.12 = 376.75$

Fig. 5.6. Standing stones, Thompson, Connecticut (Drawing by Kalpana R. Shah, after Byron Dix)

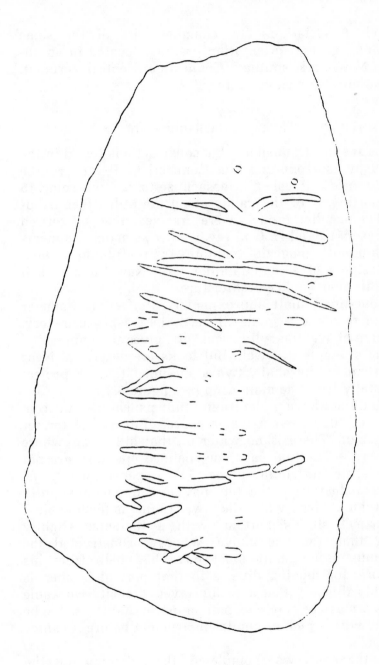

Fig. 5.7 Stone found in Weston, Massachusetts, in the 1890s by Cornelia Horsford. A scientist from the United States Geological Survey confirmed that the markings on the stone were definitely cut by a man sometime before the natural weather erosion commenced. The markings appear to be related in style to those found on the Inwood Stone and others from the New York and Vermont area. The latter inscriptions could be an ancient form of Ogam, a script that may have been used in Iberia during Carthaginian times. (Horsford, *An Inscribed Stone*)

Research Association. The chambers are of the same design and general orientation as those located in southeastern New York, southern Connecticut, central Vermont, and southern New Hampshire.

1. Stone Tunnels, Goshen, Massachusetts

Perhaps the most unusual lithic constructions found in the countryside surrounding the Connecticut River are the stone tunnels of Goshen, Massachusetts, a town some 15 miles northwest of the valley along the Mill River tributary. The peculiar tunnels were first described by retired stonemason, Leland H. Godfrey. Godfrey's article,[2] appearing in a popular magazine, contains the useful and provocative insights of a man familiar with New England soil and traditional Yankee architecture.

A stone-lined shaft approximately 3½ feet in diameter sinks 15 feet into a small hill near the Goshen cemetery. Seen from above, the cylindrical "pit" gives the impression of being a simple dry well. But looks are deceiving. Near the bottom of the shaft, two stone-lined tunnels project horizontally from the main drop (see figure 5.3).

Wells do not have underground tunnels leading out from them; they also need a water source. But as the former mason said, "There is no water on that hill or anywhere near there."[3] The two flagstone-spanned openings are not on the same horizontal plane. The upper tunnel opens about 11½ feet from the top, having a diameter slightly larger than 2½ feet, while the lower tunnel is flush against the vertical shaft's bottom, with a diameter slightly smaller than the one above. Whoever constructed the mysterious stone shaft must have had help from his neighbors, for digging ditches in that part of Goshen is incredibly difficult. Below a thin layer of easily workable loam is a mass of clay hardpan so dense that it has "to be loosened with a pick or similar instrument before it can be removed."[4]

Once the shaft was completed, then, digging out the

tunnels meant that each shovelful of dirt had to be relayed to the ground level, 15 feet above. Furthermore, once this exercise in mindless excavation was completed, the flagstones presently lining the structure had to be quarried from a nearby ledge, hauled to the shaft, lowered to the tunnels, and negotiated into the clay. In the absence of modern tools, the amount of work collectively involved must have been enormous. Yet there are no oral or written records of the tunnels and shaft ever having been built. The Goshen structure was buried beneath centuries of dirt when the first white men traveled up the Connecticut River.

Throughout the years a number of strange theories have been suggested to account for the shaft and tunnels. It once was thought that a Goshen farmer used the site as a root cellar. While conceding that this may have happened, Godfrey believes that "someone built it who was not connected with the owners of the property."[5] He raises the intriguing point that

> no one has ever claimed knowledge of its origin or purpose. A thing of this magnitude could never have been constructed after the first settlers arrived without someone knowing of it and telling their children about it—yet descendants of the original owners still live on the surrounding acreage after 200 years.[6]

A modern-day geologist once thought the structure was built by an enterprising pioneer for growing silkworms. One woman thought it was "obviously" part of the underground railroad which Northerners used for shipping runaway slaves to Canada. An amateur archeologist from New Hampshire seriously suggested that the underground tunnels were built by grave robbers attempting to gain access to the cemetery. A simple reading of Goshen's history, however, would have steered the New Hampshire gentleman along the right track. The cemetery was laid out many years *after* the discovery of the tunnels.

The stonework and general layout of the Goshen structure bear many of the features found among other equally mysterious structures along the countryside of the long Connecticut Valley. Just across the Connecticut River, near towns surrounding the Quabbin Reservoir, 4000-pound blocks of hewn granite have been laid up without mortar to form a number of slab-roofed chambers. It would be hazardous to state the exact number of chambers in the region, because our field crews have not yet scouted all of the innumerable hills and back roads of the region; but thus far we have telltale evidence for at least fifteen structures within a 3-square-mile area. Future workers would do well to concentrate on the land northwest of the reservoir. Our teams began surveying this region in the fall of 1977.

The Goshen tunnels, in all probability, are part of a larger complex of underground constructions yet to be found in the meadows surrounding the Mill River. To date there are no known stoneworks of colonial origin that even compare with these curious structures. But if we look to other parts of the world for analogies, we can easily see many similar types of below ground stonework.

In the foothills of the Alps, Germany, France, and Portugal, for example, many so called "ritual burial shafts" have been discovered (see figure 5.4). Sunk by the early Celts, these stone-lined shafts, ranging from 20-120 feet deep, were found to contain many votive offerings—goddess figurines, pots, jugs, plates, tree trunks, and the remains of animal and human sacrifices. To maintain the harmony of the universe, Celtic priests were obliged to preserve their contact with the many subterranean spirits. Consequently, temples were often placed near springs, wells, and bogs. These were the places where the water spirits dwelled. Earth spirits demanded more effort. Vertical tunnels had to be sunk deep into the ground. Into these ritual shafts were thrown the offerings to link man with the gods. In many parts of Western Europe, this ancient custom of leaving gifts for the earth and water spirits is still maintained. Every summer at Derbyshire, England, for example, the springs and wells are decorated with brightly colored flowers. At many an Irish crossroad well, the country folk hang bits of rag on nearby bushes after drinking some water. It is believed that this simple offering to the spirit residing in the water will cure warts.

While there is no water at the Goshen site, the resemblance to earth spirit shafts is remarkable; the similarity fades, however, when we consider the two horizontal tunnels.

Such underground construction is typical of another class of prehistoric ruins. In Scotland the underground dwelling complexes from Perth, Aberdeen, Ross, Sutherland, and the Orkney Islands often have tiny chambers accessible by horizontal, stone-lined tunnels. It is believed that these crude subterranean structures were used to store grain and to hide the populace from advancing enemies. The Goshen shaft and tunnels would be admirably adapted to these ends. Only future archeological excavation by MARC teams will expose the true function of the mysterious Massachusetts tunnels.

B. Thames River Valley and Northern Tributary

The Thames River in southeastern Connecticut is formed by a northeastern complex of tributaries. The Quinebaug, Shetucket, and Yantic Rivers unite into one waterway near the city of Norwich and flow south for about 15 miles to Long Island Sound.

1. STONEWALL COMPLEX, SLAB-ROOFED CHAMBERS, ALIGNMENTS, STONE CIRCLES, GROTON, CONNECTICUT

The town of Groton is tucked away in the southeastern corner of Connecticut. Situated on the eastern bank of the Thames River across from the town of New London, about 2½ miles north of Long Island Sound, Groton has long been a fishing community. During the last century an active whaling industry brought much wealth to this portion of the Connecticut coast. The port of Mystic, famous in days gone by for shipbuilding, lies about 8 miles to the east.

New London was founded in 1646 by John Winthrop, Jr. Noted throughout the colonies for his extensive knowledge of the geography of southeastern New England, Winthrop was sent the following letter by a gentleman residing in Springfield, Massachusetts, on 30 November 1654:

> Sir I heare a report of a stonewall and strong fort in it, made of stone, which is newly discovered atop neare Pequot. [Pequot is a hill near Groton named after the Pequot Indians, who occupied the territory between the Thames and Mystic Rivers.] I should be glad to know the truth of it from your selfe, here being many strange reports about it.[7]

Winthrop never responded to the inquiry.

Extensive field surveys performed by New England archeologist James Whittall of the Early Sites Research Society have since shown that the letter was probably referring to a peculiar arrangement of stone walls, slab-roofed chambers, enclosures, standing stones, and other lithic material strewn across a 24-acre hilltop about 2 miles east of the Thames River. Known as the Gungywamp site, the walled complex lies on top of a sheer, 30-foot cliff, 6 miles north of Long Island Sound (see figure 5.5). A 3-foot-high stone wall follows the western cliff face for about 1000 feet before meeting with several crude enclosures and other irregular stone walls. East of the cliff, the land slopes downwards towards a large swamp. A number of slab-roofed chambers and inexplicable rows of standing stones are scattered throughout the intervening acres.

In the 1960s, John E. Dodge, a resident of the nearby town of Stonington, spent several years surveying the site. He reported four chambers, two concentric stone circles, and a crude, drystone foundation within the Gungywamp complex.

Dodge believed that the chambers were root cellars. He also felt that the stone circles represented an early tan-bark mill and that the foundation was simply the remains of a colonial barn.

James Whittall visited the Gungywamp site in the early 1970s to take up where Dodge had left off. His detailed measurements of the chambers show that they are of the same design and construction as others found throughout New England. The largest chamber facing the southeast, measured over 18 feet long and 6 feet high and wide. It was unusual in that it had a small adjoining corbelled room near the entranceway. A few yards away another structure, oriented towards the east, measured 1½ feet high by 3 feet wide at the entranceway, with about 3½-4 feet of head room in the interior. The small shape of the chamber suggested to Whittall that it might have been used as a "sealed and covered" tomb.[8]

In the fall of 1973, the Early Sites Research Society began excavation of a rock formation situated within the southeastern quadrant of the complex. When the field team removed about 2 feet of mixed rocks, gravel, and dirt, they uncovered, much to their surprise, a small stone chamber with three collapsed roof-slabs. Aside from a mixed deposit of soil and an animal bone, nothing was found within the excavated structure. This lack of artifacts, typical of other excavated chambers in New England, suggested to the team that the structure might have been utilized as "a watch house shelter. From the entrance a good view down the bank covered any approach from the east to the main Gungywamp site."[9]

The double circle of stones could have been used as a primitive mill to crush hemlock bark which was used in the tanning process, as Dodge had suggested. In turn, the chambers could have been used to "process and store furs and hides."[10] But as to the people who cured the animal hides, Whittall has said: "It is possible that the [English settlers] constructed the site, but I doubt they did. The methods of tanning, suggested here, were as familiar to Iron-age man as to the early Colonists and the process has changed very little."[11]

On the eastern side of the site, an unusual row of small standing stones has been placed in the ground at regular intervals. Positioned so that each stone's long axis is parallel, they stand slightly more than 2½ feet apart. Since the tallest stone is only about 1½ feet high, it is unlikely that they were used as a wall to enclose animals. Unfortunately, the purpose of this north-northeast alignment is not yet known.

The stone walls atop the granite-ledged hilltop near Groton, Connecicut, are similar to other walled complexes found throughout New England. The meandering walls high above the cliff face are suggestive of the Ramapo site, while the adjoining slab-roofed chambers call to mind the Putnam Valley double-chamber walled complex. It is clear that whoever built the stone structures went to a lot of time and trouble; the very size of the site is indicative of a large work force. And yet, when we look for random or deposited artifacts, we find but a handful of rusting nails. The scarcity of any definitive debris emphasizes the site's unusual quality. The entire complex gives the impression of a ritualistic or ceremonial center.

2. STONE PILES, SLAB-ROOFED CHAMBERS,
THOMPSON, CONNECTICUT

On the eastern slope of a small hill outside of Thompson, near the Quinebaug River in northeastern Connecticut, about 45 miles north of Groton, an impressive cluster of conical stone piles rests on large base boulders. Covering an area of over 10,000 square yards, more than fifty of the structures are still visible. Closer inspection reveals the toppled remains of at least twenty more. About 60 yards from the cairns, at the foot of the hill, a tiny brook ebbs its way into a thick swamp.

The piles are typical of other found throughout New England in that all of them have been carefully constructed near a source of water on flat base rocks. The Thompson structures have also been placed on the eastern side of a rise in what seems to be a linear pattern. That is, the cairns are situated at intervals of about 25 yards from each other in more or less straight lines from the water source. Two stone-lined pits averaging about 4 feet in depth were found beneath the base supports of a couple of the toppled cairns. There is some evidence, in the way of chiseled caves, to suggest that small-scale copper and iron ore mining took place in the Thompson area; but at this time the information is too meager to define the time period of the shallow, mountainside troughs.

Colonial records make no mention of the Thompson stone piles. It is known, however, that around 30 miles downriver, just north of the present village of Greenville in Norwich, Connecticut, there used to be a stone heap on the western bank of the Shetucket River. The site supposedly marked the spot where an Indian sachem was captured and slain by an enemy tribe. Although it is no longer standing, eighteenth-century documents make it clear that the Greenville cairn in no way resembled the carefully built, conical stone piles of Thompson. The sachem's memorial was described as a large heap of stones thrown together by wandering Indians.

About 4 miles southeast of the Thompson site, a grouping of five slab-roofed, beehive chambers has been reported. More undoubtedly existed in the region until building activity destroyed many of them. The beehives open to the southeast, in full view of the winter solstice sunrise. They are relatively small structures, measuring approximately 10 feet in diameter and 4 feet in height. The stones have been laid with great skill.

Small, rectangular enclosures adjoin all of the chambers, ranging from 30-100 feet in length and width. Upon seeing these interesting structures, one is reminded of the prehistoric earth houses of Scotland. In parts of Aberdeenshire, for example, similar dirt and stone enclosures believed to have been constructed to pen sheep or cattle are often found next to the corbelled structures. A surface collection in the Thompson chambers exposed several chicken bones.

3. STANDING STONES, THOMPSON, CONNECTICUT

Not far from the beehive chambers, off Route 12, aerospace engineer Byron Dix has reported a group of three standing stones whose placement is indicative of the megalithic yard and the Pythagorean theorem.

After calculating the center point of the stones, which stand about 3 feet high, Dix measured the distance and angular deviation among all of them. He found that while the long axes of stones B and C were parallel, the long axis of Stone B ran through Stone A (see figure 5.6). The measurements showed that a right triangle was formed with the following dimensions: Side AB = 14.16 feet; Side BC = 13.29 feet; and Side CA = 19.41 feet.

Converting these measurements into the megalithic yard (1 megalithic yard = 2.72 feet), Dix obtained the results shown in figure 5.6.

The most intriguing aspect of this curious arrangement of stone is the formation of the Pythagorean triangle. It was Pythagoras who first observed that a constant relationship exists among all right-angled triangles: the sum of the squares of both legs equals the square of the hypotenuse (the side opposite the right angle). Mathematically, this relationship is expressed as:

$$A^2 + B^2 = C^2$$

(where A and B are the legs of the triangle and C is the hypotenuse).

At Thompson, Connecticut, if we square both sides of the triangle and take their sum, we get a figure which is incredibly close to the square of the hypotenuse:

$$AB^2 + BC^2 = AC^2$$
$$(14.16)^2 + (13.29)^2 = (19.416)^2$$
$$200.5056 + 176.6241 = 376.7481$$
$$377.1297 = 376.7481$$

Rounding off to the nearest hundredth, we get:

$$377.13 = 376.75.$$

The minor difference in values can be attributed to measurement error. It is clear that the standing stones were positioned in the ground by someone with a knowledge of Pythagorean right triangles and the megalithic yard.

The 3:4:5 ratio was significant to the ancient world because it led to the marriage of astronomy and mathematics. Understanding this relationship provided the know-how to build astronomically aligned structures, for implicit within it was the ability to make right angles on a horizontal plane. The ancient astronomers took advantage of the fact that one angle of a triangle is a right angle if the lengths of its sides are in the ratio of 3:4:5, the right angle being the angle opposite the longest side. This essential theory made it possible to then identify the shortest and longest days of the year by observing the noon shadow of a stick or standing stone in respect to the sides of a laid-out triangle.

The mathematics of the ancient world may have been in use up through the early Middle Ages. Recent work on churches from Greece, Italy, and France has shown that Pythagorean mathematical ratios and the megalithic yard were employed simultaneously. The Pythagorean ratio, known as the golden section, was a system for dividing lines into extreme and mean lengths. The Greeks utilized this relationship to insure harmonious proportions within their buildings. The method by which this formula was applied to actual construction is today unknown. But its usage must have been common knowledge to the Masonic craftsmen who built the great religious structures of Europe during the eleventh to fourteenth centuries A.D. They must have also known about the megalithic yard. The plan and proportion of many Gothic cathedrals show definite evidence of these two mathematical concepts.

The Thompson stones could very well have been utilized as a solar sitting station. The simple alignments formed could have been easily used to calculate the various positions of the sun at different times of the year. A north-south line could also have been obtained by plotting the midsection of the rising and setting points of particular stars on the horizon.

C. Charles River Valley, Massachusetts Bay

East of the Connecticut River in Massachusetts is a

wooded central plateau that is actually a geological exten-
sion of the White Mountains of New Hampshire. East of
the plateau the hills slope away to a coastal lowland. The
Charles River flows across 60 miles of eastern Massachusetts before emptying into the Massachusetts Bay at
Boston. Its shoreline is rocky in the north and sandy to
the south. Massachusetts Bay is but one example of the
deeply indented bays and inlets along the New England
Atlantic coast. The many protected harbors have made the
shoreline a favorite sailing spot for years—perhaps even
for thousands of years.

1. Inscribed Stone, Weston, Massachusetts

Along the eastern portion of Massachusetts a number of
unexplained "man-works" were described in the last century by Cornelia Horsford. According to the Massachusetts scholar, the presence of similar antiquities discovered in Rhode Island, Connecticut, and Long Island
suggested that an ancient race of men once occupied
America. Such discoveries included, among others, non-
functional waterways, retaining walls, mounds, dry
ditches, river walls, dams, cairns, and inscribed stones.

In a privately printed paper Ms. Horsford reported how
she accidentally came upon an ancient inscription.[12] During the fall of 1893, she and her sister were driving along
the back roads of Weston, a town about 10 miles west of
Boston in the Charles River Valley, when she spotted an
inscribed boulder lying in the midst of a pile of roadside
stones. Gathered by a farmer a few days earlier from an
overgrown field high atop a nearby hill, the stones were to
be used to build a couple of gateposts. The farmer had no
idea that an ancient inscription graced his collection of
field rocks. Within a few weeks the stone was eventually
purchased and moved to Ms. Horsford's Cambridge study,
where she set out to examine it in detail.

Measuring 33 inches broad, 15 inches high, and 14
inches thick, the stone was described as being a fine-
grained, igneous rock having a somewhat elongated shape

with four sides. Judging from the soil stains across two smooth sides, three-quarters of the stone must have been immersed in the ground and protected from the elements before it was hauled down the hillside. Unfortunately, the inscription had been cut along two weather-exposed sides, making it impossible to get an exact rendition of the characters. But since the markings extended into the smoother portions of the buried rock, it was concluded that the letters must have been carved before the surfaces were eroded by the elements.

Deep slashes, some of which crossed each other, had been incised along the stone's two sides. Anticipating the skepticism of her colleagues, who would surely attribute the incisions to nature's playful hand, Ms. Horsford shrewdly turned the stone over to J. B. Woodworth of the United States Geological Survey for his professional opinion. Woodworth sent back the following report:

> The upper surface and the sides are scarred by two distinct classes of markings:
> First, a few V-shaped depressions, which are connected with the disintegration of minute veins; second, broad and shallow U-shaped depressions, which run from beneath the soil line to near the ridge-like crest of the boulder. These latter are unquestionably the work of man.
> The U-shaped gouges . . . are not accordant in direction or position with any visible structures of the rock. They differ from glacial striae in their persistent direction perpendicular to the long axis of the boulder, and in their failure to occur except in the position above named. Glacial striae are more prevailing coincident in direction with the major axis. The gouges differ, too, from water-marks or rain-gouges, in that they appear to be clearly the result of mechanical abrasion and not of chemical solution and removal.[13]

Although weather erosion had so defaced the inscription as to make a decipherment impossible, Ms. Horsford nonetheless believed the last three characters were Norse runes, the mysterious letters of the early Germanic alphabet. In her analysis, Norsemen, also known as Vikings,[14] must have left the stone (see figure 5.7). Her interpretation has never been verified by other epigraphers. However, the importance of this stone, whose present whereabouts is unfortunately unknown, rests not with the preliminary observations put forth in 1895, but rather with its relationship to the enormous number of similarly inscribed stones that have since been found in different parts of America.

Three months after Cornelia Horsford transported the stone back to Cambridge, Alexander Chenworth dug up a boulder from the northwestern tip of Manhattan Island. The incisions were of the same style and character as those on the Weston stone. Eighty-five years later, MARC explorer Richard Grando uncovered a 300-pound boulder with long U-shaped incisions from the western slope of a mountain ridge near Warwick, New York. (See Chapter 3.) From central Vermont, NEARA researcher Byron Dix has reported over twelve hundred stone slabs and boulders, some of which have markings identical in cut, shape, and spacing to those from Massachusetts and New York. These teams are finding the same type of inscribed stones that have been reported over several hundred years of New World exploration and settlement. More stones must still lie buried somewhere in the vicinity of these first discoveries.

2. Inscribed Stone, Weymouth, Massachusetts

In the May 1976 *Bulletin* of the Early Sites Research Society, archeologist James Whittall reported an inscribed granite slab resting on a hill just east of the Mill River near Weymouth, Massachusetts.[15] The rectangular stone, thought to have been originally perched on two base rocks, measured approximately 6 feet long, 18 inches wide, and 9 inches broad. Several deep and shallow grooves had been incised across one of its sides in an apparently systematic fashion.

When Barry Fell was given photographs and latex peels of the chiseled markings, he eventually deciphered them as a type of script known as Iberian-Punic which was used in southern Spain during the third and fourth centuries B.C. His interpretation, however, was even more mind boggling: "Cease Trespassing. Anyone Treading (Here) Is Desecrating a Burial Place."[16] Thus, according to Dr. Fell, the inscription near Massachusetts Bay, in the United States of America, was an ancient Iberian cemetery marker!

Fell notes in his decipherment that a similar inscription appears on a gravestone from Herdade do Pego, Portugal. But the peculiar way in which one of the Weymouth letters was inscribed suggested to Fell an Arabian influence. In other words, Iberian-Punic-writing Arabs, presumably from North Africa, had probably set up the tombstone much as English Puritans two thousand years later would do for their comrades who died soon after the Mayflower dropped anchor along a coastal stretch later named Plymouth, only 20 miles southeast of where the Weymouth inscription was eventually found.

Even if Dr. Fell's interpretation is not entirely correct, we must nonetheless keep in mind that the marked slab of granite resting high above the Mill River in eastern Massachusetts is but another example of a seemingly never-ending array of inscribed stones being found in America.

6

Stone Mysteries: Northern New England, North Atlantic Coast

Table 6 and figure 6.1 indicate generally the types and distribution of structures discussed in this chapter.

A. Upper Connecticut River Valley

Central Vermont during the winter months is a fantasy world where valleys stretch away from snowcapped mountains and where granite and gneiss outcroppings make farming seem next to impossible. The warmer months, however, change the illusion strikingly. Many of the steep, precipitous hills, blanketed in shades of green and gold, have a soil fertile enough to produce an assortment of vegetables, grains, apples, pears, plums, and cherries. But getting to the soil is not easy. New rocks seem to crop up after every season's plowing. Early farmers got rid of the surplus stones with typical Yankee ingenuity: they built miles of field walls to retain their livestock and to maintain their property rights. The region had a late start in getting settled. If we believe what one

TABLE 6
Summary of Stone Structures

A. Upper Connecticut River Valley	B. St. Francois River Valley	C. Merrimack River Valley	D. Coast of Maine	E. Coast of Newfoundland
1. Underground stone chamber, Windham County, Vermont	1. Inscriptions, Sherbrooke, Quebec, (Canada)	1. Covered cairn burial site, Andover, Massachusetts	1. Inscription, Manana Islet off Monhegan Island; copper-tin projectile point, Monhegan Island, Maine	1. Norse settlements, l'Anse aux Meadows, northern Newfoundland (Canada)
2. Standing stones South Royalton, South Woodstock, Vermont		2. Mystery Hill, North Salem, New Hampshire	2. Ceramic amphorae, Castine Bay, Castine, Maine	
3. Stone wall complex, slab-roofed chamber, alignments, inscriptions, South Woodstock, Vermont				
4. Stone wall complex, alignments, slab-roofed chambers, inscriptions, South Royalton, Vermont				

man had to say about it, then it is easy to understand why. An explorer of the Ottauquechee River Valley, where the town of Woodstock is presently situated, described the land as "savage-looking." And after carefully inspecting the countryside, he concluded that the valley was so far from any road and so much out of the world that no human being, except possibly an Indian, would ever live there. Nevertheless, by the mid-1700s the first historic settlements were rooted in the central Vermont district. Evidence recently gathered by Byron Dix indicates, however, that Vermont may have been occupied much earlier than the eighteenth century A.D. For the past five years Dix has been rigorously applying his astro-engineering skills to the mysterious stone ruins found near the foothills of the Green Mountains. Thus far, he has come up with some surprising information.

Within a 600-square-mile area of the Connecticut River's western watershed, an area encompassing such towns as Woodstock, Royalton, and North Tunbridge and such waterways as the Black, Ottauquechee, and White Rivers, the engineer has recorded over twelve hundred standing stones, more than five hundred inscribed slabs, innumerable corbelled and flat-roofed chambers, buried stone waterworks, alignments, massive walled complexes, and other lithic material. It was largely Dix's indefatigable work that prompted the State of Vermont, during the summer of 1977, to launch its own full-scale investigation of the enigmatic remains. The fortunate citizens of that state are among the first people in the nation to realize the enormous implications of their backyard stoneworks.

1. UNDERGROUND STONE CHAMBER, WINDHAM
COUNTY, VERMONT

Forty-five miles north of the Goshen Tunnels, James Whittall in cooperation with Dr. Warren Cook of Castleton College, Vermont, made a preliminary sketch of a man-made circular mound 33 feet in diameter with a small 12-by-6-foot semicircular slab chamber buried in the center

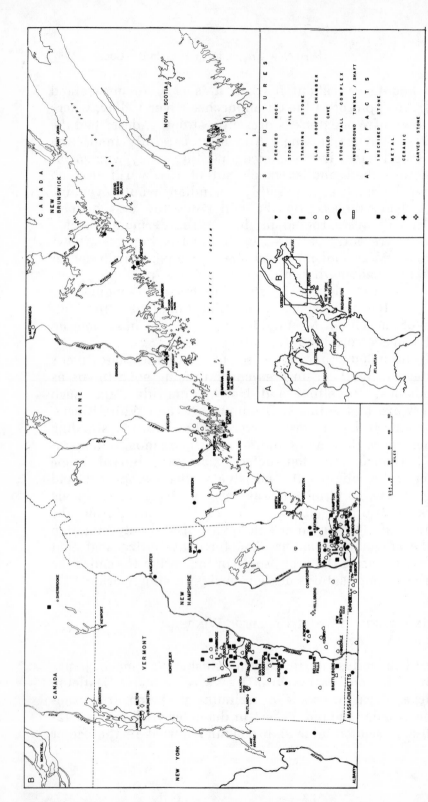

Fig. 6.1 Distribution of stone structures in northern New England and the North Atlantic coast. (Map by Kalpana R. Shah)

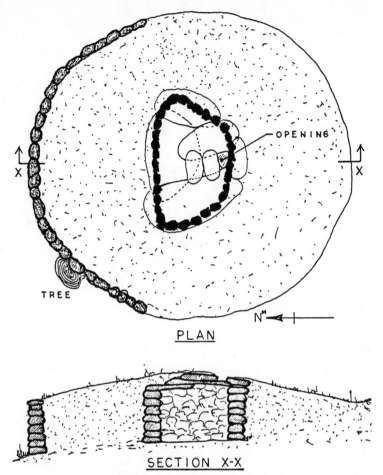

OPENING

X ← → X

TREE

N⁴

PLAN

SECTION X-X

Fig. 6.2. Underground chamber, Windham County, Vermont. (Courtesy of James Whittall and ESRS)

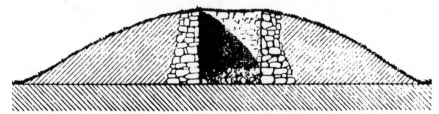

Fig. 6.3. Underground chamber within mound from southeastern Minnesota near the Iowa town of New Albin, at the confluence of the Winnebago Creek and Mississippi River. The diameter of the mound measured approximately 25 feet. Interior height of the chamber measured 6 feet. Human bones and ashes were found at the bottom of the pit. Nineteenth-century scholars believed this structure to be American Indian in origin. Scientists of today, however, who are just becoming familiarized with similar stone chambers from the northeastern part of the country, automatically attribute them to the early Dutch and English settlers. (Smithsonian Institution, *Twelfth Annual Report*)

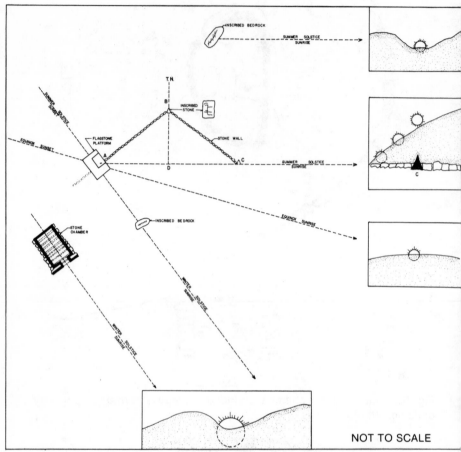

NOT TO SCALE

Fig. 6.4. Prominent stone features at South Woodstock, Vermont, site.
(Drawing by Kalpana R. Shah)

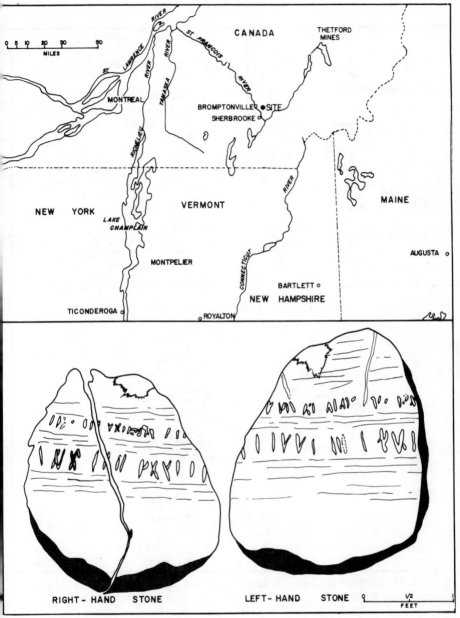

Fig. 6.5. Inscribed stones, Sherbrooke, Quebec, as displayed in the Saint Charles Boromee Museum. (Map and drawing by Kalpana R. Shah)

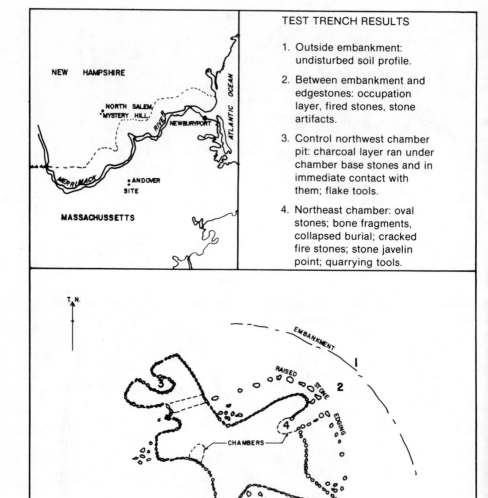

TEST TRENCH RESULTS

1. Outside embankment: undisturbed soil profile.

2. Between embankment and edgestones: occupation layer, fired stones, stone artifacts.

3. Control northwest chamber pit: charcoal layer ran under chamber base stones and in immediate contact with them; flake tools.

4. Northeast chamber: oval stones; bone fragments, collapsed burial; cracked fire stones; stone javelin point; quarrying tools.

Fig. 6.6. Covered cairn burial site, Andover, Massachusetts. (Drawing by Kalpana R. Shah after Frank Glynn)

Fig. 6.7. Norse settlement, L'Anse aux Meadows, Newfoundland, Canada (Map by Kalpana R. Shah)

(see figures 6.2 and 6.3).[1] Whittall reported that the structure appeared not to have had an original entrance; rather, one seemed to have been made by removing a roof slab sometime after the chamber had been built. A stone wall encloses part of the 4-foot-high north side of the mound, while an earth ramp leads off the south side. Detailed work on this structure is planned. Reports from Putnam Valley, New York, suggest that a similar underground chamber exists there.

2. STANDING STONES, SOUTH ROYALTON, SOUTH WOODSTOCK, VERMONT

There are an uncanny number of standing stones situated along the hillsides of Tunbridge, South Royalton, and South Woodstock, usually found in the vicinity of stone chambers and rock-cut inscriptions. As seen from ground level, they appear to be divided into two categories—small and large. But caution is advised. Until the underground length of each stone is determined, these groupings, at best, should be regarded as very tentative.

1. Small—3 to 6 feet high, 6 inches to 1½ feet wide, and thick. Usually are tapered at the base and tip. Occur in clusters several yards from each other at the base of low hills and sloping meadows, alone on ridgetops, or near the base of high hills. Source of stone varies. Some were quarried from local bedrock, while others were dragged from as far away as 2 miles.
2. Large—above 7 feet in height. The largest aboveground standing stone, which towered over 16 feet, came from South Royalton. 1½-2½ feet in base width and base thickness, 6 inches to 1½ feet in tip width and tip thickness. Tend to be cone-shaped, broader at base than tip. Found in fields, meadows, and along low hillsides. Local horizon usually quite visible.

It is obvious that this categorization leaves a lot to be desired. There really are no definite cutoff points between the two types. The stones have been grouped into a system that simply delineates the *general* size characteristics among them. Hopefully, it will serve as a preliminary guide for future field studies.

In a heavily wooded field near the town of South Royalton, a large granite standing stone has been sunk deeply into the earth (see Plate 55). Towering more than 7 feet above the ground, the conical stone, which measures about 2 feet in width and breadth at the base, tapers to about 1 by 1½ feet in width and breadth at the top. The stone very definitely has been worked with a blunt instrument, for maul markings are quite clear along its length. Its depth has not yet been determined; but as the stone is firmly implanted in its ground socket, it is safe to guess from its visible size and estimated weight that it probably extends below the surface for at least another 5 feet.

The function of this structure is unknown. Neither colonial records nor Indian legends make reference to it. In fact, it was unknown to most of the people living in the vicinity until it was found by NEARA member Elizabeth Sincerbeaux of Woodstock, Vermont. As it is situated quite a ways from the beaten track, many people are still not aware of its awesome presence.

A few miles from the stone is a grouping of six huge, southwest-facing slab-roofed chambers. Several inscribed boulders flank the structures. Behind one of the chambers situated on the MacIntosh Estate, in a field adjoining the farmhouse where the Mormon prophet Joseph Smith was born, is a series of small, saucer-shaped standing stones, averaging 1-2 feet high, 9-11 inches wide, and 4-5 inches thick. Strewn across a rolling meadow, more than ten of these curious stones have been placed into the ground at intervals of 50-100 yards from each other. Invariably the long axes of these stones are parallel. Hundreds of similar groupings of small standing stones having triangular to parabolic shapes have been reported by Byron Dix.

It is important to recall that the site lies not too far from the White River, whose headwaters originate in the western Green Mountains and flow eastward across central Vermont before emptying into the Connecticut River. English explorers penetrated the wilderness by traveling the natural valley of the White River. Ancient groups of explorers in search of the region's extensive mineral deposits might have done likewise. Perhaps the small stones were left as memorials or trail markers (see Plate 56).

On a hilltop near South Woodstock stands a medium-sized long stone. It projects 6 feet above the ground and measures approximately 2 feet in width by 1½ feet in thickness at the center. The stone narrows to 1 foot by 1 foot at both the top and base. A few yards away is one of the largest slab-roofed chambers yet recorded in New England. Some of the capstones weigh several tons. On the face of a field rock outcropping a few hundred yards from the standing stone is a complex arrangement of horizontal and vertical slashes that have since been interpreted as figures in the Celtic Ogam alphabet. Across the field, which slopes along the side of a hill, many other long stones have been found next to faint ground depressions, implying that at one time these recumbent stones were standing upright. In the distance, Byron Dix has mapped out an assortment of small and medium standing stones that were apparently set up to take full advantage of certain astronomical events like the summer and winter solstices.

The South Woodstock standing stones are not isolated phenomena. They appear to be an integral part of a sophisticated calendrical observation station which may have been used by small bands of early settlers to map out the position of the sun during the course of a year (See Plate 57).

3. STONE WALL COMPLEX, SLAB-ROOFED CHAMBER, ALIGNMENTS, INSCRIPTIONS, SOUTH WOODSTOCK, VERMONT

Byron Dix was first led to the South Woodstock stoneworks (known in the literature as the Calander II Site) by NEARA member Elizabeth Sincerbeaux. Impressed by the assortment of man-made structures, Dix spent the next eighteen months meticulously surveying the hilltop. After a detailed site map had been drawn up, Dix suspected that various features were in line with the sunrise at different times of the year. He thereby calculated the local horizon position of the sun during the solstices and equinoxes and then plotted the theoretical results onto the map. His suspicions were well founded—prominent stone features did indeed suggest a solar alignment pattern.

Prompted by these calculations, Dix ingeniously designed a sophisticated optical instrument known as an equatorially mounted theodolite to test in the field what he had proven on paper. In the late hours of the night the engineer carefully set up his equipment on the hypothetical "observation" spot and nervously awaited the sun. The first glint of sunlight changed the blue gray hue of dawn strikingly—a shifting of shadows, indefinable shades of purple, cool reds, orange, then the burning power of yellow. It was the morning of the winter solstice. Not only did the sun rise directly in line with the laid-out instruments, but it also rose from a natural cleft between the distant hills—a horizon notch.

Additional work later revealed three main areas where the sun could be observed during its major onsets: a massive slab-roofed chamber, a large flagstone platform, and a rock outcropping marked with inscriptions.

On December 21 the sun's rays directly penetrated the length of the huge slab-roofed chamber. Anyone sitting within it on that day would behold the awesome spectacle of a midwinter sun illuminating the dank crevices of the 19-by-10-foot-wide structure (see figure 6.4). Measurements taken from within also showed that the extreme rising and setting positions of the moon during its 18.61 year cycle (known as the Major and Minor Standstills) correlated with the length, width, and height of the chamber. In other words, the builders may have utilized detailed lunar observations to lay out the structure. If these calculations prove true for the area's remaining chambers, it will mean that whoever the astronomer-builders were, they lived in central Vermont for a very long time, keeping track of a heavenly body that other peoples in different lands often worshipped as a god.

A short distance from the chamber Dix found a 32-by-23-foot-wide flagstone slab. Incorporated within this "platform" was a smaller rectangular slab (a subplatform). Two walls extended from both sides of the flat stone area. At first glance the platform seems quite ordinary. In fact, historical documents show that it was used in the 1850s as a mere house platform. But detailed measurements of this mundane, simple-looking feature seem to indicate a much more exciting and probably older origin. The long axis of the larger platform is in direct alignment with the distant horizon notch above which the sun rises on the winter solstice. As in the nearby chamber, an observer standing at this site during the morning of December 21 would see the sun drift up from a very specific land formation.

Along the solstice "pathway" Dr. Barry Fell, without knowing anything about Byron's research, had independently identified a marked portion of bedrock as being a Celtic Ogam inscription. His translation alluded to a "winter observation pillar." Thus, at the same locale, within a few hundred feet there appear to be two observation areas aligned towards the same horizon point.

But there is more. The long axis of the same platform, extending in a northwesterly direction rather than in the southeasterly direction of the winter solstice sunrise, is aligned towards the summer solstice sunset (see figure 6.4). One pair of corners of the platform is *exactly* aligned towards the equinox sunrise/sunset. It is very possible that a settler could have accidentally oriented his house foundation towards the winter solstice sunrise—but that he would simultaneously hit upon the exact length-width proportions of the base flagstone so that the corners are directly positioned towards the equinox sun is difficult to attribute to chance alone. It is apparent that a significant amount of foresight was involved in laying out this structure.

About 200 feet northeast from the platform is a large triangular monolith that's been incorporated into a stone wall. Declination measurements taken from the flagstone subplatform to this stone show that on the morning of the summer solstice the sun hovers along the slant of horizon mountainside and then rises *directly* over the alignment formed by the subplatform and monolith. In other words, the monolith had been placed so that an observer standing on the subplatform could watch the sun rise above it on the longest day of the year.

A couple of hundred feet from the monolith is another outcropping of bedrock incised with markings that have been identified as Ogam. From this spot the sun can be seen rising from another horizon notch during the summer solstice. Several long stones lie along the fringes of the sloping hillside. Byron Dix has been able to illustrate via extensive site survey that if the stones were standing upright they would be in line with the sun's rising and setting points at regular intervals during the year. In other words, the stone structures spread across the eastern side of a long rolling hill in South Woodstock, Vermont, could very well have been used to record the annual passage of time by means of the sun. It may have been an intricate calendrical system.

Among the other features which suggest complex astronomical sightings are the two stone walls intersecting the flagstone platform and the summer solstice monolith. The walls join each other at a triangular-shaped, inscribed boulder. The markings on the boulder seem to delineate a symbol used by many societies in the ancient world to represent the "eye of god." Variations of this peculiar symbol have frequently been found in the Mediterranean basin, the Indus Valley, and eastern Asia. Its presence in central Vermont is startling, but nonetheless in accordance with the other indications of ancient American contact we have already pointed out.

Measuring along the two stone walls (see figure 6.4) from the subplatform's long-axis-stone-wall intersection to the triangular-shaped boulder (AB), and from the same point on the boulder to the monolith stone (BC), Byron Dix found that each wall was 136 feet long, or 50 megalithic yards. Furthermore, the summer solstice alignment line extending from the subplatform to the monolith (AC) formed the base of a huge stone triangle. Now, the most intriguing aspect of this arrangement is that the apex of the triangle (the inscribed boulder B) is pointing zero degrees north; and from this stone a due north line (BD) dropped to "base" AC divides the stone arrangement into two 3:4:5 Pythagorean right triangles. In other words, the stone walls, platform, monolith, and inscribed boulder seem to have been laid out with a calculated regard for each other. As we have seen, the Pythagorean triangular plan for stone layout appears elsewhere in New England.

Within a two-mile radius of this site are several indicative examples of past population activity. A nearby stone quarry has huge slabs only partially exposed. It is odd that whoever went to all the trouble to hack through several feet of granite along two or three sides of a slab failed to finally remove the chunk from its bedding plane. It seems as though the people quarrying the stones stopped work one day and never finished.

Along the many footpaths leading through the surrounding hills, Byron Dix has found hundreds of small inscribed stones. The symbols have been identified as an early alphabet used by a people in the western Mediterranean. Significantly, slab-roofed chambers are often found in direct association with the inscriptions. The ongoing research project supervised by Byron Dix will no doubt bring to light more lithic material from the South Woodstock area.

4. STONE WALL COMPLEX, ALIGNMENTS, SLAB-ROOFED
CHAMBERS, INSCRIPTIONS, SOUTH ROYALTON, VERMONT

About 20 miles almost due north of the South Woodstock site, within walking distance of the White River, Byron Dix and his co-workers have mapped out another stone wall site known as Calendar I which may also have been used to mark the annual position of the sun.

Near the top of a 1,300-foot hill, within a vast, bowl-shaped depression that looks as though it had been scooped out by a giant shovel, Dix has found a flagstone "platform" similar to that at South Woodstock. From this spot, key horizon features seem to define various horizon points of the sun during the year. Specifically, it's been shown that long monolithic stones have been placed so that an observer standing on the same platform area could watch the sun rise and set from the above surrounding hillsides during the summer and winter solstice and the equinox. Furthermore, Dix found that seven intermediate stone features had been placed between the hillside horizon and the central observation area in such a way that the sun could be observed at equal intervals between the major solar events. In other words, the South Royalton site could very well have acted as a huge calendar.

A number of intriguing inscribed stones were found at the site. Along a north-south wall, three elongated boulders had been placed adjacent to each other. On two of these boulders some prominent gridlike, or checkerboard, designs had been carved. Measuring approximately 2½ inches wide by 3½ inches long, the grids were made by carefully chiseling vertical and horizontal grooves into the surface of the stones. Three significant facts have emerged since the designs were first reported by Dix. Firstly, they appear on intermediate stone features from which the summer solstice can be sited from the central observation point; secondly, the long axes of all three boulders face due north; and thirdly, the very same checkerboard motif has long been associated with sun worship in other parts of the world (see Plates 58, 59, and 60). The checkerboard design has since been found throughout New England, and usually a solar alignment of stones is nearby. Its presence at the South Royalton site is interesting, for it might be related to similar, prehistoric European grids (See Plates 61 and 62).

Within the walled site is a long, narrow, partially collapsed, slab-roofed chamber. On the morning of the equinox, a person seated within the structure would see the sun rise from a prominent horizon stone. On the ceiling of the chamber near the entranceway, a gridlike symbol has been carved. There have been numerous attempts to explain the significance of this symbol, all of which are still tentative. Some have related it to post-glacial paintings found in the caves of France and Spain, while others say it is nothing more than a colonial ma-son's symbol. What is important here is that similar gridlike markings have been found in many of New England's slab-roofed chambers; and nearby many of these chambers is an assortment of flat stones that have been inscribed with a writing system believed to be over three thousand years old. About a mile from the South Royalton site, hundreds of small inscribed stones have been found dispersed within field walls. The markings are stylistically similar to those found in New England.

The abovementioned features are only a few of the most obvious at the South Royalton site. The work carried out thus far by Dix and others has since revealed many more intricate lithic features which appear to be related to sites found elsewhere in the Northeast. Future comparative work is planned. For example, a few miles from the South Royalton site, near the town of North Tunbridge, many underground slab-roofed chambers have been recently exposed by the farmer's plow. A few of them are uncan-nily similar in style, construction, and orientation to the megalithic passage graves of northern Europe (see Plates 63 and 64).

Although many of the stone features at South Royalton are aligned with the major events of the solar year, there are, nevertheless, a few inherent problems with the astro-nomical calendar hypothesis. The most obvious, of course, is the general location of the site. The bottom of a natural amphitheater would seem to be the most unlikely place in which to set up a solar observatory when so many hilltops are in the immediate vicinity. Also, because of the sighting angle of the "observation point," during the solstices and equinox, the sun would be visible long after the initial moments of sunrise. Similarly, sunset during those days would be premature. One would think that a people aware of key astronomical events would have chosen a better locale. This said, it still cannot be denied that certain stones were indeed placed to take advantage of the general position of the sun. The location of the grid symbols also appears to support this supposition.

B. Saint Francois River Valley

The Saint Francois River flows for about 90 miles in a northwesterly direction from a small glacial lake in southern Quebec before emptying into the Saint Lawrence River at a point about 70 miles north of Montreal. The passage it forms has long provided a natural route for southbound travelers seeking access to the numerous river valleys of the New England region. In turn, early explorers leaving the Connecticut Valley found a way north to Canada's great mineral deposits by trekking along the Saint Francois's path. The length of time men have been walking the route is the subject of much heated debate, but a rock inscription that's been rediscovered in the last few years may hold some of the answers.

1. INSCRIPTIONS, SHERBROOKE, QUEBEC

Sometime in the nineteenth century a Canadian farmer was working his land near Bromptonville, Quebec, a small town about 80 miles southeast of Montreal, when he uncovered two flat-faced stones in a field beside the Saint Francois River. The stones remained in the puzzled farmer's possession until the early 1900s when they were acquired by the Saint-Charles Borromée Seminary in Sherbrooke, a community about 5 miles south of Bromptonville. Turn-of-the-century scholars believed the v-shaped incisions were Norse runes. By the 1920s, however, as American interest in antiquities shifted to the Lower Nile and the spectacular discoveries of Lord Carnarvon and Howard Carter at the Tomb of the Egyptian Kings, the Sherbrooke stones, as well as other New World inscriptions, faded into oblivion.

But in the fall of 1966, Dr. Thomas E. Lee, professor of archeology at the University of Laval, strolled into the

Museum of the Saint-Charles Borromée Seminary In Sherbrooke and peered into a glass display case. Within the
case were two 800 pound slabs of limestone measuring
about 3 feet long by ½-1½ feet in width and breadth. A
quick analysis of the four rows of markings cut deeply
into both stones told Dr. Lee that the script was in no way
related to Norse runes, as the yellowing display placard
insinuated. The Sherbrooke inscriptions had been rediscovered after an inexcusable delay of almost fifty years
(see figure 6.5). Since then, the stones have been subjected
to intensive study by James Whittall, Barry Fell, and Dr.
Lee in conjunction with retired Laval University lingui-
tics professor Dr. George Sotiroff. There is bitter disagree-
ment over their meaning.

Upon analysis of photographs and rubber mold copies
(latex peels) of the markings, Dr. Fell issued a report in
the *Bulletin* of the Early Sites Research Society stating
that the script was Libyan, with a tentative date of 500
B.C.[2] With the aid of bilingual tombstones of Roman
soldiers found in North Africa and inscribed in Latin and
Libyan, the Harvard professor made the following translation: Top line—"Thus far our expedition travelled in the
service of Lord Hiram, to conquer land." Lower line—
"This is the record of Hanta, who attained the great-river.
And these words cut on stone."[3] The great-river reference
was presumably to the St. Lawrence.

Thus, according to Fell, the Sherbrooke stones represented the written records of ancient Mediterranean explorers in America. With this introduction Professor Sotiroff and Professor Lee spent the next several months
analyzing the markings. They concluded that the Sherbrooke inscription was not in any way related to Libyan.
Libyan, according to Dr. Sotiroff, contains certain elements which are not found on the Sherbrooke inscription.
Instead, the markings seemed to match an obscure script
found on a cave wall in southern Bulgaria.[4] Even more
remarkable, the two Laval University scholars postulated
that if the markings on the Quebec stone were genuine,
they could mean that an as yet unknown Old World
people preceded a Carthaginian-Libyan exploration of

North America by at least a millennium; the Bulgarian script appears to predate the development of the Phoenician alphabet in the Mediterranean by at least five hundred years!

It will take many decades of study before we know the provenance of the people who carved the Sherbrooke inscriptions. Future scholarly disputes over exact translations are inevitable. In fact, they seem to be part of the job. But this should not concern us. What is important is to first recognize that the two incised rock slabs housed in a seminary museum in southern Quebec are indicative of a little known writing system used perhaps twenty-five or thirty-five hundred years ago by a people not indigenous to North America.

C. Merrimack River Valley

Starting near the town of Franklin in south-central New Hampshire, at the confluence of the Pemigewasset and Winnepesaukee Rivers, the Merrimack River flows southward into Massachusetts where it turns northeast, twisting along the corner of the state before emptying into the Atlantic Ocean at Newburyport. Its 110-mile course covers a drainage area of over 5000 square miles. The lower Merrimack is a broad estuary that is navigable only by small boats for about the first 15 miles. The main features of the middle and upper parts of the waterway during post colonial times were the many rapids and waterfalls. Scores of textile mills built along churning water brought great wealth to the area. Fortunes were made from gristmills as well.

The enormous quantity of stone ruins found along this water route and its tributaries tends to be much better known to the general public than some of the other structures we have examined elsewhere.

1. COVERED CAIRN BURIAL SITE, ANDOVER, MASSACHUSETTS

Four miles south of the Merrimack River just outside the town of Andover, Massachusetts, the late Connecticut archeologist Frank Glynn carried out a detailed examination of a large stone mound complex. Known locally as the Effigy or Turtle Mound, this carefully laid-out conglomeration of boulders lies on top of a small hill. Incorporated into the 100-by-60-foot array of cobbles and boulders are three slab-roofed chambers, one of which is corbelled, while the other two are flat-roofed. The mound has been known to area archeologists for decades, but it wasn't until 1951 that Frank Glynn spent a season digging the site. It was well worth the effort, for the results of his systematic investigation may provide us with another clue to the identity of early inhabitants of America.

Four test trenches were sunk, two along the outer margin of the stones and two within the chambers. One of the outer pits had telltale evidence of an occupation site. A thick layer of black, greasy soil with lots of fired stone present was found beneath an undisturbed layer of dark brown and gray white earth. The coloration of the undisturbed layer as well as its well-stratified composition indicated to Glynn that the black soil layer beneath it had been buried for a considerable length of time. In essence, what Glynn found was the trash of a group of people who had been living and cooking at the site a long time ago.[5]

The other two trenches revealed a combination of stone artifacts and the remains of a chambered burial (see figure 6.6). Within the northeast chamber about one foot below ground level, a number of stones had been placed in the ground, forming an oval pattern with the long axis pointing north-south. Glynn's meticulous removal of each horizontal layer of ground soil within the center of the oval revealed small traces of material believed to be human bone. Eventually it became evident from soil discoloration, charred stone artifacts, and the collapsed nature of the interior stratum that a body at some time in the past had been laid out, covered over with a thin layer of dirt, and subjected to the intense heat of a large fire. Furthermore, the foundation stones of the overhead slab-roofed chamber completely enclosed and were in direct contact with the oval buried stones. In other words, the stone chamber, which is constructed exactly like the other chambers we have seen throughout the Northeast, was erected soon after the corpse of some ancient person was laid in the ground. It was a stone tomb built by America's mysterious early inhabitants.

Who were these people? How old is the Andover burial site? Unfortunately, the excavations were carried out in 1951, a time when radiocarbon dating was in its infancy and therefore prohibitively expensive to use as an archeological tool by dedicated individuals like Frank Glynn. We can, however, put together a crude picture of the cultural level of the people who constructed the burial cairn by examining the recovered artifacts. All but two of the artifacts were uncovered in the excavated northeast chamber. They were all made of stone. Included among them were a javelin point found within the oval chamber burial, axeheads, an octagonal ball, hammerstones, drills (straight and single-shouldered), mauls, a pestle, rectangular pendants, and a polished celt (a hafted axelike stone commonly known as a tomahawk head). Polished celts are almost invariably more than six thousand years old. In fact, all of the stone material found within the burial chamber points to a date as early as 3000 B.C.

Similar stone artifacts have been found all over the United States at established American Indian archeological sites. The early tribes in this country made and utilized an enormous quantity and variety of lithic tools. This cannot be denied. The artifacts may well have Indian origins, but there are only a few sites that suggest that Indians *constructed* chambered tombs. The evidence is wanting.

In prehistoric Europe, however, during the Neolithic period, stone mauls, pestles, axes, pendants, and polished celts were being used by many communities. The people at that time also had a peculiar way of burying their dead—they erected giant stone cairns over the deceased. They constructed chambered burial tombs, dolmens, mounds of earth, or stone-lined pits into which the body was deposited. In parts of Sweden and Norway, for example, Neolithic farmers placed their dead within elliptical rings of stone before covering the body with magnificent arrangements of surface cobblestones and boulders. Why they went to all this trouble is unclear. Presumably a person of great importance was buried beneath the stone.

The Andover site is incredibly similar in design and layout to Neolithic West European burials. Both the artifacts and the stone cover strongly suggest this, but the artifacts could also be interpreted as American Indian. We are, therefore, confronted by two exciting and thoroughly testable hypotheses: that the burial cairn site was constructed by an unknown group of northeast Indians who worked in stone, or that the cairn was built by prehistoric Old World travelers to America.

If the first hypothesis is correct, then we had all better get on the ball and reevaluate our present theories about native American independent cultural evolution. If the second hypothesis has any substance, then we had better rethink our concepts about ancient sea travel. The antiquity of the site as evidenced by the association of stone artifacts could mean that, long before even the most ardent supporter of diffusionism thought possible, people were sailing to America and establishing settlements. Although the time period when this may have been done— between six thousand and five thousand years ago— absolutely boggles the mind, the possibility that it indeed happened is very real.

Aside from weekend excursions by curiosity seekers and the like, the Andover site has not been carefully examined by competent archeologists since 1951.

2. MYSTERY HILL SITE, NORTH SALEM, NEW HAMPSHIRE

About 14 miles northwest of the Andover site across from the Merrimack River, atop a wooded rise outside of North Salem, New Hampshire, an intriguing complex of granite walls, drystone chambers, underground passageways, standing monoliths, alignments, and inscriptions is spread over a 24-acre fenced hilltop. Known as Mystery Hill, the site has long fascinated the layperson and disgusted the professional archeologist, in part because of its long history of exploration by inept researchers.

The first person known to be associated with the site was a Jonathan Pattee, who built a house amidst the stone ruins in 1826. Over the next twenty-five years Pattee managed to sire thirteen children—eleven daughters and two sons—as he successfully farmed the nearby valley. In the mid 1850s, however, a fire destroyed his brick farmhouse, forcing the family to settle elsewhere in the community. Left to the elements, the charred remains were eventually covered over with years of plant growth.

The hilltop was well known throughout the town. Residents referred to the stone structures adjoining the house foundation simply as Pattee's Caves. They erroneously assumed that the nineteenth-century farmer had a penchant for stone construction equaling his love for children. Hunters used to hide within the chambers and wait for passing buck. And many a young boy spent a summer afternoon exploring the overgrown man-made "caves."

That Jonathan Pattee utilized the stone structures strewn about his property cannot be denied. Many early nineteenth-century artifacts in the way of rusted nails, kitchen utensils, and broken china are scattered all over the surface of the site. That Jonathan Pattee erected all of the monstrous chambers is quite another matter and is the subject of an ongoing debate.

The first person to challenge local folklore was William B. Goodwin, a wealthy insurance executive from Hartford, Connecticut, who purchased the former Pattee property in the 1930s and set out to show the world that a Christian monastery had been built there in the tenth century A.D. by a band of Irish Culdee monks. Understandably, a slew of outraged archeologists and historians on both sides of the Atlantic published scathing rebuttals of Goodwin's weak premises. When the dust finally settled, one sticky problem remained, namely, who built the stone chambers and underground passageways?

In 1945 Dr. Junius Bird of the New York Museum of

Natural History (the same place where the Inwood Stone is housed) was invited to conduct the first professional investigation of Pattee's Caves. The results of his five-day excavation, admittedly a short time to dig, were contradictory. He wrote, "There is the suggestion of age antidating Colonial times from the charcoal distribution in the soil in the hill slopes;" but at the same time the data from a slab-roofed chamber implied an historic date.[6]

Dr. Bird did note something which archeologists today still fail to comprehend when they claim that no information can be obtained from a site which has been meddled with for so many years. He stated that "no structure could have been so thoroughly cleared or disturbed in recent times as to completely obliterate the evidence of several centuries' abandonment if they were constructed in pre-Colonial times. Even if the builders left no artifacts, there should be evidence of occupation, at least charcoal, which should be separated from subsequent material by sterile dirt."[7] He was enthusiastically in favor of future research.

About a decade later a Yale archeology graduate student undertook six weeks of digging at the North Salem site. He concluded, on very thin evidence, that the *entire* stone complex was initially constructed sometime between the late seventeenth and early eighteenth centuries and that Jonathan Pattee was probably the principal "reconstruction" architect in the nineteenth century.

During the next few years the property was purchased by Robert Stone, an electrical engineer who lived nearby. Stone eventually changed the name of the place from Pattee's Caves to Mystery Hill and subsequently established the first ongoing research project at the site. It is largely through the dedication of this farsighted man that Mystery Hill has been preserved from the bulldozer.

Throughout the 1960s and '70s, however, Mystery Hill acquired a bad reputation. Each year a new investigator saw something else in the confusing array of stone structures. As new strides in European megalithic archeology were taken, the enthusiastic people who visited North Salem quickly applied the fundamental concepts of the megalithic data to the site's buildings in an effort to explain them. Thus, a few years after the British astronomer Gerald Hawkins shocked archeologists throughout the world with his impressive analysis of Stonehenge, Mystery Hill earned the dubious title of "giant megalithic astronomical complex." When Alexander Thom's high-powered statistical arguments for a standard megalithic unit of measurement finally filtered down into popular literature, the megalithic yard and all its variations were found in every nook and cranny at North Salem. When Barry Fell pointed out in 1975 that a number of slabs at the site appeared to have markings which resembled Iberian Punic script, suddenly Mystery Hill was *proven* to be a *major* outpost of Celtic-Iberian people.

Mystery Hill should be studied not in isolation, but with an eye on the association of similar stone traits dotting parts of northeast America and elsewhere. It is clear that it and other impressive complexes of stone were laid out under the same conceptual framework. The mystery at Mystery Hill is its persistent ability to confuse what should be a relatively straightforward answer to a simple archeological question: was it built since the early sixteenth century A.D. or not?

No definite colonial artifacts are known to have been recovered *in situ* within an undisturbed section of the main complex. But there were supposedly hundreds of seventeenth- and eighteenth-century implements found on the surface by William Goodwin in the 1930s. The lack of colonial artifacts from undisturbed ground soil within a few of the slab-roofed structures is the very same pattern we have observed elsewhere, in particular at the Gungy-wamp site in southern Connecticut and at the Ramapo site in New York.

A trench sunk by James Whittall over the so-called Oracle Chamber drain revealed tiny specks of charcoal from under one of the capstones. The results of a radiocarbon test yielded a date of 520 A.D. (± 135 years). From another excavation, on two separate occasions, Whittall obtained charcoal from *between* the slabs of a drystone walling. One sample gave a date of 1045 B.C. (± 180 years), the other a date of 1525 B.C. (± 210 years).

The people at Mystery Hill quickly released these remarkable dates and waited for the praise. Unfortunately it never came. Archeologists criticized the radiocarbon dates, reasoning that when the walls were constructed in *colonial* times some charcoal and dirt from an earlier *Indian* occupation site on the hill must have mixed in with the stone slabs. In other words they discounted the hill's antiquity on the basis of the assumption that it simply could not be older than the early sixteenth century, at the extreme, because ancient European or Mediterranean man never made it to America. Therefore any charcoal from fires must be Indian and any stonework must be from the colonial or postcolonial period. This sort of reasoning goes nowhere. In fact, it has acted as a major blindfold for America's archeologists. Continuing to spout established dogma without a detailed personal investigation of the site is to impede scientific progress.

Mystery Hill is intriguing. The fenced section comprises only a tiny portion of a site that rambles on for over 150 acres. Along the many infrequently traveled trails surrounding the hilltop is some impressive evidence of wedge and fire stone quarrying (methods of quarrying without the use of metal tools). On a high ridge a few hundred yards from the so-called Sacrificial Table, a series of long stone slabs lies amidst a patch of poison ivy plants. Some of these rectangular blocks are up to 15 feet long and 5 feet wide. Standing among them, one is left with the impression that whoever was pounding away to remove them must have left, never to return to complete the task. Most of the slabs have only been partially removed from the bedrock.

The quarry site has never been excavated. In fact, it was only recently discovered by the site's general manager, Osborn Stone. Future workers would do well to concentrate on exposing the area around the slabs. Estimates of the quantity of stone removed would be helpful in calculating the amount of manpower involved. It is important to stress that this spot bears no resemblance to colonial quarries. The early settlers had no time to bash stone on stone to remove slabs. They had metal implements and oxen to help them lift and pull slabs out. The Mystery Hill stones were apparently all removed by a combination of bashing, wedging, and heating.

The frequency of large, recumbent, triangular monoliths is astounding. During a recent visit to the Hill, Osborn Stone showed me over ten similarly sculpted stones. Some of them measured up to 20 feet long by 10 feet wide. These stones are not naturally shaped glacial debris. Systematic maul markings and chipping along the edges are quite clear and impressive. A few of them stand upright in the midst of colonial field walls. Thus far there is absolutely no evidence that early English settlers had any reason to quarry such material for their walls. The impression one gets is that the tall planes of stone were initially standing upright and were therefore simply made part of a field wall. There is a rapidly growing body of data which suggests that this may indeed have been what happened.

Over the past year or two Mystery Hill has undergone an extensive examination with reference to possible astronomical alignments. Previous maps of the site have been discarded in place of a highly detailed survey pinpointing most of the outlining field walls and standing stones. The meticulous and oftentimes tedious work has paid off, for it seems that a number of major standing stones (more than one would expect by chance alone), when viewed from a particular spot, line up with key solar events such as the solstice and equinox sunrise/sunsets. If future work establishes that these alignments are indeed true, then Mystery Hill, ironically, could be what its present owners have claimed it is—a crude observatory. It is obvious that the site holds a lot more secrets which can only be explained if a first-rate nonbiased team of astro-archeologists undertake a thorough examination of the complex and exciting data.

Barry Fell visited the site in mid-1975 and was soon

able to identify a triangular tablet as having been marked in Iberian-Punic script. His translation spoke of the Phoenician god Baal. A few months later several other inscribed stones came to light. These turned out to bear a form of Ogam, and their translations were similar. They read, "Dedicated to Bel" (the Celtic sun god). On this basis Dr. Fell inferred that Baal and Bel were, in fact, the Celtic and Phoenician names for the same god. In other words, Mystery Hill seems to have been visited by both the Celts and the Phoenicians. As more inscriptions were found, the period of visitation as determined from the style of writing was placed between 800 and 600 B.C. According to this theory, the Celts may have stayed in North Salem a good many centuries longer. One tablet suggested a data as late as 45 B.C.

What do we make of all this? It is obvious that some serious chronological and methodological problems still, and probably always will, exist at Mystery Hill until a major excavation is mounted. The radiocarbon dates suggest a thirty-five-hundred-year-old legacy, a time that would fit in very nicely with the megalithic style construction apparent throughout the entire 150 and more acres of hilltop. As the radiocarbon dates are not accepted by everyone, it will be necessary to gather more samples from areas that have not been disturbed by construction in order to determine the oldest actual Indian occupation of the locale. Then it will be important to open up a number of test trenches across and under several stone structures to see if charcoal and artifacts of the same date crop up.

Barry Fell's decipherments speak of a people occupying the site at least a thousand years later than the radiocarbon dates imply. It is perfectly possible that the Celts erected the structures for their own use. The data from other sections of the Northeast seems to suggest that these people had a good deal to do with slab-roofed chambers. Then again, it is also perfectly feasible that the structures were already standing if and when the ancient Celts arrived in America. The tentative results of Frank Glynn's excavations at the Andover burial cairn site would appear to support this supposition.

Even if all of the above turns out to be nonsense, we are still faced with some serious questions. Why in the world would Scottish and English pioneers labor to first cut down giant hardwood trees at the base of so many hilltops across the Northeast and then set up enormous stone structures? Did early America harbor a crazed yet sophisticated cult of settlers bent on imitating the script and ancient ruins of their homelands? Did our immediate ancestors simply like to work with stone instead of wood? Perhaps. The material is out in the fields. It demands positive identification and a thorough explanation.

D. Coast of Maine

Maine is a study in contrasts. Inland a heavy cover of pine trees graces rugged mountains as crystal blue lakes dot a countryside sometimes called "the last wilderness frontier in the east." Towns are few in the isolated northwest where giant mills pulverize trees into paper and toothpicks. Along the rockweed coastline the Atlantic pounds against granite sea ledges. Raging storms called northeasters sometimes keep vessels docked for days as they rip into high coastal headlands.

In the sixteenth century, soon after Europe realized that Columbus had not reached India, other explorers were employed to search for a northwest passage to the wealth of the Orient. Many of these adventurers sailed past Maine into the Bay of Fundy before discovering their passage was blocked by a land mass that would eventually be called New Brunswick and Nova Scotia. While they all failed to find a waterway across the new frontier, they did manage to find, near the northeastern coast, one of the world's richest fishing grounds. Thriving seaports naturally grew as sailors forgot about spices and instead turned to fishing. Shipping fish to the markets of Spain and Europe became a major export business returning handsome profits for all involved.

By 1657, attracted by the region's economic potential, pioneers had migrated into the Kennebec River Valley and established the first settlements. But as the settlers cut down and cleared the woodland once believed impenetrable, the vestiges of an earlier age were brought to light. British farmers found the remains of "chimneys and mouldered ruins which had been overgrown by the forest."[8] These stone structures, at one time thought to be the shelters of seventeenth-century fishermen, have since been found in practically every part of northeastern America. Furthermore, several other types of remains consistently found in the Maine region over the past two centuries have led some scholars to suspect that the rock-clad coastline may have harbored boats and sheltered fishermen thousands of years before a certain Genoan claimed he had sailed to India.

1. INSCRIPTION, MANANA ISLAND OFF MONHEGAN ISLAND, ME.

During the summer of 1971, a man strolling along the shore in Popham Beach State Park in southeastern Maine found three runic stones in a gravel bank near the seaside. The stones contained characters that were used by tenth-century Norsemen. They were eventually turned over to the State Museum in August, where they were analyzed and proclaimed authentic. How they got to Maine, however, is still a question that puzzles American archeologists unfamiliar with our newly emerging past. It is automatically assumed that since the stones are original they must therefore have been brought to Maine since colonial times. This need not be the explanation, for as we have seen in preceding chapters, the vast number of inscribed stones found throughout the Northeast suggests that they were, in fact, deposited long before the fifteenth century.

About 25 miles east of Popham Beach are two islands that may have been used as trading stops even before Vikings sailed west of Iceland. Monhegan Island is little more than 1½ miles long and ¾ miles wide. Across a tiny harbor on its southwestern end is Manana Island, which is even smaller, ranging less than ½ mile in length and ¼ mile in width. Both islands figure in the seventeenth-century history of the Maine coast, for they were used by fishermen as docking stations before their catches were transported to Europe.

In the mid-1850s Dr. Augustus C. Hamlin of Bangor, Maine, found an inscription carved along the face of a weathered rock outcropping near a high hilltop on Manana Island (see Plate 65). Dr. Hamlin presented his finding at a scientific meeting in Albany, New York, where the general consensus among scholars was that the markings resembled "pointed Runic characters." For many years afterwards antiquarians proudly pointed to the Manana Island inscription as definite proof of early Viking contact. By the late nineteenth century, however, opinions had changed. A geologist traveled to the island and declared the so-called inscription to be a folly of nature. This feeling was reaffirmed in 1971 by an authority from the Carnegie Museum in Pittsburgh who interpreted the carvings as a mere erosion phenomenon.[9]

In 1975, archeologists James Whittall and William Nisbet relayed latex peels and photographs of the markings to Barry Fell for study. Fell's analysis was far different from those of past scholars. He claimed that the seemingly random slashes and grooves from Manana Island were in reality examples of an unrecognized Celtic script known as Hinge-Ogam. It differed from the seventy well-known varieties of Irish Ogam recorded in an eight-hundred-year-old manuscript known as the *Book of Ballymote* in that it lacked symbols for vowels. Past epigraphers apparently had failed to understand these differences and therefore had seen runes or natural erosion instead. Barry Fell had, in essence, cracked the code of a previously unknown writing system.

Reading from right to left, he made the following translation: "Long-ships from Phoenicia: Cargo-lots (and) landing-quay."[10] In other words, the symbols seemed to be a message to Phoenician merchant-sailors that Manana

Island was a place to pick up merchandise, presumably fish. The fact that it was written in a style of Ogam only recently identified along the Iberian Peninsula by Jim Whittall suggests that Iberian Celts were the people who left the message. The inscribed stones from northern Portugal and southern Spain, having been dated on the basis of associated archeological assemblages, imply that the Manana inscription was composed around 400 B.C.

Across the harbor on the larger island of Monhegan, a tiny arrowhead, or possibly a small dagger, was recovered from an excavation of a rubbish heap by the island's archeologist. A C^{14} test of the organic material associated with the deposited metal artifact gave an approximate date of 1800 B.C. For some unknown reason, no one until William Nisbet of the Early Sites Research Society thought of testing the composition of the metal. This is odd, for the radiocarbon dating was conducted at the University of Maine. We can only assume that the scientists in charge of the study did not think it was necessary.

During the summer of 1975 Nisbet submitted a tiny fragment of the artifact to a laboratory for analysis. The results were shocking.[11] The seemingly insignificant arrowhead was composed of copper and tin. There are no tin deposits in either the eastern or middle states of America. The closest mines are in Bolivia, but these deposits were not worked in 1800 B.C. We must look elsewhere to explain how a copper and tin artifact found its way into an island trash pile that had lain undisturbed for perhaps over three thousand seven hundred fifty years.

Tin in the form of its alloy, bronze, was widely used in the Old World during ancient times. Tin mining was reported in central Europe as early as 2000 B.C., and later in Iran, Spain, France, and the British Isles. The Phoenicians are credited with spreading the bronze culture throughout the Mediterranean due to their tin trade. Phoenician ships, as early as 1300 B.C., regularly sailed from their Cornish and Spanish tin mines to all parts of the known world.

If we accept the Manana Island translations of Dr.

Plate 28. Roger Riley near stone A at perched rock site, Greenwood Lake, New York. (Photo by S. M. Trento)

Plate 29. Inscribed stone, Bellvale, New York. (Photo by S. M. Trento)

Plate 30. Close-up of Bellvale inscription. (Photo by S. M. Trento)

Plate 31. Kalpana Shah sitting near an inscribed hearthstone in Riverside, Connecticut. The markings, unknown to previous owners of the eighteenth-century house, were rediscovered in 1973 by a ten-year-old boy. (Photo by S. M. Trento)

Plate 32. Cast of the Riverside hearthstone (Photo by S. M. Trento)

Plate 33. The inscription on the Riverside hearthstone appears to be a variety of Old World Script. (Photo by S. M. Trento)

Plate 34. Southern corner of Putnam Valley stone wall complex, partially hidden by spring foliage, towers 16 feet above Richard Grando. (Photo by S. M. Trento)

Plate 35. Mid-nineteenth-century engraving of a stone enclosure in Paint Creek Valley, Ohio. Radiocarbon dating of works from other parts of Ohio, Kentucky, and Georgia ranges from 5000 B.C. to 2285 B.C. The technical features found there—massive ramparts with multiple revetments, cairns, and nearby "guard chambers," echoed in the New York enclosures and in Celtic Iberian, French, German, and British hill forts—may suggest a common cultural influence or an intriguing analagous relationship. (Baldwin, *Ancient America*)

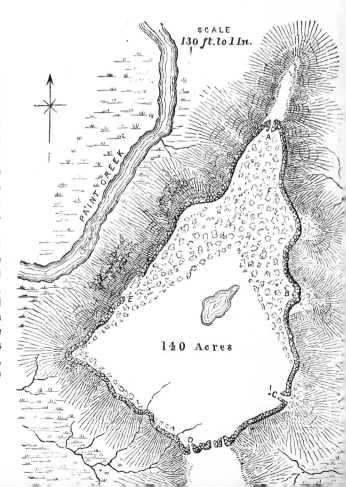

SCALE
130 ft. to 1 In.

PAINT CREEK

140 Acres

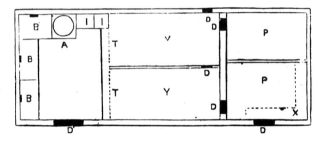

Plate 36. Plan of an 1847 piggery. The Vermont farmer who submitted the design for publication in *Transactions of the New York State Agricultural Society* recommended that wooden "boards be put on in a rough state, and white washed with a composition of stone lime and water lime." He also mentioned that a pig house should be "put up, on a tasteful and cheap scale, within the reach of every thriving citizen in our State." The cost of the project was about $40. " 'Millionaires' may require something more expensive, but this is sufficiently spacious for the common citizens of Vermont," he added. It is stretching the fiscal imagination to believe that the enormous number of stone chambers, whose construction involved much more time, labor, and money, were built by the struggling farmer of nineteenth-century New England. As pointed out elsewhere, design plans for every type of farm building have been found by our researchers; but we have yet to come across *any* plans which speak of slab-roofed chambers.

Plate 37. Passage grave, Anto do Silval, from southwestern Portugal, circa 3700–2500 B.C. These giant slabbed burial vaults, towering above long approaching passages, occur in the copper-rich areas of Portugal, suggesting that the ore was important to the early builders. They also occur near the rich grain fields of the southwest. Interestingly, the American stone vaults discovered in the 1890s were also situated near vast copper deposits and the rolling meadows which would eventually become the breadbasket of modern America. (Courtesy of Jacquetta Hawkes)

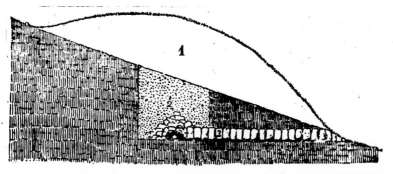

Plate 38. In the late 1800s, east of Dunleith, Illinois, several earthen mounds were found to contain long double rows of flat stones set up on edge about a foot apart, leading to corbelled burial vaults. They were assumed to be American Indian in origin. Their design and layout, however, suggest certain parallels with the 5000-year-old megalithic passage graves of southwestern Portugal. (Smithsonian Institution, *Twelfth Annual Report*)

Plate 39. Corbelled, slab-roofed chamber with enclosing mound cover,
near New Albin, Iowa. Early nineteenth-century fur trappers traveling
the Mississippi River found great numbers of similarly styled stone wall
structures upon the terraces overlooking the river. Within these burial
vaults, the white pioneers found stone hatchets, copper chisels,
charcoal ashes, and burned human bones. Before Cyrus Thomas
examined the above chamber on behalf of the Smithsonian Institution,
he noted that its diameter exceeded 15 feet and that the walls were over
4 feet in thickness. The stones were dragged into place from a nearby
quarry.

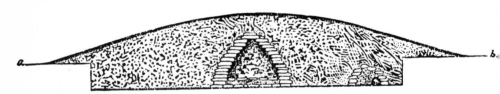

Plate 40. Slab-roofed burial chamber from northwestern
Pennsylvania, near the town of Irvine. (Smithsonian Institution,
Twelfth Annual Report)

Plate 41. Three slab-roofed chambers from Kent Cliffs, New York. (Photos by S. M. Trento)

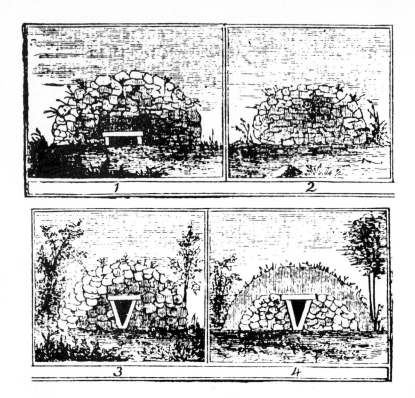

Plate 42. Stone chambers from Frederic County, Virginia, circa 1812. At the time they were reported, timber of several centuries growth was rooted in the structures, which were believed to be aboriginal cemeteries. (Pidgeon, *Traditions of Dee-coo-dah*)

Plate 43. Balanced rock, North Salem, New York. The placement, orientation, and conical shape of the limestone supports indicate the 90-ton granite capstone was perched by man. Nearby ground disturbance patterns visible as circles only from the air, the presence of an equinox-facing chamber, and an ancient European inscription suggest this structure may be a magalithic tomb. (Photo by Kalpana Shah)

Plate 44. A mound of earth originally covered this megalithic tomb from Proleek, County Louth, Ireland. The base stones support a 90,000-pound boulder. Similar Irish tombs were built around 3000 B.C. (W. C. Borliss, *The Dolmens of Ireland,* London: Chapman and Hall, 1897)

Plate 45. Northeast view of the triangular arrangement of base slabs. The support stones were spaced in intervals of the megalithic yard. (Photo by S. M. Trento)

Plate 46. Dolmens were actually repositories for the dead. In a megalithic tomb from the Channel Islands just off the coast of Normandy, France, two skeletons were found beneath the capstone. (W. C. Lukis and W. C. Borliss, *Prehistoric Monuments of the British Isles*, London, 1895)

Plate 47. Dolmen from North Wales, Great Britain, known locally as Maen-y-Bardd, the Poet's Stone. Erosion has worn away the mound cover.

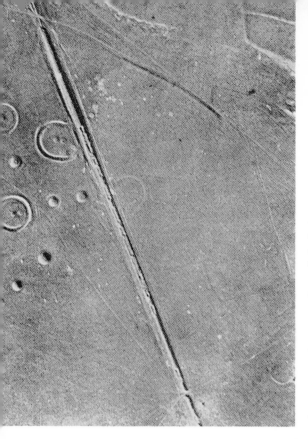

Plate 48. Aerial view of Oakley Down, Dorset, Great Britain. To the left of the diagonal line (an old Roman road) are several circular early Bronze Age (3000 B.C.) graves. On the right are the faint impressions of a prehistoric farming field. (Photo courtesy of O. G. S. Crawford and A. Keiller, *Wessex from the Air*, Oxford University Press, 1928)

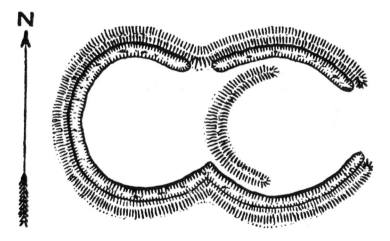

Plate 49. A double circular embankment from the Kanawha Valley, West Virginia. When Cyrus Thomas surveyed the site in the late nineteenth century, the two concentric walls, measuring 295 feet at the outer diameter, were separated by a 20-foot-wide ditch that was barely visible due to years of accumulating rubbish. The architects of this curious feature, which is strangely reminiscent of the North Salem ground impressions as well as the early Bronze Age barrows from Europe, are unknown. (Smithsonian Institution, *Twelfth Annual Report*)

Plate 50. Aerial view of two tangential, circular ground impressions found in a field east of the Balanced Rock, North Salem, New York. The approximate diameter of the left circle is 290 feet while the one on the right is 330 feet. The width of the band is 50 feet. Though the field was recently plowed at the time of this photo, the patterns could still be seen from the air. The impressions represent the obliterated outlines of a circular enclosure that was standing long before the farmer cleared the land for agriculture. Stones inscribed with markings believed to be ancient script have been found alongside the field walls near the tree in the left-hand part of photo. About a mile away is a grouping of massively constructed, equinox-facing slab-roofed chambers. (Photo by Laurel Marx)

Plate 51. Bronze Age mound with enclosed megalithic tomb, Denmark. Many dolmens were originally covered over by earth mounds. (Du Chaillu, *Viking Age*)

Plate 52. Iron Age cist chamber, Denmark. Early American scholars were amazed by the similarity between the Algonquin Indians' stone graves (particularly the ones found along the banks of the Delaware River near the ancient copper mines) and those from northern Europe. On the basis of these parallel burial methods, many savants assumed there was some type of European contact in ancient America. (Du Chaillu, *Viking Age*)

Plate 53. One of several stone graves excavated in the nineteenth century along the Mill Creek in Illinois (Smithsonian Institution, *Twelfth Annual Report*)

Plate 54. Stone Pile, Washington, Massachusetts. On the northern side, not shown, is a large protected base opening which resembles a fireplace. A few yards away lies a stone circle with a center quartz boulder that matches the top stone of the pile. Wadsworth R. Pierce stands nearby. (Photo courtesy of Wadsworth R. Pierce)

Plate 55. One of the largest single standing stones was discovered by Elizabeth Sincerbeaux outside South Royalton, Vermont. Local geologists claim similar stones are the result of natural weather erosion. (Photo by William E. Lovering)

Plate 56. Close-up of the lower left side of the South Royalton inscribed barn stone clearly shows the incisions are neither glacial scratches nor plow markings. They are the organized symbols of an as yet undetermined script. (Photo by William E. Lovering)

Plate 57. The top two standing stones are from the central Vermont region, while the bottom illustration is a similarly styled standing stone from northern Scotland. All are in full view of the local horizon. Near the Vermont stones an enormous number of inscriptions have been reported. (Photos by S. M. Trento, drawing from Daniel Wilson, *Prehistoric Annals of Scotland*)

Plate 58. Byron Dix poses next to a checkerboard design carved into a boulder at the South Royalton, Vermont, site. Behind the boulder at the bottom of a bowl-shaped depression is an equinox-facing stone chamber with a grid marking incised onto its ceiling slab. The checkerboard motif, carved on standing stones and field slabs throughout New England, is well illustrated in Europe, the Mediterranean, and Asia. In the ancient world, for example, the sign was associated with the Egyptian sun god, Aton. It is possible that the pattern represented a cultivated field grid with irrigation canals (Totten). If so, the connection with the sun (for crop production) would be understandable. Its presence in the New World, up until very recently, has been completely neglected or overlooked by American archaeologists. (Photo by S. M. Trento)

Plate 59. Close-up of the South Royalton, Vermont, checkerboard motif (Photo by S. M. Trento)

Plate 60. Three-thousand-year-old sandstone slab with checkerboard design from a German megalithic burial (Courtesy of S. R. Gnamm, Munich)

Plate 61. A gridlike sign appears on the ceiling slab of a stone chamber within the South Royalton, Vermont, site. The same type of sign has been found in other New England chambers. (Photo by S. M. Trento)

Plate 62. Portion of the fresco ceiling of the long Axial Gallery cave at Lascaux, France. These and other well-composed scenes of Upper Paleolithic hunting life from southwestern France and northwestern Spain are likely to date anywhere from 8000 B.C. to 5000 B.C., although some may extend back to 35,000 B.C. Of interest is a rectangular symbol apearing between the three cows and the horse. The same type of design appears on the ceilings of many New England stone chambers. (Courtesy of Caisse Nationale des Monuments Historiques, France)

Plate 63. A Neolithic pasage grave from Denmark. The overall dimensions of this southward-facing chamber, which dates to at least the fifth millennium, are analagous to some of the underground chambers of central Vermont. (Du Chaillu, *Viking Age*)

Plate 64. An underground slab-roofed, corbelled chamber from South Royalton, Vermont. Until the entranceway was partially excavated by Jim Whittall of the E. S. R. S., entrance to the chamber was through the tiny opening at the top. Behind this structure, near the farm of the Mormon prophet Joseph Smith, are several small standing stones. Script-like markings have been found in abundance in the surrounding fields. (Photo by S. M. Trento)

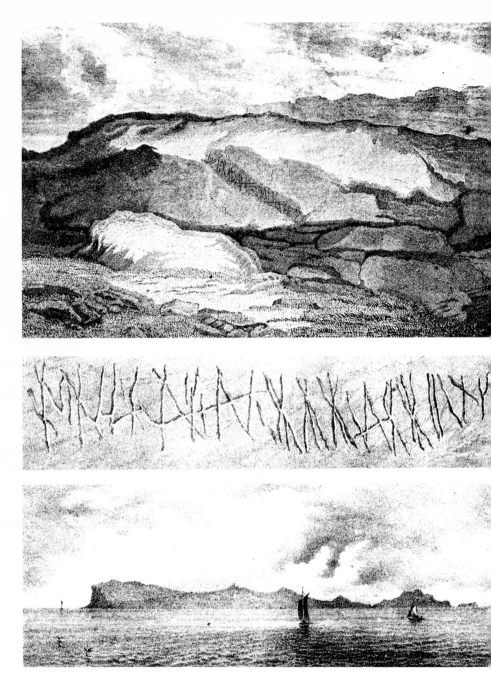

Plate 65. Mid-1850s illustration of Manana Islet inscription and Monhegan Island (Schoolcraft, *History of the Indian Tribes*)

Barry Fell, then the copper-tin projectile point takes on a whole new meaning. It may have been left by a Phoenician merchant who stopped at the landing quay to pick up his stock of merchandise.

We can only wonder how many other "copper" artifacts are lying untested in the museums of America. Detailed compositional analysis of these seemingly aboriginal cultural remains may very well reveal that they are the handiwork of a society quite familiar with the tin deposits of ancient Europe.

2. CERAMIC AMPHORAE, CASTINE BAY, CASTINE, MAINE

If there really was active sea trade between North America and the Mediterranean over two thousand years ago, then surely there must be tangible and recognizable artifacts scattered along the coastal region. Something more substantial than a message from Manana must be brought to light. Five years prior to Barry Fell's suggestion that scientists would do well to search the seabed between Monhegan Island and the shore for the remains of cargo ships that may have capsized in ancient times, a scuba diver made a remarkable discovery.

In the summer of 1971, Norman Bakeman was pleasure diving in the Bay of Castine, about 50 miles northeast of Monhegan Island along the Maine coast, when at a depth of about 40 feet he noticed what looked like the side of a jar. After clearing away the encrusted mud, he saw he was right. Pleased with his luck, he continued searching the shallow seabed. Within moments he spotted another small vessel of similar design. It turned out to be an off-white ceramic jug exactly like the one he had just found. After returning to shore, he unsuccessfully tried to classify the weird-looking objects. He had never seen anything like them, and neither had any of his friends or associates. For a while they were on display at the University of Maine.

Word of the discovery eventually reached Boston, where James Whittall and Malcom Pearson, expedition photographer for the Early Sites Research Society, traveled to Maine to photograph Bakeman's find. Whittall promptly issued a report on the jugs in the Society's *Bulletin* stating that identical ceramic amphorae (as they are known in the Mediterranean) had been found off the coast of Portugal in the late 19th century.[12] At the time Portuguese archeologists had classified them as coming from the first century B.C. or later. According to Whittall's analysis, the volume of the Maine amphorae matched identically a standard Roman unit of measurement, the sextarius. Furthermore, he noted that the composition and consistency of the jar's clay was similar to ceramics he had excavated in Portugal and Spain.

Another amphora discovered in Jonesboro, a town about 66 miles northeast of Castine along the Maine coast, convinced the Early Sites Research Society to mount a major underwater expedition during the summer of 1977 to search for any telltale debris that might explain the unusually shaped jugs of which only fourteen are known to exist, all of them dating back to Roman times and found along the coast of Iberia. Future work is planned.

E. Coast of Newfoundland

Newfoundland is roughly triangular in shape and is separated from the Canadian mainland by the Strait of Belle Isle, the Gulf of Saint Lawrence, and the Cabot Strait. The Labrador coast extends northwards from the Strait of Belle Isle. The island is basically a rough, eastward-sloping plateau whose surface shows clear signs of the last Ice Age, such as deep lake basins and v-shaped, indented valleys. The coastline is jagged and indented on the east and south, while relatively straight on the west. Air masses from the west give Newfoundland a decidedly continental climate. However, the cold Labrador current flowing southward along the east coast prevents high seasonal temperatures. Fog is an ever present feature along the southeast coast due to the Labrador Current meeting the warm Gulf Stream.

The wealth of codfish off the southern coast was long known to fishermen before the English explorer John Cabot made his North Atlantic voyage in 1497. By the early sixteenth century, English, French, Basque, and Portuguese sailors were fishing regularly off Newfoundland. Throughout the 1500s the fishing grounds attracted extensive maritime expeditions from Europe. Frequent mercantile conflicts during the late seventeenth and early eighteenth centuries, as well as England's policy not to permit permanent settlement, postponed colonization of the island until the late 1700s.

If the fishermen of the fifteenth through eighteenth centuries had ventured inland or to the northern parts of Newfoundland they might have noticed stone ruins left by men who had sailed to the island hundreds of years earlier.

1. NORSE SETTLEMENTS, L'ANSE AUX MEADOWS, NEWFOUNDLAND, CANADA

By the late 1890s there was a concerted effort on the part of America's learned men to classify every newly found inscription as Norse. Practically everything uncovered, be it an earth embankment or a vaulted chamber, was attributed to the exploits of ninth to twelfth century A.D. Vikings. The Smithsonian's voluminous *Twelfth Annual Report* had much to do with this changed attitude. It largely silenced the pre-Indian supercivilization fanatics, and the mysterious mound builders were instead transformed by well-meaning antiquarians into Leif Ericsson and crew.

Scholars pored over Norwegian sagas searching for telltale references to the New World. Much to their delight they found a host of allusions to North America. There were comments about "Northern Hunting Grounds" found west of Iceland and called Helluland, Markland, and Vinland. Around the turn of the century, the whereabouts of these "countries" settled by Vikings changed every month. At yearly scientific meetings a new paper would inevitably be read by some enterprising scholar giving his indisputable "proof" of the identity of these Norse locales. Finding Vinland became the new American craze. As one might expect, a crop of books hit the stores, each with a story wilder than some of the mound builder nonsense. Among other places, Vinland was thought to be Maine, Massachusetts, New York, or New Jersey. Some writers even suggested Central America.

By the 1930s most serious scholars had abandoned any hope of getting firm clues from the admittedly terse sagas. Besides, a different explanation was circling the halls of academia. The accounts were reexamined in terms of a newly emerging theory of legend analysis. The collective myths of entire societies, both past and present, were relegated to the world of fantasy. The early Norse were seen as an adventurous but highly romantic breed of people, given to weaving yarns about nonexistent voyages to nonexistent lands. Viking society, so the psychological anthropologists said, needed elaborate cultural supportive devices to cushion the emotional shock of the uncanny numbers of sailors who never returned home from raids. Thus, thanks to the prevailing psycho-anthropological theories of the time, the Norse sagas were plucked from the realm of the possible and cast into the ambiguous domain of the imagination. They were regarded as folktales, nothing more.

In 1969 Norwegian archeologist Helge Ingstad stunned the academic world by establishing beyond any doubt that an eleventh-century Norse settlement had thrived for many years on the northern coast of Newfoundland. Eight years of excavation had revealed that an extensive community of Vikings had indeed visited and settled North America long before Columbus was born.

Near the fishing village of l'Anse aux Meadows, on the isolated tip of an old beach terrace (see figure 6.7) a few yards inland from the cold Labrador Current and the warm Gulf Stream, Ingstad and his teams found the stone foundations of rectangular long houses, smaller dwelling units, several fireplaces, and circular cooking pits filled with cracked rocks and charcoal. Other important artifacts recovered included such items as a bronze ringheaded pin, pieces of copper, a stone lamp, and a typically Norse soapstone spindle whorl. On a small hill the remains of several stone piles were found. Although it wasn't possible to determine if the cairns were associated with the occupation site, Professor Ingstad did mention that Norsemen often built cairns near their homes in order to tell time. They would line up the well-constructed conical piles with various points on the horizon in order to judge the position of the sun and, thereby, the amount of time before sunset.

Iron ore dispersed in the sod of a nearby bog had apparently been melted down and utilized by the Norse community. This fact alone suggested to Ingstad that the settlement had definite plans to stay in its newfound home, its Vinland, for the highly skilled Viking blacksmith was an essential element to Norse colonization. His services were invaluable for the survival of a new settlement.

Radiocarbon dating showed that most of the remains went back to around 1000 A.D. Sometime after, however, the community vanished. The obvious question of where they went is at present an archeological mystery, but Professor Ingstad does suggest that the constant Indian and Eskimo threat to the small, yet successful, group must have been an important factor. He wisely notes that the Vikings, although savage in their own right, were no match for the multitude of Indians probably attacking in guerrilla style. In any event, for some unknown reason, Newfoundland was abandoned hundreds of years before Spain, France, and England blazed a trail through the Western Hemisphere with the help of the gun.

The l'Anse aux Meadows findings are an incredible achievement for many obvious reasons. It should be excitingly clear that *some* of the sagas were, in fact, referring to North America. The Viking legends *must* contain tidbits of truth. How right were the turn-of-the-century antiquarians who sensed what many of their less imaginative colleagues scoffed at!

Given the extensiveness of the Newfoundland site, it follows that more sites must still exist in the Northeast and elsewhere. If this is so, perhaps we ought to reconsider some of the all too frequently overlooked Indian tales of white men settling parts of America in "ancient" times (see Chapter 3). The white men may very well have been blond-haired marauders from Iceland, Greenland, and Norway. It is possible, of course, that the white god legends originate in the American Indian collective feelings of alienation and racial grief prompted by the colonial intrusion. This anthropological theory may sound fine and proper at an annual meeting or in a scholarly journal, but it does very little to help us synthesize the array of pre-Columbian European settlement debris we have been finding in the Northeast. It is a stagnant theory unable to cope with a revisionist interpretation of American prehistory.

Future excavations throughout the Canadian maritime provinces and the rest of the Atlantic coast will probably expose many examples of Viking occupation. And, judging from the widely scattered material collected by private archeological societies over the past several years, it wouldn't be surprising to someday hear one of my more conservative academic cronies solemnly state that "we have evidence which suggests that people from Europe and the Mediterranean explored and partially settled North America in ancient times."

We need not wait for the day whose arrival is still a long time coming, for at this very moment the tangible remains of early settlements lie partially hidden throughout America. All we have to do is learn how to see them.

7

Some Final Words

Today the roads and byways of some parts of rural America are so infrequently traveled that occasionally it's possible to kick over a flintlock that has rested undisturbed for more than three hundred years. Many corroded artifacts lie scarcely below the roots of trees, waiting to be found. It is within these backwoods that we are recording the intricate but unsuccessful attempts of an ancient generation of people to settle North America. More than anything else, the Indian was probably a constant and powerful deterrent to any long-standing colonization. Only in modern times did a new crop of white men from across the ocean, with their sophisticated firearms, manage to permanently and brutally eliminate this "problem" and thereby settle a land mass others tried to subdue so many centuries earlier.

Near the banks of the Susquehanna, Delaware, and Hudson Rivers, in the countryside surrounding the Upper Croton, Housatonic and Connecticut River Valleys, along the sculptured shoreline of Maine and Canada's Maritime

Provinces, as well as from other major river valleys, tributaries, and shorelines across the nation, we are uncovering the obscure remains of a long-gone, seagoing people. If we plunge headfirst into the murky sea of Indian mythology, we come face to face with the ever present white god legends. Swimming back to the world of the profane, we are impressed by the great numbers and general similarity of stone piles, dolmenlike altar stones, cist chambers, rock-cut inscriptions, giant walled enclosures, underground tunnels, copper mines, and smelted artifacts over wide stretches of America. All this testifies to active, though small and widely scattered, communities of Old World traders.

The mass of data is still confusing. Some of it implies an 800 B.C. Celt-Iberian or 400 B.C. Libyan legacy. Some of it speaks of first millennium Phoenicians, while other stonework and burials make sense only if we assume that a five-thousand-year-old megalithic community lived on this continent. Only time and continued study will straighten out this problem. For now, however, we must simply recognize the stone ruins of America for what they are rather than for what they are not.

It is often said, "So what. Why should we bother with old stones and bones? Who gives a damn about yesterday anyway?" The truth of the matter is, not many people care about the past. This is odd when we consider that every living person has an infinitely long line of ancestors to thank for successfully transmitting their genetic code from one generation to the next. If only one person, one hominid, one amoeba cell mucked up, you and I wouldn't be here right now.

Nevertheless, our indifferent attitude towards the past, which in part had its beginnings with the Industrial Revolution, continues to plague us today. Since that time human progress has been equated with and measured by the relative sophistication of machine technology. Because we have split the atom, sent men to the moon, because we have mastered the art of doing things, surely we are the epitome of all past civilizations. After all, didn't the ancients have an equal chance in their time to reach the glorious achievements of today? Modern society, with its awesome capacity to erect towering skyscrapers and (thank you Carl Sagan) to send intergalactic inscriptions—the aesthetic equivalent of standing stones and rock-cut slabs—is certainly superior to a four-thousand-year-old community that cavorted about dragging 10-ton stones into place—isn't it?

No. The concept that West European-American culture is at the most progressive end of a linear scale of society is part of an antiquated philosophy that should have been shoved down the throats of the first Victorians who uttered it. It is nonsense to think that societies evolve as do organisms. An increasingly vocal Third World made this obvious to industrial governments and anthropologists long ago. Curiously, this philosophy can still be detected when archeologists describe ancient cultures. It is assumed, a priori, that early Old World peoples not only lacked the technology and the skill to cross an ocean but that they also had no desire to do so—they were frightened by legends of sea monsters and a flat earth.

This book has only touched upon the enormous changes that are taking place in our world view. Their repercussions will be felt in history, genetics, anthropology, philosophy, mathematics, and engineering. If Old World peoples actually settled in scattered, low-density villages along the waterways of the Western Hemisphere and moved giant slabs of stone without mechanical power, then America before Columbus must not and cannot be viewed in isolation from the rest of the world as a sociobiological laboratory free from genetic and cultural admixture. The quantity of stone ruins and inscriptions lying in the forest suggests that intentional and frequent voyages had been going on for quite some time before Columbus sailed here. Once we concede that a basis for population settlement existed in early America, we are forced to look beyond our New World pioneer syndrome and into the obscure and buried past.

Recently charges of racism have been brought against

individuals professing to have data suggesting even limited trans-Atlantic contact before Columbus. Critics say
that the disciples of diffusionism fail to consider the
American Indian's ingenuity and capability. They claim
that it is ridiculous to look to other shores for the builders
and scribes of America's monuments and inscriptions
when the entire country was populated by aboriginal
tribes who could very well have left the stone material.

Perhaps diffusionists, in their enthusiasm, have been a
trifle simplistic concerning the outstanding achievements
of the native American. Judging from the present archeological record, we can see that an extraordinary number of
cultures existed among the prehistoric Indians. Such diversity naturally was expressed in unique methods of
agriculture, hunting, and in some cases, building with
earth. Furthermore, it cannot be denied that the quality of
tribunal justice and social order, at least among the
eastern Algonquins, was far more understanding and
humane than the brash, egocentric beliefs of the sixteenth-
century Europeans who brutally raped North America.

The data presented in this book should not be clouded
up with bigoted thinking. The purpose has not been to
make a case for any people monopolizing this country in
pre-Columbian times. Rather, it has been simply to point
out that a variety of stonework and script exists here
which appears to have more in common with Old World
ancient cultures than with known Indian and historic
European societies. To confuse these points is to remain
ignorant of our exciting prehistory.

To all my ruffled colleagues who are nauseated by
another book which appears intellectually deluded, I
simply suggest that you take to the woods for twelve to
eighteen months. Walk trails that haven't been walked in
a hundred years. Climb cliffs known only to the birds. Get
two hundred or more graduate students to assist you in
this exercise in academic "folly" and see the material
yourselves. Come to your own conclusions. You're in for a
surprise far more complex than you may have imagined.

Since its glorious beginnings as an experiment in

democracy, America has been first in everything, be it manpower, technology, or science. There is a certain irony in our being one of the last countries in the world to recognize and appreciate the history of the land we occupy. But we are still young with growing pains. Reflection requires a certain level of maturity where there is time to pause, to look back on where we've been rather than where we're going. Let us hope the day is near when we need not fear the unknown, when we can finally rip off our conceptual blinders and fully tackle the incredible mystery of America's stone ruins. By recognizing the products of human labor many years removed from us, we may be able to intuitively reach into the past as did Heinrich Schliemann and "commune with the old workers." Although many of the structures were erected at a time when life was quite different from today, they were nonetheless built by real people who lived, laughed, and loved, just as we do. Somehow they found time in their struggles to record precious moments of their existence. These people, turned to dust hundreds if not thousands of years before Christ, with a language we are just beginning to notice, call out to us from monuments standing mysteriously in the hills—the fabric of a timeless scene. Everything speaks of them.

Perhaps by studying the remains of their structures, by reading their inscriptions, by walking the same valleys and cliffsides where they must have worshiped, we will be in much better position to see and feel what these people did so very long ago. Maybe not, but one thing is certain— we won't know until we try.

Appendix 1
The How, When, and Where of Exploring Early America

How

BODY FITNESS

The most important asset to a field explorer is a healthy body. Before taking to the woods make sure you are in good shape. Sometimes it takes a couple of hours of sustained backpacking to reach a site. So before attempting to set a world record for mountain climbing, spend about two weeks toning up your muscles. Jogging is, by far, the best way to simultaneously build strong legs and increase endurance.

EQUIPMENT

The main thing to remember is to travel light but well. A small backpack with an aluminum frame should be sufficient for an exploratory romp through the forest.

Good boots are a must. When you're out in the middle of God's country miles from the closest dirt road, a comfortable pair of boots can make the difference between the excitement of discovery and the misery of aching feet. Winter hikes should always be started with thick, heavily insulated boots waterproof above the ankle. On a winter field trip to Vermont, I once mistakenly packed a pair of thin-walled, flat-soled summer shoes instead of the usual insulated winter footwear. Our schedule demanded sixteen-hour-days of climbing and descending snow-covered hills. Needless to say, it was torture. Cold feet are no fun regardless of what's out in the field. But more importantly, the danger of frostbite becomes imminent.

For summer walks, a light, above-the-ankle leather shoe with sturdy rubber cleats should be sufficient. By all means do not use flat-soled work boots or construction boots. While adequate for walking on city pavements, the soles of these shoes are worthless for backpacking. They fail to give sufficient traction when climbing up dirt slopes.

The amount of clothing should depend on the season, but remember, always pack a jacket. Even if it's 110 degrees F at 8 A.M., when you're out in the woods, a thunderstorm could suddenly bring the temperature down to 50 degrees F. If you're stuck on top of a mountain peak decked out in a tank top and shorts, you're running the very real and dangerous risk of exposure. Every summer someone in America dies due to a lack of foresight. It is best to always wear a long pair of pants, especially if the terrain is covered with poison ivy.

People often ask what kind of food they should bring along. The best foods are those providing high energy in a concentrated form. Powdered protein is excellent. It's light to carry and jam-packed with an assortment of body building amino acids. A 6-ounce plastic container of this marvelous stuff should get you through midafternoon hiking fatigue. A small amount of honey or raisins should also be packed away. These naturally charged foods provide the body with an immediate supply of energy. A medium-sized canteen filled with *water*—not soda or liquor—should be sufficient for a day's hike.

The type of physical equipment one takes into the field depends upon the quality and quantity of information one expects to gather. If the trip is merely of a sightseeing nature, then a camera, a sturdy compass, and a good field map will do. More elaborate plans, however, make it necessary to invest more time and effort in securing the proper instruments.

Topographic maps are invaluable to the explorer, for they translate the countryside into easily understandable graphic symbols. Geological features such as wooded ridges, mountain peaks, fields, waterways, and the like are all clearly depicted. Most large sporting goods stores, especially in areas with an active hunting season, stock local maps. They can also be purchased directly from the government at the following addresses: east of the Mississippi River—Branch of Distribution, U.S. Geological Survey, 1200 South Eads Street, Arlington, Virginia 22202; or west of the river—Branch of Distribution, U.S. Geological Survey, P.O. Box 25286, Federal Center, Denver, Colorado 80225. Prices vary between $1.25 and $2.00 depending on the type of map required. Indexes showing plans for each state are available free on request at the same addresses. If you've never used these charts, then by all means also request the free booklet entitled *Topographic Maps*. It explains practically everything you need to know about them. Local trail guides, sometimes available from hunting clubs and hiking associations, should be used to supplement the topographic map.

Our teams found that a covered vinyl clipboard worked well for outdoor note taking. The cover saved many a site-survey sheet from the ravages of early morning dew and late afternoon showers. For field recording, it is best to write in pencil, preferably a # 2½ or harder. Ink tends to smear and is difficult to erase.

A 35-mm camera is the handiest and most economical way to keep a photographic record of stonework and inscriptions. Unless you have a specific task in mind, costly lenses and additions are not necessary, although it is helpful to keep an inexpensive horizon filter on the camera lens at all times. Furthermore, though you can get by very nicely without it, a wide-angle lens sometimes comes in handy in tight situations.

Having the proper film can make all the difference between recording a structure on the first attempt and having to try again at a later date. Remember, many of these sites are way up on top of mountain peaks. To spend a couple of hours climbing a ridge during a sunny morning and then have it turn overcast and gray by noon can spoil your photographic endeavors if you're not prepared. Always take both high and low speed, color, and

TABLE 7   Site Information Sheet

MIDDLETOWN ARCHEOLOGICAL RESEARCH CENTER, INC.

1. Site Name _____ 2. Previous Name _____

3. Survey Map _____ 4. Site Coordinates_____ 5. Elevation____

6. Road or Route _____ 7. Town _____ 8. County _____ 9. State _____

10. Soil _____ 11. Rock Type _____

12. Local Vegetation _____ 13. Cultivation _____

14. Structures:

	Number	Large	Medium	Small	Length	Width	Height	Depth	Circumference	Diameter	Type	Floor	Field Orientation	True Orientation	Pecked	Scratched	Incised	Rubbed	Painted	Other
Cairn																				
Perched Rock																				
Stone Circle																				
Stone Semicircle																				
Circular Impression																				
Standing Stone																				
Chamber																				
Wall Complex																				
Earth Embankment																				
Inscription																				
Chiseled Cave																				
Other:																				

15. Description _____

_____

_____

_____

_____

16. Remarks _____

_____

17. References _____

_____

18. Photos BW, CLR.   19. Available sunlight _____

20. Please attach photos, sketch, rubbing, or latex peel

21. Recorded by _____   22. Date _____

Month/Day/Year

black and white film with you. A film with a high A.S.A. of 400, for example, is particularly useful in low light situations, such as the one in the interior of a slab-roofed chamber, while one having a lower A.S.A. of, say, 124 or 64 is useful in ordinary lighting situations. Kodak puts out a wide variety of reliable films at modest prices. They also publish handy information sheets which describe the best types of film to use for every conceivable lighting condition. Most camera stores pass this information along to their customers.

The only way to get accurate information from a site's layout is to have a professional survey team map out the structures—preferably a crew that has had experience working in rural areas. In any event, there are a number of methodological problems that must be considered before attempting to amass detailed information from a site. People interested in these problems should consult both the Bibliography and Appendix 2 of this book, where references to the literature and research organizations familiar with these survey techniques have been listed.

Our teams found it helpful to carry walkie-talkies in the field. Adequate communication between groups, especially when hiking over unfamiliar terrain, saves a lot of time and needless trouble.

Plastic bags, aluminum foil, a scrub brush, and quick-drying liquid rubber should be packed in every knapsack. The bags are important for storing bits of stone, soil, or ceramics when surface collecting. Aluminum foil is used to record an inscription while in the field. The following technique is the simplest and most efficient way of recording an inscribed stone that cannot be taken back to the laboratory.

First clean the suspected inscription of any dirt or plant growth that might be lodged within the incisions. Once this is done, wrap the surface of the stone with a large sheet of thin-weight foil, making sure that all the markings have been covered. Then take a medium-hard plastic scrub brush and gently rub the foil until the underlying impressions become visible and well defined. When all of the incisions seem to be represented, gently peel the foil from the rock surface, carefully checking to see if all of the marks have been copied. If so, then store the aluminum peel, as it is called, in a safe place. It is always a good idea to make at least four peels of the same stone, to insure against transportation damage or inaccurate rubbings. At home, plaster of Paris poured over the negative image of the foil markings should produce a fairly accurate impression of the original inscription.

However, the best way by far to record a field inscription is to apply several coats of quick-drying liquid rubber. If done correctly, the resulting mold should be an exact negative copy of the original. The beauty of this technique is that a virtually endless number of plaster casts can be reproduced from this one master. Liquid rubber, also known by its popular trademark, Latex, can be purchased in most hobby stores.

It is best to have several detailed photographs of the inscription as well. Splashing water on a dry stone helps to bring out the shadows and depth of the incised grooves.

When

SUMMER

If you live in the Northeast, the worst time to scamper off into the woods in search of "new" stone mysteries is during the summer. Lush green plants, wildflowers, and shrubbery have a remarkable way of hiding the works of man, both modern and ancient. Moss creeps over boulders; lichen camouflage inscriptions; clinging vines wind around standing stones; and even the boldest cairns melt into the forest. I once spent two days trying to find a giant 10-foot-high pile I had visited many times during the winter.

Summer is, however, the season when archeologists dust off their spades and take to the fields: sites are surveyed, grids are laid, trenches are sunk, soil is sifted, and the past is given another chance to tell its story to an eager crowd. The summer months are used to reevaluate and reexamine known lithic sites.

June through August are the best months to walk along

the banks of rivers, tributaries, and brooks. As the water level is usually lower or altogether nonexistent— intermittent streams affording the best example—it is easy to spot flat-faced slabs that may have an eroded inscription pecked across their mud-caked surfaces.

If the summer is the only season available for exploration and if mountain ridges hold your fascination, then be on the lookout for snakes. As one prominent hiker has said, as soon as you step off the asphalt road into the forest you are "an immediate and vulnerable part of nature's ecosystem." A forest trail is not Main Street in some American town. It is a dangerous place where man must be on his constant alert for danger. Over the past few years copperheads and rattlers, for some inexplicable reason, have been multiplying at a phenomenal rate in the woods of northeastern America, particularly in the southern New York-western Connecticut region. During hot July days it is not uncommon to find the reptiles sunning themselves on the faces of bold summits. The bites from these snakes can be deadly, especially if you are a few miles into the woods away from the beaten track. High leather boots are a definite must for walking along the cracks and crevices of this area. It is best to contact your local park commissioner to determine the extent of the snake threat.

Remember that the summer solstice is during this season—June 21 or 22. If you think you've spotted a potential summer solstice alignment pattern, the best way to test it is to get up before sunrise on this date, hike out to your spot, and wait for the sun. Don't forget your camera.

Fall

Late autumn, when the trees have shed their leaves and before the first snowfall covers their crisp brown shells, is the best season to walk the ridges and valleys of the Northeast in search of early America. A forest without its cover gives up its most precious secrets to all who are sensitive enough to see. Stones that were hidden by the green of summer suddenly stand naked before you. Take advantage of this brisk time of year.

Aerial surveys should be performed after the autumn harvest. If roots of field crops have penetrated any underlying ground structures, then their outline should be quite visible from the air. Photographs of rock inscriptions should also be taken during this season and compared with summer photos in order to detect the visual change, if any, produced by lichen cover.

Don't forget the autumn equinox on September 21 or 22.

WINTER

Winter is also a good season for forest site survey. If you're fortunate enough to live in snow-belt country, then snowshoes are about the best way to get up and down slopes. Since there can't be much surface collecting with several feet of snow on the ground, it's probably a wise move to limit yourself to examining known aboveground lithic features such as stone chambers.

The winter solstice is on December 21 or 22.

SPRING

Spring is an excellent season to carefully observe the subtle color changes in fields, meadows, and shrubbery. For example, if within a row of hedges there's one section that's greener or of greater stature than the surrounding bushes, chances are there's probably some rich organic matter beneath the soil, like a burial site or a trash pit. "Plant archeology" is a new and exciting tool for the prehistoric researcher.

Spring rains often wash away ample sections of country riverbanks, especially at tributary confluences. After a heavy shower, be sure to examine such places for telltale artifacts of past activity.

And don't forget that March 21 or 22 is the vernal equinox.

Where

DOCUMENTS AND ORAL REPORTS

The best place to start looking for "curious stone structures" is the local history section of the local library. Try
to secure copies of the earliest written records of the land
you wish to explore. Major libraries usually keep map
rooms which have the first exploration reports and surveys of an area. These documents should be carefully
scrutinized, for the seemingly insignificant "stone room" of
the eighteenth-century woodsman may be a slab-roofed
chamber complete with ceiling inscription; or the balanced
rock conveniently used as a boundary marker may in fact
be an example of a boulder perched by man.

The older residents of a community, particularly those
living in the more rural sections of the Northeast, are an
excellent source to tap. It's not uncommon to learn that
many of these people have lots of stories about peculiar
stones in the woods. They usually start off with "Why
back 'round fifty years ago, I recall seein' . . ." It'll be your
job to follow through on the lead to see if it goes anywhere.

Farmers with deep family roots in one locale should
always be approached. During the course of a few generations many artifacts have probably surfaced during plowing. Items displayed on a farmhouse mantel will usually
attest to this.

FIELD EXPLORING

Before you go tromping through some fellow's cornfield,
make sure you've first obtained permission to do so. A
simple introduction and explanation will usually suffice,
and common courtesy will insure permission for another
day. If you are unsure of the landowner, then stay out of
the area, regardless of whether a "posted" sign appears or
not. Cardboard "No trespassing" signs have a marvelous
way of dissolving into meaningless globs of wet tissue
paper after a rainy summer season. Asking at the nearest

farmhouse or courthouse will probably turn up the needed information.

Given the following conditions, stonework will probably be present along the eastern and western crests of hillsides: a nearby stream, bog, or lake, and an unobstructed view of the distant horizon. Always check the high summits of natural valley passes or places where a river has cut an opening through a ridge. Study the topographic map while in the field and try to imagine the easiest way to get from one place to another. Chances are you'll find yourself drawn to the river valleys and their tributaries. The earliest explorers of America quickly realized that penetrating an impenetrable forest meant trekking along north-south waterways. Consequently, while walking along a riverbed or tiny creek, watch for long flat slabs that may be protruding from a rain-washed riverbank. You might see an inscription.

The best places to look for possible inscribed stones are along the oldest colonial field walls and mill foundations. If our prevailing hypothesis is correct, it is very likely that many settlers simply picked up usable field stones and laid them up as their first property divides and gristmill walls. In all probability some of these stones were incised with organized markings. Thus, carefully scrutinize each flat stone for designs similar to those depicted in this book.

Don't be afraid to spend many hours in the woods searching for that elusive rock. Leave no stone unturned, but watch out for snakes. And by all means try not to get discouraged if your sixteen-hour day brings you nothing but fatigue and frustration. It takes sustained effort and infinite patience. Whatever you do, please try to remain as levelheaded as possible. Quite often the excitement of discovery impedes the researcher from making objective field assessments of a possible inscription.

An obvious question now arises. When in the field, how do you tell natural weather markings or chain-link scars from legitimate organized markings? If you've taken the time to read the preceding chapters, the answer should be equally obvious. Unless you've had epigraphic training or have worked with similar material, it is unusually difficult to tell. Latex peels and photographs of the markings should be brought back to the laboratory for study. The stone should also be moved from the field to a locale where high-powered microscopic examination and thin-section analysis of the markings can be carried out. These physical tests and the opinion of epigraphers should pretty much answer any questions about the status of a marked stone.

Unless you are a member of a competent archeological organization with sufficient excavation funds or have had adequate field training, it is best to leave the digging to others and stick to preliminary site-location work. Digging up the ground without knowing how to go about it or what to do is a one-way ticket to nowhere. Once a site is disturbed, the knowledge to be gained from it is most likely gone forever. Any attempt to replace an artifact in the ground or "reconstruct" a burial doesn't count. So please be careful—especially if you own a metal detector and have a penchant for savagely removing ground soil every time your machine starts buzzing away.

Finally, if you come across or know about an interesting but inexplicable stone structure, and its mystery is driving you nutty, then drop us a line enclosing a photograph, if possible, and a short description of the structure, following the format of the sample site-information sheet shown in Table 7. Send it to: MARC, Inc., P.O. Box 761, Middletown, New York 10940. We'll get a team on it immediately and let you know the outcome as soon as possible.

Appendix 2
Research Organizations

References to specific sites in New England and elsewhere can be obtained directly from a number of operating research societies. On the following pages a short synopsis of each group's objectives is accompanied by a brief summary of the type and quality of available data. I've also listed a few organizations that offer expeditions to various archeological sites in the world. It is by no means complete. Listings are in alphabetical order.

The American Indian Archaeological Institute (AIAI)
Box 85
Washington, Connecticut 06793

Purpose. The AIAI was established as a nonprofit educational and research organization in order to compile information on the prehistory of western Connecticut.

Membership. Annual dues are $5 for students and $10 for nonstudents. Members receive a quarterly publication as well as periodic information on the Institute's research progress.

Data Available. A quarterly newsletter entitled *Artifacts* is published along with a series of work report monographs on western Connecticut archeology. Recently an archeological bibliography of northeast New England has been compiled by Director of Research Roger Moeller.

The Institute contains several workrooms where ongoing projects are systematically studied. Archeology training sessions, including graduate-level courses and field survey work, are also offered at the facility by a professional staff. People interested in an objective look at the American Indian prehistory of New England should write directly to the AIAI for further information.

Archaeological Institute of America (AIA)
260 West Broadway
New York, New York 10013

The AIA annually publishes a valuable list of world-wide archeological programs. People interested in a concise report which describes such useful information as available field schools, participant archeology schools, programs in foreign countries, and staff positions should send $1 to the above address for the publication *Fieldwork Opportunities Bulletin*; or £2 to: Archaeology Abroad Service, 31-34 Gordon Square, London W.C. 1, England, for the publication *Archaeology Abroad*.

Early Sites Research Society (ESRS)
R.F.D. 2
Danielson, Connecticut 06239

Purpose. ESRS is a nonprofit organization established to achieve a fuller understanding of the nature, origin, history, and purpose of unidentified stonework or other unexplained antiquities in New England.

Membership. Annual dues are $10. Students may join for $1 and institutional members may join for $4. Members receive a year's subscription to the Society's journal, the *Bulletin*, as well as a periodic newsletter.

Data Available. ESRS has access to extensive field notes and records of an earlier research society that was active in the 1950s. Selections of these valuable reports are usually published in the *Bulletin*. This journal is published on an occasional basis, whenever enough primary research has been completed to release it (usually one to three issues a year). Articles tend to be detailed, well-referenced, and of exceedingly high caliber. A concerted effort has been made by the contributors to keep the data as descriptive and objective as possible. Excellent illustrations, site-survey maps, and clear photographs with scale usually accompany most articles.

The Society also publishes an important indexed series entitled *Work Reports*, which includes short progress reports of ongoing research around the New England area. Issues of the *Work Reports* must be purchased individually, as membership does not cover them. The cost is nominal.

Back issues of the *Bulletin* are available at $2 per copy. Inquiries should be addressed to William D. Nisbet in care of the ESRS address. A list of past *Bulletin* articles is available upon request. The journal enjoys very limited distribution to a few New England university libraries. It is wise to contact the Society directly for article information.

ESRS is one of the most professional and consistently active organizations in New England. People with specific archeological interests or problems should address themselves to Chief Archeologist James P. Whittall II, in care of ESRS.

Earthwatch
10 Juniper Road
Box 27
Belmont, Massachusetts 02178

Earthwatch is a clearinghouse designed to make scientific expeditions accessible to interested members of the public. It offers a wide variety of programs throughout the world under the direction of professional scientists. All members work as a team, and each expedition has objectives to be accomplished and problems to be solved.

Earthwatch represents an innovative means of furthering field research, much of which might otherwise be left undone for lack of funding. Contributions, which range from approximately $500 to $1000, help cover the expenses of the scientific team and all necessary logistical support such as tools, equipment, field gear, and supplies. The cost also covers meals, accomodation, ground transportation during the expedition, scientific instruments, and preparatory curriculum materials. Write directly to Earthwatch for its catalogue of worldwide expedition programs.

The Epigraphic Society (TES)
6 Woodland Street
Arlington, Massachusetts 02174

Purpose. The Epigraphic Society is a nonprofit publishing society concerned with finding and preserving ancient inscriptions and communicating the meaning and implications of the ancient texts to persons of different fields and backgrounds.

Membership. TES is an organization which does not hold meetings. Purchase of its journal *Occasional Publications* entitles one to membership.

Data Available. TES publishes detailed epigraphic articles in a bound journal entitled *Occasional Publications.* Each volume costs $10 and usually comes out once a year. No general index has been compiled, but content sheets of past volumes are available upon request. Under separate title the Society will soon be publishing a dictionary of ancient languages.

The Society distributes to forty-five of the fifty states and to twenty-six countries, including the Soviet Union. Many of the world's leading universities subscribe to the journal. Although some of the articles are highly technical, most are comprehensible and enjoyable to the nonspecialist. Most of the reports are well documented and neatly indexed. The methods of epigraphic analysis are given in detail.

The Epigraphic Society's *Occasional Publications* provides a forum for thought on ancient inscription. Presently it is the only publication of its kind that is confronting the enormous problem of deciphering and interpreting inscriptions in America and the world.

Institute of Comparative Studies (ICS)
Deya Archeological Museum Foundation
    and Research Center
Deya de Mallorca
Baleares, Spain

The Institute of Comparative Studies is a branch of the Deya Archeological Museum Foundation and Research Center. It is primarily concerned with undergraduate and graduate training in field archeology, geology, and paleontology of the Balearic Islands. Tuition varies, depending upon the length of stay and the type of research facilities required. Make inquiries directly to the Institute.

The Institute's facilities include a library, study rooms,

workrooms, a photographic laboratory, drafting rooms, and a permanent museum collection of artifacts gathered by field teams, on display and available for detailed study.

The Deya Archaeological Museum Foundation conducts field and laboratory projects on a yearly basis. Several excellent monographs on Balearic prehistory have been privately printed by the Foundation. Most can be purchased directly from the Museum.

The Mediterranean Expedition Institute (MEI)
(Overseas Division of the Middletown Archeological
   Research Center)
Soller, Mallorca
Baleares, Spain

MEI is the overseas facility of the Middletown Archeological Research Center, a nonprofit research society. The Institute offers special programs on the history and prehistory of the western Mediterranean, specializing in the Balearic Islands. Lectures, seminars, and excursions conducted by an American and European faculty provide on-site training and experience in historical and archeological procedure.

The MEI consists of two adjoining villas located at the base of a mountainside in the city of Soller. Lecture rooms, libraries, and outdoor workshops are used in conjunction with research facilities situated in the field. Tax-deductible contributions average around $750 and include room, board, museum and field expeditions, sailing excursions, and transportation throughout the Balearics.

For further information write to MARC.

The Middletown Archeological Research Center, Inc.
(MARC)
Box 761
Middletown, New York 10940

Purpose. MARC is a private, nonprofit field organization concerned with the origin and function of unexplained stone structures in both the Americas and Europe.

Membership. People with background experience in archeology, anthropology, surveying, history, or library science are encouraged to participate in seasonal Ameri-

can and European expeditions. Open membership is determined upon individual capabilities. Interested volunteers
must be ready to spend two to four consecutive weeks in
an intensive field training session where the techniques of
data collection, site survey, and document retrieval are
taught. For specific information on our regional liaison
offices, please write to the above address.

Data Available. Articles will be issued in various professional journals. A running file and index of site reports
is scheduled for publication sometime in 1979.

New England Antiquities Research Association (NEARA)
4 Smith Street
Milford, New Hampshire 03055

Purpose. NEARA is a nonprofit organization dedicated
to a better understanding of the history and prehistory of
the New England and surrounding areas, especially in
relation to the unexplained stone structures and markings
found throughout the Northeast.

Membership. Dues are $10 per year, and members must
be at least eighteen years of age. The rights of membership include voting, holding office, having access to
NEARA files, and writing articles for its journal, subject
to editor's approval. Members are urged to submit official
NEARA site reports and to assist in archeological excavations.

Data Available. NEARA has published continuously,
since 1966, a useful quarterly journal appropriately called
the *NEARA Journal* (originally titled *NEARA Newsletter*).
The articles are of mixed quality. Some have obviously
been thoroughly researched and are well written and
brimming with insight, while others tend to ramble on
about nothing. Nonetheless, on the whole, some terribly
important research has been compiled between its collective covers. In recent years the quality of the articles has
consistently improved.

An extremely useful index covering the first ten years of
the NEARA Newsletter/Journal is available for $3 from
Marjorie Chandler, Averill Road, Brookline, New Hamp-

shire 03033. Subscription to the journal costs $4 per year. Back issues may be obtained, when available, at $2 each.

One of the most important and exciting projects NEARA is presently working on is the compilation of detailed state site location maps. These sheets will eventually list all the stone sites, presently on file at NEARA headquarters, that have been collected since the organization was founded.

The Society for the Investigation of the Unexplained
(SITU)
R.D. 1
Columbia, New Jersey 07832

Purpose. SITU is a nonprofit organization of both professionals and laypeople dedicated to collecting and investigating reports of unexplained phenomena, exploring their causes, effects, and occurrences, and reporting their findings and those of others to their membership. SITU's long-range goal is to understand and explain that which "orthodox" science, for one reason or another, does not or will not study.

Membership. Membership is $10 per year. Society members receive all issues of SITU's journal, *Pursuit,* plus any special publication.

Data Available. The Society publishes an indexed quarterly journal called *Pursuit* in January, April, July, and October. *Pursuit* contains an assortment of excellently written comprehensive articles on both current and historical unexplained phenomena. It also includes book reviews and acts as a forum for idea exchange between members.

SITU has a well-stocked library and reference files which include original reports, newspaper and other clippings, correspondence, audio tapes, films, photographs, drawings, maps, and actual specimens. Library and reference files are open only to members, who may visit SITU headquarters in New Jersey by appointment or make inquiries by mail or telephone.

For people interested in a different slant on scientific explanation, membership in SITU is recommended.

The Sourcebook Project
c/o William R. Corliss
Box 107
Glen Arm, Maryland 21057

The Sourcebook Project collects and organizes scientific anomalies—those observations of nature not easily explained by prevailing scientific hypotheses. Thousands of articles from reputable scientific publications have been analyzed, reprinted, and compiled into serial, ring-bound *Sourcebooks*. The *Sourcebooks* run about 280 pages each, with illustrations and careful indexes. There are six series of *Sourcebooks*, one series for each of six major branches of knowledge: *Strange Universe* (curious astronomical observations), *Strange Life* (the mysteries of organic nature), *Strange Planet* (unusual geological facts), *Strange Phenomena* (unusual natural phenomena), *Strange Artifacts* (ancient man), and *Strange Minds* (unusual mental phenomena). Additional volumes in each series are published as data accumulates.

Appendix 3
Listing of Stone Sites

Listing of the major stone sites in North America. Nearest village, town, city, or county used as reference.

	Stone Piles	Perched Rocks	Standing Stones	Slab-roofed Chamber	Inscriptions	Circle, Semicircle of Boulders	Stone Tunnels	Stone Wall Complex	Artifacts: Bronze, Copper	Artifacts: Carved Stone	Artifacts: Ancient Coins	Chiseled Cave
Alabama												
Desoto Falls								X				
Phoenix City										X		
Arizona												
Clarkdale								X				
Tucson					X							
Arkansas												
Clarksville Bluff					X			X				
Independence County	X											
Johnson County					X							
Canada												
Bromptonville, Quebec					X							
Yarmouth, Nova Scotia					X							

	Stone Piles	Perched Rocks	Standing Stones	Slab-roofed Chamber	Inscriptions	Circle, Semicircle of Boulders	Stone Tunnels	Stone Wall Complex	Artifacts: Bronze, Copper	Artifacts: Carved Stone	Artifacts: Ancient Coins	Chiseled Cave
Connecticut												
Avon	X											
Bridgewater	X											
Bulls Bridge	X											
Chesterfield	X											
Colchester				X								
Danbury				X	X							
Danielson	X		X	X								
Devon	X											
East Hampton												X
Essex									X			
Groton			X	X		X		X				
Haddam				X								
Hamburg	X											
Kent					X							
Lyme				X				X				
Macedonia	X											
Milford	X											
Montville				X								
Moodus	X											
New Haven	X											

	Stone Piles	Perched Rocks	Standing Stones	Slab-roofed Chamber	Inscriptions	Circle, Semicircle of Boulders	Stone Tunnels	Stone Wall Complex	Artifacts: Bronze, Copper	Artifacts: Carved Stone	Artifacts: Ancient Coins	Chiseled Cave
New London	X			X								
New Milford	X											
New Preston	X	X	X		X	X						
North Salem				X								
Old Lyme	X											
Plantsville									X			
Quaker Hill		X		X								
Riverside						X						
Salem				X								
Southport	X											
Still River	X											
Thompson	X		X	X								X
Washington			X		X							
Waterford				X								
Westbrook	X											
Windsor									X			
Florida												
Black Hammock	X											
Georgia												
Columbus											X	
Fort Mountain								X				

	Stone Piles	Perched Rocks	Standing Stones	Slab-roofed Chamber	Inscriptions	Circle, Semicircle of Boulders	Stone Tunnels	Stone Wall Complex	Artifacts: Bronze, Copper	Artifacts: Carved Stone	Artifacts: Ancient Coins	Chiseled Cave
La Grange					X							
Spalding County								X				
Illinois												
Carbondale	X							X				
Champaign											X	
Chicago										X		
Cobden	X							X				
Crescent City	X											
Dellwood	X							X				
Dunleith				X								
Eddyville	X							X				
Effingham	X											
Highland								X				
Karbers Ridge	X							X				
Makanda								X				
Mill Goreville	X							X				
Mounds	X											
Naples								X				
New Athens	X											
Ozark	X							X				

	Stone Piles	Perched Rocks	Standing Stones	Slab-roofed Chamber	Inscriptions	Circle, Semicircle of Boulders	Stone Tunnels	Stone Wall Complex	Artifacts: Bronze, Copper	Artifacts: Carved Stone	Artifacts: Ancient Coins	Chiseled Cave
Raum	X							X				
Salem	X											
Sparta	X											
Thebes	X											
Indiana												
Attica	X											
Lafayette	X											
Rising Sun	X											
Salem	X											
Terre Haute	X											
Iowa												
Davenport					X					X		
La Valley						X						
New Albin				X								
Kentucky												
Clay City											X	
Fleming			X									
Flemingburg	X				X							
Garrett	X											
Hopkinsville											X	

	Stone Piles	Perched Rocks	Standing Stones	Slab-roofed Chamber	Inscriptions	Circle, Semicircle of Boulders	Stone Tunnels	Stone Wall Complex	Artifacts: Bronze, Copper	Artifacts: Carved Stone	Artifacts: Ancient Coins	Chiseled Cave
Lexington											X	
Louisville	X										X	
Muses Mills			X									
Owensboro	X											
Portsmouth				X								
Maine												
Castine					X							
Cushing				X								
Dennyville	X											
Harrison	X											
Mattawamkeag	X											
Monhegan Island					X					X		
North Berwick	X											
Pemaquid		X		X								
Pittston				X								
Quimby	X											
Sebasco				X								
Massachusetts												
Abington					X							
Andover				X						X		

	Stone Piles	Perched Rocks	Standing Stones	Slab-roofed Chamber	Inscriptions	Circle, Semicircle of Boulders	Stone Tunnels	Stone Wall Complex	Artifacts: Bronze, Copper	Artifacts: Carved Stone	Artifacts: Ancient Coins	Chiseled Cave
Berkley					X							
Bourne					X							
Cheshire			X									
Gill									X			
Goshen							X					
Greenfield			X									
Groveland					X							
Hardwick			X									
Harvard				X								
Hopkinton				X								
Housatonic	X											
Hyannis	X											
Lawrence										X		
Lenox			X									
Leominster		X										
Leverett			X	X								
Littleton				X								
Martha's Vineyard	X	X	X		X							
Mendon		X		X								
Merrimackport									X			

	Stone Piles	Perched Rocks	Standing Stones	Slab-roofed Chamber	Inscriptions	Circle, Semicircle of Boulders	Stone Tunnels	Stone Wall Complex	Artifacts: Bronze, Copper	Artifacts: Carved Stone	Artifacts: Ancient Coins	Chiseled Cave
Millbury									X			
Newbury Port				X								
North Salem		X										
Oxford				X		X		X				
Pelham				X								
Pepperell									X			
Petersham				X								
Plymouth	X											
Quabbin				X								
Rowley	X											
Sheffield	X											
Shelburne Falls	X											
Shutesbury			X	X						X		
Taunton		X		X								
Tyngsborough							X					
Upton		X		X								
Washington	X					X						
Webster		X		X								
Wendell				X								
West Port		X										

	Stone Piles	Perched Rocks	Standing Stones	Slab-roofed Chamber	Inscriptions	Circle, Semicircle of Boulders	Stone Tunnels	Stone Wall Complex	Artifacts: Bronze, Copper	Artifacts: Carved Stone	Artifacts: Ancient Coins	Chiseled Cave
Worchester	X	X		X								
Michigan												
Atlanta	X											
Cheboygan	X											
Flatrock	X											
Gaylord	X											
Isle Royale												X
Ithaca	X											
Marquette												X
Mesick	X											
Niles	X											
Tecumseh	X											
Missouri												
Doe Run									X			
Flat River	X											
Franklin County												X
Greenville	X											
Hillsboro					X							
Holcomb	X											
Lutesville	X											

	Stone Piles	Perched Rocks	Standing Stones	Slab-roofed Chamber	Inscriptions	Circle, Semicircle of Boulders	Stone Tunnels	Stone Wall Complex	Artifacts: Bronze, Copper	Artifacts: Carved Stone	Artifacts: Ancient Coins	Chiseled Cave
New Hamphsire												
Acworth	X	X		X								
Atkinson				X								
Bartlett	X	X										
Derry										X		
Gilmanton												X
Hampton Falls					X							
Hillsboro										X		
Hinsdale				X								
Jackson					X							
Lancaster	X											
Londonderry					X							
New Ipswich							X					
Newton				X								
North Pelham	X											
North Salem			X	X	X			X		X		
Plaiston		X										
Raymond		X		X	X	X						
Sullivan				X								
Surry				X								

	Stone Piles	Perched Rocks	Standing Stones	Slab-roofed Chamber	Inscriptions	Circle, Semicircle of Boulders	Stone Tunnels	Stone Wall Complex	Artifacts: Bronze, Copper	Artifacts: Carved Stone	Artifacts: Ancient Coins	Chiseled Cave
Windham		X		X								
New Jersey												
Allendale	X											
Barnegat									X			
Cape May									X			
Delaware Water Gap					X					X		
Fairfield			X									
Frenchtown	X											
Millbrook					X							
Milford										X		
Paquarra Township												X
Pemberton					X							
Ringwood		X										
Sandystone Township				X								
New Mexico												
Carrizozo								X				
Deming											X	
Gobernador								X				
Largo								X				
Los Lunas					X							

	Stone Piles	Perched Rocks	Standing Stones	Slab-roofed Chamber	Inscriptions	Circle, Semicircle of Boulders	Stone Tunnels	Stone Wall Complex	Artifacts: Bronze, Copper	Artifacts: Carved Stone	Artifacts: Ancient Coins	Chiseled Cave
Mimbres Valley					X							
Taos								X				
New York												
Barryville	X											
Bellvalle					X							
Binghamton									X			
Brewster				X								
Callicoon	X											
Carmel				X								
Comstock	X											
Cornwall	X	X										
Croton-on-Hudson	X											
Deerpark		X			X							
Ellenville												X
Fleischmanns	X											
Glens Falls	X											
Grahamsville	X											
Greenwood Lake		X			X	X						
Guymard												X
Harriman		X										

	Stone Piles	Perched Rocks	Standing Stones	Slab-roofed Chamber	Inscriptions	Circle, Semicircle of Boulders	Stone Tunnels	Stone Wall Complex	Artifacts: Bronze, Copper	Artifacts: Carved Stone	Artifacts: Ancient Coins	Chiseled Cave
Haverstraw									X			
Hudson	X											
Hunter	X											
Inwood					X							
Kerhonkson	X											X
Kent Cliffs				X				X				
Kingston												X
Ladentown		X										
Lake Carmel				X								
Mahopac				X								
Marbletown	X											
Middletown										X		
Mountaindale	X											
Mt. Hope					X							
North Salem		X		X								
Nyack	X											
Orient (Shelter Island)	X		X		X							
Otisville												X
Patterson				X								
Pawling			X	X								

	Stone Piles	Perched Rocks	Standing Stones	Slab-roofed Chamber	Inscriptions	Circle, Semicircle of Boulders	Stone Tunnels	Stone Wall Complex	Artifacts: Bronze, Copper	Artifacts: Carved Stone	Artifacts: Ancient Coins	Chiseled Cave
Phoenicia	X											
Plattekill								X				
Putnam Valley				X	X			X				X
Ramapo	X							X				
Roscoe	X											
Roxbury	X											
Shrub Oak				X								
Sloatsburg	X	X										
Somers		X		X								
Spring Glen	X											X
Suffern	X											
Summitville	X											X
Tompkins County								X				
Wappingers Falls			X		X							
Waterford	X											
Watertown	X							X				
Warwarsing	X											
Westbrookville	X											
West Harrison				X								
Wurtsboro	X	X										X

	Stone Piles	Perched Rocks	Standing Stones	Slab-roofed Chamber	Inscriptions	Circle, Semicircle of Boulders	Stone Tunnels	Stone Wall Complex	Artifacts: Bronze, Copper	Artifacts: Carved Stone	Artifacts: Ancient Coins	Chiseled Cave
North Carolina												
Black Mountain											X	
Blowing Rock	X											
Charlotte	X											
Patterson	X											
Roxboro	X											
North Dakota												
McLean County			X		X							
Ohio												
Frankfort				X								
Hopeton				X				X				
Lebanon	X											
Paint Creek Valley	X			X				X				
Spruce Hill				X								
Troy	X											
Oklahoma												
Bache					X							
Cimarron County					X							
Gowen					X							
Heavener					X							

	Stone Piles	Perched Rocks	Standing Stones	Slab-roofed Chamber	Inscriptions	Circle, Semicircle of Boulders	Stone Tunnels	Stone Wall Complex	Artifacts: Bronze, Copper	Artifacts: Carved Stone	Artifacts: Ancient Coins	Chiseled Cave
Leflore County					X							
Tulsa					X							
Warner					X							
Oregon												
Hay Creek				X				X				
Pennsylvania												
Gibson		X										
Harrisburg	X											
Hellertown	X											
Huntington			X									
Irwine				X								
Lackawaxen					X					X		
Mechanicsburg					X							
Millrift	X											
Perkasie	X											
Pleasant Mount				X	X							
Trout Run				X								
Wilkes-Barre	X											
Tennessee												
Agee								X				

	Stone Piles	Perched Rocks	Standing Stones	Slab-roofed Chamber	Inscriptions	Circle, Semicircle of Boulders	Stone Tunnels	Stone Wall Complex	Artifacts: Bronze, Copper	Artifacts: Carved Stone	Artifacts: Ancient Coins	Chiseled Cave
Bedford County								X				
Carthage	X											
Charlotte					X							
Chatata					X							
Cumberland Gap	X											
Fayetteville											X	
Lebanon	X											
Loudon	X				X							
Lynchburg	X											
Manchester	X		X					X				
Nashville					X							
Savannah	X											
Vermont												
Bellows Falls					X							
Brattleboro				X								
Ludlow	X											
Milton										X		
Norwich	X											
Reading	X				X						X	
Royalton		X										

	Stone Piles	Perched Rocks	Standing Stones	Slab-roofed Chamber	Inscriptions	Circle, Semicircle of Boulders	Stone Tunnels	Stone Wall Complex	Artifacts: Bronze, Copper	Artifacts: Carved Stone	Artifacts: Ancient Coins	Chiseled Cave
Rutland	X					X						
South Reading	X		X									
South Royalton			X	X	X					X		
South Tunbridge			X	X								
South Woodstock			X	X	X			X				
Strafford					X							
Sunderland	X											
Swanton									X			
White River				X								
Woodstock	X		X	X								
Virginia												
Bath County				X								
Cumberland				X								
Frederic County				X								
Goshen	X											
Lovingston	X											
Salem	X											
Sperryville	X											
Wadesville				X								
Wheeling				X								

	Stone Piles	Perched Rocks	Standing Stones	Slab-roofed Chamber	Inscriptions	Circle, Semicircle of Boulders	Stone Tunnels	Stone Wall Complex	Artifacts: Bronze, Copper	Artifacts: Carved Stone	Artifacts: Ancient Coins	Chiseled Cave
Winchester				X								
West Virginia												
Braxton County					X							
Big Creek	X											
Charleston	X							X				
Fayette County	X			X								
Grave Creek (Moundsville)					X							
Huntington	X											
Mount Carbon	X							X				
Ripley	X											
Wisconsin												
Bay Field									X			

Notes

Introduction

1. A note on terminology and dating:

Bronze Age. A cultural time period (3500 to 1000 B.C.) when bronze, an alloy of copper and tin, was the most widely used and important material in the making of weapons and tools in the Old World. Bronze metallurgy was unknown in the Americas except for two confined locales, Argentina and Peru, where it began around 1000 B.C.

B.C. Before Christ, used as a shorthand chronological reference point.

A.D. From the Latin, *anno domini*, in the year of our Lord.

B.P. Before the present, indicates actual number of past years.

Radiocarbon Dating. (also listed as carbon-14 or C^{14}). A dating method to determine the approximate age of organic material (bone, charcoal, shell, cloth, etc.) from the amount of C^{14} it contains. All living things contain equal amounts of the radioactive isotope C^{14} and the inert C^{12}. Upon death, C^{14} disintegrates at a fixed rate. The analysis of the proportion of C^{14} to C^{12} in archeological remains gives an approximate date of death (up to 50,000 years B.P.). The date obtained is expressed as plus or minus (±) a certain amount of years. Recent testing of the technique, using known historical documents, indicates flaws: most C^{14} dates are too low. For example, a date of 1500 B.C. should actually be 300 years earlier (1800 B.C.); 3000 B.C. should be 500 to 1000 years earlier (3500 or 4000 B.C.).

2. In John Wesley Powell, *The Twelfth Annual Report of the Bureau of Ethnology to the Smithsonian Institution*, pp. xlvi, xlvii.

3. Paul N. Perrot 1976: personal communication on file at MARC office (Emphasis added.)

Chapter 1—Good-bye Columbus, Hello Hanno

1. Quoted in Donald B. Harden, *The Phoenicians*, p. 17.
2. Quoted in ibid.
3. Quoted in Henriette Mertz, *The Wine Dark Sea*, pp. 59-60.
4. Ibid., p. 60.
5. Quoted in Gerhard Herm, *The Celts*, p. 4.
6. *The Geography of Strabo*, bk. 1, sec. 1.18; bk. 1, sec. 3.2.
7. Diodorus of Sicily, *Library of History*, 5; 19-20 (Emphasis added.)

8. Samuel Eliot Morison, *Admiral of the Ocean Sea*, p. 94.
9. Ibid., p. 97.
10. Quoted in ibid., p. 105. (Emphasis added.)
11. Garcilaso de la Vega, *The Florida of the Inca*, p. 314.
12. Morison, *Admiral*, p. 183.
13. Ibid., p. 187
14. Ibid., p. 196.
15. Julius E. Olson and Edward Gaylord Bourne, eds., *The Northmen, Columbus and Cabot, Nine Eighty Five to Fifteen Three*, pp. 100-101. (Emphasis added.)
16. Ibid., p. 101.
17. Ibid.
18. Ibid., p. 128. (Emphasis added.)
19. Ibid., p. 121.
20. James P. Whittall II, "The Inscribed Stone from Comassakumkanit [Bourne Stone, Massachusetts]."
21. James D. Baldwin, Ancient America in Notes on American Archaeology, pp. 43-44.
22. Ibid., p. 44.
23. Ibid., pp. 45-46.
24. Henriette Mertz, *Atlantis: Dwelling Place of the Gods*, p. 65.
25. Ibid., p. 70.

Chapter 2—The Structures: Shapes of Time Past

1. James Adair, *History of the American Indians*, p. 194.
2. Dennis N. Bertland, Patricia M. Valence, and Russell J. Woodling. *The Minisink*, pp. 67-68.
3. Jerome Wyckoff, *Rock Scenery of the Hudson Highlands and Palisades*, p. 85.
4. John Finch, "On the Celtic Antiquities of America."
5. Henriette Mertz, *Atlantis: Dwelling Place of the Gods*, pp. 50, 52.
6. Cornelia Horsford, *An Inscribed Stone*, p. 6.
7. Henry David Thoreau, *Walden and Other Writings*, p. 35.
8. Ibid.
9. Quoted in *NEARA Journal*, vol. 5, No. 3, September 1970, p. 57. (Emphasis added.)
10. Horsford, *Inscribed Stone*, p. 7.
11. Ibid., p. 6.
12. "The Newton, N.H. Stone Structure No. 3."
13. "New Ipswich, N.H. Stone Structure."
14. Maurice Pope, *The Story of Archaeological Decipherment*, p. 7.
15. Neolithic indicates the "New Stone Age," when farming, semipermanent villages, and animal breeding displaced nomadic hunting.

16. Basque is an ancient, poorly understood language still spoken by the Basques, a people living in the northwestern Pyrenees on the Iberian peninsula.

17. Andrew E. Rothovious, "The Celt-Iberian Culture of New England, First Millennium B.C."

18. Cyrus H. Gordon, *Riddles in History*, p. 155.

19. Ibid., p. 145.

20. Cyrus H. Gordon, *Before Columbus*, p. 187.

21. Henry Rowe Schoolcraft, *History of the Indian Tribes of the United States*, p. 610.

Chapter 3—Stone Mysteries: Northeastern Pennsylvania, Northern New Jersey, Southern New York

1. John Witthoft, "Alleged Phoenician Inscriptions from York County, Pennsylvania."

2. Ibid.

3. Ibid.

4. Ibid., p. 93.

5. Robert E. Stone, "The Mechanicsburg Stones—Two Distinct Types."

6. Vernon Leslie, *Faces in Clay*.

7. Quoted in Thomas Ewbank, "Alleged Inscribed Stone Axe."

8. James P. Whittall II, "An Inscribed Celt."

9. Edward J. Lenik, "Petroglyphs from the Upper Delaware Valley."

10. Ibid.

11. James M. Allerton, *The Hawks Nest, or the Last of the Cahoonshees*, pp. 5-6.

12. Doug Hay, "A 'Stonehenge' Mystery on the Hawks Nest." p. 3.

13. "The Hawley Stone: Newest Discovery of a Possibly Pre-Columbian Inscription."

14. "James Knapp, Pleasant Mount, Finds Stone with Strange Characters, Drawing on it," *The Wayne Independent*.

15. Barry Fell, personal communication.

16. Leslie, *Faces in Clay*, p. 238.

17. Ibid., p. 240.

18. Ibid, p. 243.

19. William L. Stone, *Life of Joseph Brant-Thayendanega*, p. 484.

20. Cited from W. Mead Stapler, "A Pre-Colonial Wall in Manhattan?"

21. Cornelia Horsford, *An Inscribed Stone*, p. 14.

22. Edward J. Lenik, "The Riddle of the Prehistoric Walls, Ramapo, New York."

23. Ibid.

24. Philip H. Smith, *Legends of the Shawangunk*, p. 168.

Chapter 4—Stone Mysteries: Southeastern New York, Southwestern Connecticut

1. William J. Blake, *The History of Putnam County, New York*, p. 40.
2. Daniel Wilson, *Prehistoric Annals of Scotland*, 1:147.
3. Quoted in Xenophon's *Memorabilia*.
4. Bruce Anderson, *The Solar Home Book*, p. 80.
5. Ibid., p. 59.
6. John Finch, "On the Celtic Antiquities of America."
7. Ibid.
8. Ibid.
9. Ibid.
10. Blood type is determined by who mates with whom. An individual inherits one blood group gene from each parent, resulting in six statistically predictable variations of blood type in the A-B-O system.
11. Quoted in John Wesley Powell, *Twelfth Annual Report of the Bureau of Ethnology to the Secretary of the Smithsonian Institution*, p. 691.
12. Ibid., p. 19.
13. Ezra Stiles, *Extracts from the Itineraries and Other Miscellanies of Ezra Stiles*.
14. Edward J. Lenik, "Ancient Inscriptions in Western Connecticut."
15. Quoted in Garrick Mallery, *Picture-writing of the American Indians*, 1:75-76.
16. Lenik, "Ancient Inscriptions."
17. Wadsworth R. Pierce, "Monument Poses Mystery in the Berkshires."
18. Ibid.

Chapter 5—Stone Mysteries: Southern New England

1. Mary Kingsbury Talcott, *The Talcott Papers*, 4:6.
2. Leland H. Godfrey, "The Goshen Stone Mystery."
3. Personal communication.
4. Godfrey, p. 223.
5. Personal communication.
6. Godfrey, p. 219.
7. Quoted in James P. Whittall II, "The Gungywamp Complex, Groton, Connecticut."
8. Ibid.
9. Ibid.
10. Ibid.
11. Ibid.
12. Cornelia Horsford, *An Inscribed Stone*.

13. Quoted in ibid., p. 18-19.

14. Viking is a term used to describe Scandinavian sailor-warriors who conquered other lands from about A.D. 800-1100.

15. James P. Whittall II, "The Mill River Inscription."

16. Barry Fell, quoted in ibid.

Chapter 6—Stone Mysteries: Northern New England, North Atlantic Coast

1. James P. Whittall II, "Stone Chamber: Windham County, Vt."

2. James P. Whittall II, "The Inscribed Stones of Sherbrooke, Quebec."

3. Barry Fell, "Decipherment of the Bifacial Sherbrooke Stele."

4. Thomas E. Lee, "The Sherbrooke Inscriptions."

5. Frank Glynn, "The Effigy Mound, A Covered Cairn Burial Site."

6. Junius Bird, "Excavation Report: North Salem, New Hampshire (1945)."

7. Ibid.

8. Quoted in Henry Rowe Schoolcraft, *History of the Indian Tribes of the United States*, p. 608.

9. Geoffrey Ashe, et al. *The Quest for America*, p. 161.

10. Quoted in James P. Whittall II, "The Monhegan Inscription."

11. James P. Whittall II, "Copper/Tin Projectile, Monhegan, Maine."

12. Whittall, "Anforetas Recovered in Maine."

13. Helge Ingstad, *Westward to Vinland*.

Bibliography

While extensive, this bibliography is far from exhaustive. It includes only the most important and/or accessible of the sources used in the preparation of this volume.

Adair, James. *Adair's History of the American Indians.* London, 1775. Reprint edited by Samuel Cole Williams. New York: Promontory Press, 1930.

Adams, Herbert B., and Henry Wood. *Columbus and His Discovery of America.* Tenth Series, vols. 10, 11. Baltimore: Johns Hopkins, 1892.

Albright, William Foxwell. *The Archaeology of Palestine.* Baltimore: Penguin Books, 1963

Allerton, James M. *Hawks Nest, or the Last of the Cahoonshees: A Tale of the Delaware Valley and Historical Romance of 1690.* Port Jervis, N.Y.: Gazette Book and Job Print, 1892.

Anderson, Bruce. *The Solar Home Book.* Harrisville, N.H.: Cheshire Books, 1976.

Aristotle. *Minor Works.* Edited by W. S. Hett. Cambridge: Harvard University Press, 1955.

Arribas Palav, Antonio. *The Iberians.* London: Thames and Hudson, 1964.

Ashe, Geoffey et. al. *The Quest for America.* New York: Praeger, 1971.

Asher, Maxine. "Digging into the Past with E.S.P." *Psychic Magazine* 7, no. 2 (June 1976): 9-14.

Bailey, James. *The God-Kings and the Titans.* New York: St. Martin, 1973.

Bailyn, Bernard. *The New England Merchants in the Seventeenth Century.* New York: Harper and Row, 1955.

Baldwin, James D. *Ancient America in Notes on American Archaeology.* New York: Harper and Bros., 1872.

Beach, Lewis. *Cornwall.* Newburgh, N.Y.: E.M. Ruttenber and Sons, Printers, 1873.

Bertland, Dennis N., Patricia M. Valence, and Russell J. Woodling. *The Minisink.* Monroe and Pike Counties, Pa.; Sussex and Warren Counties, N.J.: Four County Task Force on the Tocks-Island Dam Project, March, 1975.

Bingham, Alfred. "Squatter Settlements of Freed Slaves in New England." *Connecticut Historical Society Bulletin* 41, no. 3 (July 1976): 65-80.

Bird, Junius. "Excavation Report: North Salem, New Hampshire (1945)."*Early Sites Research Society Work Report 3, no 27* (1977).

Blake, William J. *The History of Putnam County, New York.* New York: Baker and Scribner, 1849.

Bolton, Reginald Pelham. *Indian Life of Long Ago in the City of New York.* New York: Harmony, 1972.

Booth, Malcolm A. *A Bicentennial History of Orange County.* New York: Greentree Publishing Corp., 1975.

Borland, Charles Michael. *They All Discovered America.* New York: Pocket Books, 1961.

Bradford, William et al. *Homes in the Wilderness.* New York: William R. Scott, 1939.

Brennan, Louis A. *Artifacts of Prehistoric America.* Harrisburg, Pa.: Stackpole, 1975.

Brinckerhoff, T. VanWyck. *Historical Sketch and Directory of the Town of Fishkill.* Fishkill, N.Y.: Dean and Spaight, 1866.

Buchanan, Donal B. "An Iberian Inscription in the Altamira Cave." *New England Antiquities Research Association (NEARA) Journal* 11, no. 2 (Fall 1976): 29.

Burl, Aubrey. *The Stone Circles of the British Isles.* New Haven: Yale University Press, 1976.

Butler, Eva L. "The Brush or Stone Heaps of Southern New England." *Archaeological Society of Connecticut Bulletin,* no. 19 (1946): 2-12.

Casson, Lionel. *The Ancient Mariners.* New York: Macmillan, 1959.

Corliss, William R., comp. *Strange Artifacts: A Sourcebook on Ancient Man,* Vol. M-1, M-2. Glen Arm, Md.: W. R. Corliss, 1976.

Covey, Cyclone. *Calalus: Roman Jewish Colony in America from the Time of Charlemagne through Alfred the Great.* New York: Vantage, 1975.

Cumming, W. P. et. al. *The Exploration of North America: 1630-1776.* New York: Putnam, 1974.

Dana, Henry Swan. *History of Woodstock, Vermont.* Boston: Houghton Mifflin, 1889.

Daniel, Glyn Edmund. *The Megalith Builders of Western Europe.* London: Hutchinson and Co., 1963.

———. *Megaliths in History.* London: Thames and Hudson, 1972.

Davis, Richard W. "Beads." *Artifacts* 5, no. 1 (September 1976): 3-4, 10.

DeVries, David. *Voyages from Holland to America, A.D. 1632 to 1644.* Translated by H. C. Murphy. Reprint. 1853. Millwood, N.Y.: Kraus Reprint, 1971.

Diodorus of Sicily. *Library of History.* Vol. 3. Edited by C. H. Oldfather. Cambridge: Harvard University Press, 1952.

Dix, Byron E. "An Early Calendar Site in Central Vermont." *Occasional Publications of the Epigraphic Society* 3, no. 51 (August 1975): 1-3.

———. "Possible Evidence of the Megalithic Yard at Calendar Site II, Vermont." *NEARA Journal* 11 no. 2 (Fall 1976): 25-28.

———. "A Second Early Calendar Site in Central Vermont." *Occasional Publications of the Epigraphic Society* 3, no. 61 (September 1976): 1-18.

Doe, Brian. *Southern Arabia.* New York: McGraw-Hill, 1971.

Dolls, Charles G. "Geology of the Memphremagog Quadrangle and the Southeastern Portion of the Irisburg Quadrangle, Vermont." *Bulletin No. 3.* 1951. Reprint. The Vermont Development Commission and the Vermont Geological Survey, 1968.

DuChaillu, Paul B. *The Viking Age.* 2 vols. New York: Scribner, 1889.

Emerson, N. J. *Intuitive Archaeology: The Argillite Carving.* Department of Anthropolgy, University of Toronto: private printing, March 1974.

Ewbank, Thomas. "Alleged Inscribed Stone Axe." *Bulletin of the American Ethnological Society* 1 (1861): 44-47.

Farley, Gloria. "The Gowen Bluff Shelter." *Occasional Publications of the Epigraphic Society* 3, no. 68 (September 1976): 1-2.

———. "Inscriptions from Mid-America." *Occasional Publications of the Epigraphic Society* 3, no. 69 (September 1976): 1-10.

Feldman, Mark. *Archaeology for Everyone.* New York: Quadrangle, 1977.

———. *The Mystery Hill Story.* North Salem, N.H.: Mystery Hill, 1977.

Fell, Barry. *America B.C.: European Settlers in the New World.* New York: Quadrangle, 1976.

———. "Ancient Arabic Script and Vocabulary of the Algonquian Indians." *Occasional Publications of the Epigraphic Society* 3, no. 54 (September 1976): 1-3.

———. "An Arabic Dialect in Ancient Moroccan Inscriptions." *Occasional Publications of the Epigraphic Society* 3, no. 48 (September 1976): 1-12.

———. "A Celtiberian Funeral Stele in Navarra, Spain, Inscribed in Ogam." *Occasional Publications of the Epigraphic Society* 3, no. 58 (September 1976): 1-2.

——— "A Celtiberian (Gadelic) Law-Tablet from Ourique, Portugal." *Occasional Publications of the Epigraphic Society* 3, no. 55 (September 1976): 1-3.

——— "Celtic Iberian Inscriptions of New England." *Occasional Publications of the Epigraphic Society* 3, no. 50 (August 1975): 1-5.

———. "Decipherment of the Bifacial Sherbrooke Stele." *Early Sites Research Society Bulletin* 4, no. 1 (May 1976): 33-38.

———. "Epigraphy of the Susquehanna Steles." *Occasional Publications of the Epigraphic Society* 2, no. 45 (May 1975): 1-8.

———. "The Etymology of Some Ancient American Inscriptions." *Occasional Publications of the Epigraphic Society* 3, no. 76 (September 1976): 1-5.

———. "A Fifth-Century Moroccan Emigration to North America." *Occasional Publications of the Epigraphic Society* 3, no. 46 (September 1976): 1-10.

———. "An Iberian-Punic Stele of Hanno." *Occasional Publications of the Epigraphic Society* 2, no. 44 (May 1975): 1-3.

———. "The Romano-Celtic Phase at Mystery Hill, New Hampshire, in New England." *Occasional Publications of the Epigraphic Society* 3, no. 67 (September 1975): 1-3.

Fernandez-Armesto, Felipe. *Ferdinand and Isabella.* London: Weiderfeld and Nicolson, 1975.

Finch, John. "On the Celtic Antiquities of America." *American Journal of Science* 7 (1824): 149-161.

Fleming, Andrew. "Megalithic Astronomy: A Prehistorian's View." *Nature* 255, no. 5 (June 19, 1975): 575.

Forlong, James C. R. *Faiths of Man: Encyclopedia of Religion.* London: Bernard Quaritch, 1906.

Formosa, Gerald J. *The Megalithic Monuments of Malta.* Vancouver, Can.: Skorba Publishers, 1975.

Funk, Robert E.; George R. Walters; and William F. Ehlers, Jr. "The Archeology of Dutchess Quarry Cave." *Pennsylvania Archaeologist* 39, nos. 1-4, (December 1969): 7-22.

Gibbero, Frederick. *The Architecture of England: From Norman Times to the Present Day.* Westminster, Eng.: The Architectural Press, 1953.

Gibson, Frances McKinley. *The Seafarers: Pre-Columbian Voyages to America.* Philadelphia: Dorrance and Co., 1974.

Gloag, John. *The Architectural Interpretation of History.* London: Adam and Charles Black, 1975.

Glynn, Frank. "The Effigy Mound, A Covered Cairn Burial Site," *NEARA Journal* 4, no. 4 (December 1969) 75-79.

———. "Excavation of the Pilot Point Stone Heaps." *The Archaeological Society of Connecticut Bulletin,* no. 38 (August 1973): 77-89.

Godfrey, Leland H. "The Goshen Stone Mystery." *Yankee Magazine* 35, no. 11 (November 1971): 218-223.

Goodwin, William B. *The Remains of Greater Ireland in New England*. Boston: Meador, 1946.

Gordon, Cyrus H. *Before Columbus: Links between the Old World and Ancient America*. New York: Crown, 1971.

———. *Forgotten Scripts*. New York: Basic Books, 1968.

———. *Riddles in History*. New York: Crown, 1974.

Grant, Campbell. *Rock Art of the American Indian*. New York: Thomas Y. Crowell Co., 1967.

Gwynne, Peter. "Hi, Columbus! Like the Trip?" *Newsweek*, 26 May 1975, pp. 81-82.

———. "New York View: Who Was First?" *New Scientist*, 29 May 1975, pp. 517-518.

Hadingham, Evan. *Circles and Standing Stones: An Illustrated Exploration of Megalith Mysteries of Early Britain*. New York: Walker and Co., 1975.

Harden, Donald B. *The Phoenicians*. Baltimore: Penguin Books, 1971.

Harris, Harold. *Treasure Tales of the Shawangunks and Catskills*. Ellenville, N.Y.: private printing, 1955.

Hawkes, Jacquetta. *The Atlas of Early Man*. New York: St. Martin, 1976.

"The Hawley Stone: Newest Discovery of a Possibly Pre-Columbian Inscription." *NEARA Newsletter* 5, no. 4 (December 1970): 88.

Hay, Doug. "A 'Stonehenge' Mystery on the Hawks Nest." *Union-Gazette* (Port Jervis, N.Y.), 31 May 1975, p. 3.

Haywood, John. *The Natural and Aboriginal History of Tennessee*. Nashville: George Wilson, 1823.

Hencken, Hugh. "The 'Irish Monastery' at North Salem, New Hampshire." *New England Quarterly* 12 (1936): 428-442.

Herm, Gerhard. *The Celts*. New York: St. Martin, 1976.

Herodotus. *History*. Vol. 4. Translated by A.D. Godley. Cambridge: Harvard University Press, 1963.

Hertzberg, Ruth; Beatrice Vaughan; and Janet Greene. *Putting Food By*. Brattleboro, Vt.: Stephen Greene Press, 1974.

Hine, Charles Gilbert. *The Old Mine Road*. 1909. Reprint. New Brunswick, N.J.: Rutgers University Press, 1963.

Honoré, Pierre. *In Quest of the White God.* London: Futura Publications, 1975.

Horsford, Cornelia. *An Inscribed Stone.* Cambridge, Mass.: private printing, 1895.

Hull, Richard W. *People of the Valleys.* Warwick, N. Y.: Historical Society, 1975.

Ingstad, Helge. *Westward to Vinland.* Translated by Erik J. Friis. New York: St. Martin, 1969.

Irving, Washington. *The Legend of Sleepy Hollow and Other Stories.* New York: Magnum Books, 1968.

"James Knapp, Pleasant Mount, Finds Stone with Strange Characters, Drawing on It," *The Wayne Independent* (Honesdale, Pa.), 22 March 1977, p. 1.

Jett, Stephen C. "Diffusion vs. Independent Development: The Bases of Controversy." In *Men Across the Sea: Problems of Pre-Columbian Contacts,* edited by Carroll L. Riley et al. Austin: University of Texas Press. 1971.

Jett, Stephen C., and George F. Carter. "A Comment on Rowe's 'Diffusionism and Archaeology.'" *American Antiquity* 31, no. 16 (October 1966): 807-870.

Jodin, André. *Les établissements du roi Juba II aux îles Purpuraires (Mogador).* Tangiers (Tanger): Centre National de la Recherche Scientifique, 1967.

Keeler, Clyde E., and Bennett E. Kelley. "Ancient Iron-Smelting Furnaces of Ohio." *NEARA Newsletter* 6, no. 2, (June 1971): 28-32.

Kraft, Herbert C., ed. *A Delaware Indian Symposium.* Harrisburg: Pennsylvania Historical and Museum Commission, 1975.

Ladd, Richard. *New Hampshire, Past and Present.* Seabrook, N.H.: Withey Press.

Leask, H. G. *Irish Churches and Monastic Buildings.* 3 vols. Dundalk, Ireland: Dundalgan Press, 1955-60.

Lee, Thomas E. "The Sherbrooke Inscriptions." *NEARA Journal* (eleven), no. 1 (Summer 1976): 6-7.

Lehner, Ernst, and Johanna Lehner. *How They Saw the New World.* New York: Tudor Publishing Co., 1966.

Leisner, V. *Die Megalithgraber der Iberischen Halbinsel: I. Der Western.* Berlin: Madrider Forschungen, 1/3, 1965.

Lenik, Edward J. "Ancient Inscriptions in Western Connecticut." NEARA Journal 11, no. 3 (Winter 1977): 34-38.

———. "Petroglyphs from the Upper Delaware Valley." Pennsylvania Archaeologist 47, no. 1 (April 1977): 14-18.

———. "The Riddle of the Prehistoric Walls, Ramapo, New York." New York State Archeological Association Bulletin, no. 63 (March 1975): 1-14.

———. "The Sandystone Chamber in New Jersey." NEARA Newsletter 7, no. 3 (September 1972): 56-57.

Leslie, Vernon. Faces in Clay. Middletown, N.Y.: T.E. Henderson, 1973.

Lobeck, A.K. The Physiography of the New York Region. Maplewood, N.J.: Hammond Inc., 1930.

MacCracken, Henry Noble. Old Dutchess Forever! New York: Hastings, 1956.

McKusick, Victor A. Human Genetics. 2d ed. Englewood Cliffs, N.J.: Prentice-Hall, 1969.

Madariaga, Salvador de. Christopher Columbus: Being the Life of the Very Magnificent Lord, Don Cristobal Colon. New York: Ungar, 1967.

Mallery, Garrick. Picture-Writing of the American Indians. 2 vols. New York: Dover, 1972.

Martel, Warren R., Jr. "Astronomical Alignment Research at Mystery Hill." NEARA Newsletter 6, no. 2 (June 1971): 22-23.

Martin, Paul S. "The Discovery of America." Science, 9 March 1973, pp. 909-974.

Mertz, Henriette. Atlantis: Dwelling Place of the Gods. Chicago: private printing, 1976.

———. The Wine Dark Sea. Chicago: private printing, 1964.

Moran, Hugh A., and David H. Kelley. The Alphabet and the Ancient Calendar Signs. 2d ed. Palo Alto, Calif.: Daily Press, 1969.

Morison, Samuel Eliot. Admiral of the Ocean Sea: A life of Christopher Columbus. Vol. 1. Boston: Oxford University Press, 1942.

———. Christopher Columbus, Mariner. New York: Mentor Books, 1956.

Moscati, Sabatino. "A Carthaginian Fortress in Sardinia." *Scientific American* 232, no. 2 (February 1975): 80-87.
———. *The World of the Phoenicians.* London: Sphere Books, 1973.
"New Ipswich, N.H. Stone Structure." *NEARA Newsletter* 4, no. 4 (December 1969): 73.
"New Radiocarbon Dating Indicates an Even Greater Antiquity for North Salem Megalithic Site." *NEARA Newsletter* 6, no. 2 (June 1971): 40.
"The Newton, N.H. Stone Structure no. 3" *NEARA Newsletter* 6, no. 4 (December 1971): 80.
New York Walk Book. Garden City, N.Y.: Doubleday, Natural History Press, 1971.
Oedel, David. "Atnakuna Motifs on Egyptian Figurines." *Occasional Publications of the Epigraphic Society* 3, no. 59 (September 1976): 1-3.
Olson, Julius E., and Edward Gaylord Bourne, eds. *The Northmen, Columbus and Cabot, Nine Eighty Five to Fifteen Three.* 1906. Reprint. New York: Barnes and Noble, 1959.
O'Riordan, Sean P., and Glyn E. Daniel. *New Grange and the Bend of the Boyne.* New York: Praeger, 1964.
Pericot-Garcia, Luis. *The Balearic Islands.* London: Thames and Hudson, 1972.
Phillips, Philip. "The Role of Trans-Pacific Contacts in the Development of New World Pre-Columbian Civilizations." In *Handbook of Middle American Indians.* Vol. 4, pp. 296-315 Austin: Univ. of Texas Press, 1966.
Pidgeon, William. *Traditions of De-coo-dah and Antiquarian Researches: Comprising Extensive Explorations, Surveys, and Excavations of the Wonderful and Mysterious Earthen Remains of the Mound Builders in America; the Traditions of the Last Prophet of the Elk Nation Relative to Their Origin and Use; and the Evidences of an Ancient Population More Numerous Than the Present Aborigines.* New York: Thayer, Bridgman and Fanning, 1853.
Pierce, Wadsworth R. "Monument Poses Mystery in the Berkshires," *The Springfield Union* (Mass.), 17 July 1969. p. 31.

Piggott, Stuart. The Druids. New York: Praeger, 1975.

Plato. Dialogues. Translated by R. G. Bury. Cambridge: Harvard University Press, 1961.

Pliny. Natural History. Translated by H. Rackham. Cambridge: Harvard University Press, 1938-63.

Plutarch's Moralia. Vol. 10. Translated by Harold North Fowler. Cambridge: Harvard University Press, 1960.

Pohl, Frederick. The Viking Settlements of North America. New York: Potter, 1972.

Pomfret, John E. Founding the American Colonies, 1583-1660. New York: Harper and Row, 1970.

Pope, Maurice. The Story of Archaeological Decipherment. New York: Scribner, 1975.

Powell, John Wesley. The Twelfth Annual Report of the Bureau of Ethnology to the Secretary of the Smithsonian Institution. Washington, D.C.: Government Printing Office, 1894.

Quinlan, James Eldridge. History of Sullivan County. Liberty, N.Y.: G. M. Beebe and W. T. Morgans, 1873.

Renfrew, Colin. Before Civilization: The Radio Carbon Revolution and Prehistoric Europe. New York: Knopf, 1974.

Riley, Carroll L. et. al., eds. Man Across the Sea: Problems of Pre-Columbian Contacts. Austin: Univ. of Texas Press, 1971.

Ritchie, William A. "The Pre-Iroquoian Occupations of New York State." Rochester Museum Memoir No. 1, Rochester, N.Y.: Rochester Museum, 1944.

Rosello-Bordoy, Guillermo, and William H. Waldren. "Excavaciones en el Abrigo de Bosque de Son Matge Valldemosa, Mallorca)." Noticiano Arquelogio Hispanico, Prehistoria II. Madrid: Langa y Cia, 1973.

Rothovius, Andrew E. "The Celt-Culture of New England, First Millennium B.C.." NEARA Journal 10, no. 2 (Summer-Fall 1975): 2-6.

Rowe, John Howland. "Diffusionism and Archaeology." American Antiquity 31, no. 3 (January 1966): 334-337.

Ruttenber, Edward M. History of the County of Orange. Newburgh, N.Y.: E.M. Ruttenber and Sons, Printers, 1875.

———. *History of the Indian Tribes of Hudson's River.* 1872. Reprint. Port Washington, N.Y.: Kennikat, 1971.

Ruttenber, E. M., and L. H. Clark, comps. *History of Orange County, New York.* Philadelphia: Everts and Peck, 1881.

Ryder, Antonia. *Charles Darwin, Early Views.* Mimeographed. Middletown Archeological Reseach Center, Middletown, New York, 1977.

Savory, H. N. *Spain and Portugal: The Prehistory of the Iberian Peninsula.* New York: Praeger, 1968.

Schoolcraft, Henry Rowe. *History of the Indian Tribes of the United States.* Philadelphia: J. B. Lippincott, 1857.

Shuster, Alvin. "Discovery of an Ancient City In Syria called Sensational." *New York Times,* 25 October 1976, p. 8.

Sloane, Eric. *Our Vanishing Landscape.* New York: Ballantine, 1975.

Smith, Philip H. *Legends of the Shawangunk.* Pawling, N.Y.: Smith and Co., 1887.

Smith, W. Robertson. *The Religion of the Semites: The Fundamental Institutions.* New York: Schocken, 1972.

Squier, E. G. "Aboriginal Monuments of the State of New York." *Smithsonian Contributions to Knowledge* 2, no. 2 (1850).

Squier, E. G. and E. H. Davis. "Ancient Monuments of the Mississippi Valley." *Smithsonian Contributions to Knowledge* 1, no. 1 (1848).

Stapler, W. Mead. "A Pre-Colonial Wall in Manhattan?" *NEARA Newsletter* 9, no. 2 (Summer 1974): 40.

Stieglitz, Robert A. "An Ancient Judean Inscription from Tennessee." *Occasional Publications of the Epigraphic Society* 3, no. 65 (September 1976): 1-5.

Stiles, Ezra. *Extracts from the Itineraries and Other Miscellanies of Ezra Stiles, 1755-1794, with a Selection from His Correspondence.* New Haven: Yale University Press, 1916.

Stone, Robert E. "The Mechanicsburg Stones—Two Distinct Types." *NEARA Newsletter* 5, no. 3 (September 1970): 53.

———. "Mystery Hill and NEARA Research Progress

Report—1975." *NEARA Journal* 10, no. 2 (Summer-Fall 1975): 7-13.

Stone, William L. *Life of Joseph Brant-Thayendanega.* New York: Alexander Blake, 1838.

Strabo. *The Geography of Strabo.* Translated by H. L. Jones. Cambridge: Harvard University Press, 1961.

Swigart, Edmund K. *The Prehistory of the Indians of Western Connecticut, Part I, 9000-1000 B.C.: A Research Report of the Shepaug Valley Archaeological Society, Volume I.* Washington, Conn.: Shepaug Valley Archaeological Society, October, 1974.

Tacitus. *Dialogus, Agricola, and Germania.* Translated by W. Hamilton Fyfe. New York: Oxford University Press, 1908.

Talcott, Mary Kingsbury, ed. *The Talcott Papers: Correspondence and Documents (Chiefly Official) during Joseph Talcott's Governorship of the Colony of Connecticut, 1724-41.* 2 vols. Hartford: Collections of the Connecticut Historical Society, 1892-96.

Taylor, H. M., and J. Taylor. *Anglo-Saxon Architecture.* Cambridge: at the University Press, 1965.

Tom, Alexander. "The Geometry of Megalithic Man." *The Mathematical Gazette: The Journal of the Mathematical Association* 45, no. 353 (May 1961): 83-93.

——. "The Megalithic Unit of Length." *Journal of the Royal Statistical Society* 225, part 2 (1962): 243-251.

——. "A Statistical Examination of the Megalithic Sites in Britain." *Journal of the Royal Statistical Society* 118, part 3 (1955): 275-295.

Thoreau, Henry David. *Walden and Other Writings of Henry David Thoreau.* Edited by Brooks Atkinson. New York: Modern Library, 1950.

Thucydides. *History of the Peloponnesian War.* Edited by Benjamin Jowett. New York: Oxford University Press, 1900.

Timlow, Herman R. *Ecclesiastical and Other Sketches of Southington, Connecticut.* Hartford: Press of the Case, Lockwood and Brainard Co., 1875.

Tooker, William Wallace. *The Indian Place-Names on Long Island* 1911. Reprint. Port Washington, N.Y.: Kennikat, 1962.

Torbrugge, Walter. *Prehistoric European Art.* New York: Abrams, 1968.

Totten, Norman. "The Eye of God and the Agricultural Grid." *Occasional Publications of the Epigraphic Society* 4, no. 86 (October 1976): 1-11.

———. "The First European Colonists in New England." *Occasional Publications of the Epigraphic Society* 3, no. 49 (August 1975): 1-5.

Transactions of the New York State Agricultural Society. 3 (1847).

Trumbull, James Hammond. *Indian Names of Places, etc. in and on the Borders of Connecticut.* Hartford: Lockwood and Brainard, 1881.

Tuck, James A., and Robert J. McGhee. "An Archaic Indian Burial Mound." *Scientific American* 235, no. 5 (November 1976): 121-129.

United States Department of Agriculture. *Home Freezers, Their Selection and Use.* Home and Garden Bulletin No. 48. Washington D.C.: Government Printing Office, 1973.

———. *Storing Vegetables and Fruits in Basements, Cellars, Outbuildings and Pits.* Home and Garden Bulletin No. 119. Washington D.C.: Government Printing Office, 1973.

Vega, Garcilaso de la. *The Florida of the Inca.* Edited by John Varner and Jeanette Varner. Austin: University of Texas Press, 1951.

Vivian, John. *Building Stone Walls.* Charlotte, Vt.: Garden Way Publishing, 1976.

Von Wuthenau, Alexander. *The Art of Terracotta Pottery in Pre-Columbian Central and South America.* New York: Crown, 1970.

———. *Unexpected Faces in Ancient America: The Historical Testimony of Pre-Columbian Artists.* New York: Crown, 1975.

Waldren, William H. "Myotragus Balearicus." *Deya Archaeological Museum, No. 5,* Deya de Mallorca, Spain: private printing, 1967.

Walters, George R. *Early Man in Orange County, New York.* Middletown, N.Y.: Historical Society of Middletown and the Wallkill Precinct, Spring, 1974.

Washburn, Wilcomb E. *The Indian in America.* New York: Harper and Row, 1975.

Whipple, Chandler. *The Indian and the White Man in Connecticut.* Stockbridge, Mass.: Berkshire Traveller Press, 1972.

Whittall, James P., II. "Anforetas Recovered in Maine." *Early Sites Research Society Bulletin* 5, no. 1 (February 1977): 1-6.

———. "Copper/Tin Projectile, Monhegan, Maine." *Early Sites Research Society Bulletin* 5, no. 1 (February 1977): 7-9.

———. "Excavation Report: Oracle Chamber Drain." *Early Sites Research Society Bulletin* 5, no. 1 (February 1977): 18-21.

———. "The Gungywamp Complex, Groton, Connecticut." *Early Sites Research Society Bulletin* 4 no. 1 (May 1976): 15-27.

———. "An Inscribed Celt." *Early Sites Research Society Bulletin* 5, no. 1 (February 1977): 9-12.

———. "The Inscribed Stone From Comassakumkanit [Bourne Stone]." *Occasional Publications of the Epigraphic Society* 2, no. 44 (May 1975): 1-3.

———. "The Inscribed Stones of Sherbrooke, Quebec." *Early Sites Research Society Bulletin* 4, no. 1 (May 1976): 28-32.

———. "The Mill River Inscription." *Early Sites Research Society Bulletin* 4, no. 1 (May 1976]: 8-10.

———. "The Monhegan Inscriptions." *Early Sites Research Society Bulletin* 4, no. 1 (May 1976): 1-7.

———. "Mystery Hill Excavations, 1969." *NEARA Newsletter* 4, no. 4 (December 1969): 80-81.

———. "Stone Chamber: North Salem, N.Y." *Early Sites Research Society Work Report* 3, no. 30 (1977).

————. "Stone Chamber: Windham County, Vt." *Early Sites Research Society Work Report* 3, no. 31 (1977).

————. "Structure XIB: North Salem, N.H." *Early Sites Research Society Bulletin* 5, no. 1 (February 1977): 22-28.

Willey, Gordon R. *An Introduction to American Archaeology. Volume 1: North and Middle America.* Englewood Cliffs, N.J.: Prentice-Hall, 1966.

Wilson, Daniel. *Prehistoric Annals of Scotland.* 2 vols. London: Macmillan, 1863.

Witthoft, John. "Alleged Phoenician Inscriptions from York County, Pennsylvania." *Pennsylvania Archaeologist* 34, no. 2 (September 1964): 93-94.

Wyckoff, Jerome. *Rock Scenery of the Hudson Highlands and Palisades.* Glens Falls, N. Y.: Adirondack Mountain Club, 1971.

Zimm, Louise Seymour (Hasbrouck) et al., eds. *Southeastern New York.* Vol. 2. New York: Lewis Historical Publishing Co., 1946.

Acknowledgments

A sense of excitement and intrigue allowed many people to work together in a massive effort to examine this country's stone ruins. This book is about their work.

To Jeff Ackerson of the American Broadcasting Company for planting the idea of a book and for making the idea a tangible reality. To Linda Ackerson for meticulous bibliographic assistance.

To Congresswoman Jean Amatucci for help in cutting through bureaucratic red tape.

To Linda Aumick of Thrall Library; Rose Capozella, Carole Demberg, Diane Dewitt, Beverly Diviriglio, Lucile Gardner, Elsie Genegel, Dennis Montagna, and Frances Wittman of the Sarah Wells Library, Orange County Community College; and Jean Sharpe of Newburgh Free Library for the many hours they spent tracking down obscure documents on local history.

To Eileen Bach, for the many historical documents and references she untiringly dug out of family archives.

To Alfred M. Bingham and the Connecticut Historical Society for permission to cite from his article on stone chambers and freed slaves.

To Tina Borchard for help in keeping the Middletown Archeological Research Center (MARC) afloat during the early months of organization, and for the many sources on colonial exploration in the New World.

To Bord Failte and Clive Brooks for help in securing material on Irish beehive chambers.

To Henry E. Bown, Associate Archivist of the Pennsylvania Historical and Museum Commission for information on Indian treaties.

To Tom Brannan, engineer and surveyor, for his detailed site map and for information about many stone structures in the mid-Hudson Valley.

To Mary Browne for guiding us to many western Connecticut stone sites.

To Caisse Nationale des Monuments Historiques for permission to reproduce a photograph of the long Axial Gallery Cave at Lascaux, France.

To Doris Chandler and Doris Cosco for typing numerous drafts of this book.

To Professor Warren Cook of Castleton State College for information about Vermont stone sites.

To Paulette Cooper for helpful organizational advice.

To Marty Coopersmith for field assistance and for his expert lectures on avoiding snake dens while in the woods.

To William Corliss of the Sourcebook Project for copies of rare reports.

To William Cuddy for providing the equipment to move 500-pound inscribed stones from the mountains to the laboratory.

To Delaware Valley Community College Service Center's Director, Tom Pivinchny, for providing a classroom forum in which to discuss archeological issues. To my students at Delaware Valley, who listened to the arguments and who offered critical counterarguments as this book took form.

To Byron Dix for permission to use his impressive astro-archeological data and for the opportunity to join him on sixteen-hour, snow-laden hikes through the mountains of Vermont.

To Dowling College's Student Union Society for hosting several speaking engagements in order to issue reports on field progress.

To the Early Sites Research Association and to James Whittall II for permission to cite many excellent reports on New England sites.

To the Epigraphic Society for permission to cite select articles; and to Professor Barry Fell for permission to incorporate his decipherments and translations into this book.

To Daniel Feldman for help during our first few months of operation.

To Mark Feldman for research details about Mystery Hill.

To Andrew Fleming of the Research Laboratory for Archaeology at Oxford for information on the detection of forgery in ceramic and metal artifacts.

To George Fluhr, historian for the town of Shohola, Pennsylvania, for historical references.

To Gerald Formosa for information on prehistoric Maltese grid symbols and for photographs from his book *The Megalithic Monuments of Malta*.

To Mrs. Walter Geiser for transcribing scholarly reports from German.

To Congressman Benjamin Gilman for valuable information about scientific agencies in the federal government.

To Professor Cyrus Gordon of New York University for helpful epigraphic material and for permission to cite from his voluminous writings.

To Richard Grando for survey assistance and for use of his comprehensive library of rare antiquarian reports and letters.

To Debbie Gust and Doris Hambly for field help.

To Hammond Incorporated for permission to reproduce a physiographic illustration of New York.

To Doug Hay for information on Delaware Valley sites.

To Tom Henderson for providing many historical references.

To James Herd for supplying important documentary material.

To Evelyn Holmes for continued support.

To Professor Norman Holub and his wife Joan for sharing endless hours of discussion and for references both in the States and in Mallorca.

To John and Ida Kelly for continued support.

To Anthony F. Kent of the National Film Board for information about Canadian inscriptions.

To Cece Kirkorian of the Archaeological Associates of

Greenwich, Connecticut, for data on an inscribed stone.

To Fred Kirsch for being both patient and critical of our findings.

To the Kiwanis Clubs of Wilkes-Barre, Pennsylvania, and Middletown, New York, for providing a forum for discussing the stone sites in the Delaware and Hudson Valleys.

To Sydelle Kramer, for her patient and rigorous editing of the many manuscript revisions. May she one day own a pair of golden scissors.

To Krauss Photo Store of Port Jervis, New York, for excellent photographic assistance.

To Albert LaVine and the Middletown Lions Club for arranging an archeology discussion.

To Edward J. Lenik, Archaeologist, New England Antiquities Research Association, for permission to quote from his numerous archeological articles and for the use of his maps.

To Professor Vernon Leslie for permission to use information from his many books on local history.

To Merrie Lloyd for field assistance.

To Claire Lofrese, MARC's graphic illustrator, for many detailed site drawings and for assistance on several excursions around New England.

To William and Dorothy Lovering for permission to use a photograph of an inscribed stone and for their warm hospitality after a hike through central Vermont.

To Gary Manoloff for field assistance during MARC's first stone site expedition.

To H. Pierson Mapes of the Ramapo Land Company, Inc., for permission to reproduce his 1845 "prehistoric walls" map.

To the MARC office secretaries Val Gilcrest, Tana Barnes, and Shawneen Wright, who admirably handled many of our initial organization problems.

To Dr. Daniel Marcellus and his brainchild, the Middletown Experimental College Association, for setting the intellectual environment for the beginning of MARC.

To Pat Marquez for transcribing scholarly reports from French.

To Laurel Marx for her excellent aerial survey prints and the weekly supply of archeological references, and also for the hours of critical discussion, many of which helped clarify muddled concepts.

To Henriette Mertz for permission to quote from her thought-provoking books and for several scholarly references.

To Robert Miller for coordinating the local and regional archive search and for donating many summer days to field exploration.

To Desmond Morris for helpful research suggestions.

To the Mystery Hill Corporation, Dan Leary, and Osborn and Robert Stone for information about their site.

To Giovanna Neudorfer, Vermont State Archeologist, for information about stone chambers and for reference material.

To the New England Antiquities Research Association (NEARA) and Andrew Rothovius, editor of the *NEARA Journal,* for supplying important data about many stone sites.

To Niel Novesky, Bruce Cohen, and Lucinda Sloane of the Educational Training Administration, for helping set up MARC as a Summer Youth Program sponsor.

To George Oliver for field and library assistance.

To Mr. and Mrs. James Ottaway, Jr., and son for continued support and for field assistance.

To Klaus Otterburig and Walter De Gruyter and Company for permission to reproduce some photographs.

To Oxford University Press for permission to reproduce a photograph.

To my parents, who gave me much support and encouragement while this book was being written.

To Mrs. Paul S. Phenix for information about a colonial estate.

To the Phi Beta Kappa Association of New York and to Marjorie May for scheduling and sponsoring an archeological lecture.

To Wayne Phillips of the Depository Trust Company for information on geological phenomena in the metropolitan New York area.

To Wadsworth R. Pierce for permission to reproduce a photograph and for information about Massachusetts stone piles.

To Generoso Pope, Jr., of the *National Enquirer* for continued interest in our archeological findings.

To Professor Maurice Pope for helpful epigraphic advice.

To Nancy Prather, my former instructor and present friend for reading early versions of this manuscript and offering many useful suggestions, but mostly for inspiring within me, while I was her student, the excitement of research and mystery.

To Judy Prinz for continued support.

To the Professional Photographic Center for supplying prints of inscribed stones.

To Michael Raab for helpful information about the mid-Hudson Valley.

To Judith Raiguel for typing.

To the Regional Economic Community Action Program of Middletown, New York, for providing summer field assistants.

To Irene Rector for information about several Kentucky stone sites.

To Dr. Donald Rickey, historian with the United States Bureau of Land Management at Denver, for professional support and data on Colorado inscriptions.

To Professor Noel Ring of Norwich University for data on high altitude aerial surveys of Vermont.

To geologist Ralph Robinson for information on mid-Hudson stone sites, for access to his extensive collection of field notes, for photographic assistance, and for fruitful discussions on America's past.

To my good friends Roger and David Rodiek for field assistance.

To Joseph Roebling of the *Union Gazette* production department for stat reproduction.

To Al Romm, editor of the *Times Herald Record*, for having the foresight to objectively listen to the arguments.

To MARC's aerial survey pilot, Rudi, for his skillful maneuvering of a plane about to eat trees.

To Jeff Seideman and Arnold Posner of North Star Productions for professional assistance in filming stone sites.

To Kalpana Shah for her meticulous drafting of the many maps accompanying this book and for creating an intellectual atmosphere necessary for creative thought.

To Louis Sherwood for field and library assistance.

To anthropology colleague Peter Shifton for continued support.

To Jamie Simpson for assistance on many field trips and for locating and typing the preliminary reference material for this book.

To Elizabeth and Robert Sincerbeaux for their kind Vermont hospitality and for supplying valuable antiquarian research papers.

To Howard Smith, Brian Van der Horst and Leslie Harrib of the *Village Voice* for their consistent interest in MARC's metropolitan New York stone sites.

To the New York chapter of the Society for the Investigation of Recurring Events and to members Susan K. Hardt, Donald D. MacAlpine, and Michael G. Zahorchak for scheduling an information-exchange archeological lecture before the Society.

To Marion Sokolinsky for access to her unpublished manuscript on ancient stone ruins.

To Barry Studin for field and photographic assistance.

To Terri Sullivan for detailed site locations of the Putnam County stone chambers.

To Selma and Dr. Edward Thaler for helpful manuscript suggestions, field contacts, and continued support.

To H. Townsend for information leading to stone curiosities in Orange County.

To Raymond W. Turmelle for photographic information on perched rocks.

To Dr. William H. Waldren for Balearic field training and methodology.

To George Walters for expert archeological opinion.

To my friend Dr. Gary Steven Wand for field and photographic assistance, but mostly for the months of enlightening critical discussion concerning the implications of our discoveries.

To Jesse and Hector Ward for continued support.

To Judith Weber for making this book happen.

To the White Mountains Recreation Association, Inc., for graciously supplying a physiographic illustration of New Hampshire's White Mountains.

To Jerome Wyckoff for permission to cite from his excellent geological writings.

To Yankee, Inc., for kindly supplying the Goshen Stone Tunnel illustration and for permission to reprint it.

Index